DATE DUE

DEC 2 1987 5115	
JAN 4 1988	
MAY 1 0 1988	
NOV 7 1988	
Nov 21	
Jun. 28, 89	
DEC 1 9 1989	
5 DEC 1989	
MAR 1 1990	
DEC 1 3 1990	
JAN - 2 1991	
FEB 2 4 1994	
MAR 2 4 1997	

BRODART, INC.   Cat. No. 23-221

INNOVATORS OF AMERICAN ILLUSTRATION

EDITED BY STEVEN HELLER

VNR Van Nostrand Reinhold Company
New York

To Louise

▐P Copyright © 1986 by Steven Heller and Push Pin Editions
All illustrations copyright © in the names of the illustrators.

Library of Congress Catalog Card Number 85-22577

ISBN 0-442-23230-6

Printed in Hong Kong

Designed by Seymour Chwast

Van Nostrand Reinhold Company Inc.
115 Fifth Avenue
New York, New York 10003

Van Nostrand Reinhold Company Limited
Molly Millars Lane
Wokingham, Berkshire RG11 2PY, England

Van Nostrand Reinhold
480 La Trobe Street
Melbourne, Victoria 3000, Australia

Macmillan of Canada
Division of Canada Publishing Corporation
164 Commander Boulevard
Agincourt, Ontario M1S 3C7, Canada

16 15 14 13 12 11 10 9 8 7 6 5 4 3 2 1

Library of Congress Cataloging-in-Publication Data

Main entry under title:

Innovators of American illustration.

   Includes index.
   1. Illustrators—United States—Interviews.
2. Illustration of books—20th century—United States.
I. Heller, Steven.
NC975.I56   1986   741.64′092′2   85-22577
ISBN 0-442-23230-6

CONTENTS

ACKNOWLEDGMENTS

Without the cooperation and encouragement of the artists interviewed, this book would not have been possible.

I would also like to thank the following people for their contributions: Dorothy Spencer, my editor at Van Nostrand Reinhold; Linda Venator, the managing editor; Martina D'Alton, the copy editor; Edward Spiro, for his photography; Ted Panken, for his transcriptions; Sarah Jane Freymann, my agent; Doris Neulinger and Caroline Ginesi, for preparation of this book; and David Sachs, for encouraging me in the early stages of this project.

INTRODUCTION

By the early 1950s, American illustration was on the brink of change. Young practitioners were leaping beyond the strictures of storybook realism, changing appearance and content. *Innovators of American Illustration* describes that evolution, being a collection of interviews with twenty-one illustrators, representing three "generations," from the benchmark period of the early fifties to the present. Each one has contributed to the modern perception of illustration, has raised the conceptual and aesthetic values of the form, and continues to make a stylistic impact on the field. Collectively they address the notion that illustration in general is in a process of continual change, not only reflecting the needs of the marketplace but also responding to the artist's personal aesthetic and philosophical needs.

In the fifties, a time when fine and applied arts were polarized between the abstract and realist dogmas, two significant events occurred in illustration: sentimentalism was neutralized and realism modernized. Robert Weaver, Robert Andrew Parker, and Tom Allen, among others, pioneered a mode of painterly expressionism. Seymour Chwast and Milton Glaser, as founders, with Ed Sorel, of Push Pin Studios, wed illustration to the broader principles of design.

Though light years apart in conceptual and stylistic methodologies, these artists practiced illustration as an end in itself. Moreover, because their works were receiving acclaim, other illustrators were encouraged to reject tired practices and experiment with concept and composition.

Not surprisingly, this "New Wave illustration" as Leo Lionni, former art director of *Fortune*, categorized it in the fifties, developed during the peak years of consumer magazine publishing. It was a time when editorial departments were independent of the marketing and advertising departments, when editorial decisions were made without the sometimes frivolous tampering of the other departments. Art directors, with mandates from astute editors, exercised unprecedented freedom. At *Esquire*, one of the major springboards for young talent, Henry Wolf, its former art director, was given four pages per issue on which to exhibit his own discoveries. In a recent interview, Wolf recalled presenting one of Weaver's paintings for approval to his editor, Arnold Gingrich, who responded, "Henry, I'm in my sixties and *don't* like it, but you're twenty-eight, and if you *do*, then it goes into the magazine." Lionni also gave illustrators inestimable license to create pictorial, journalistic essays. "Our responsibility [as art directors] is to enliven the magazine as a whole," wrote Lionni in a catalog for an exhibition of *Fortune* art, "and to give it a sense of personal involvement which art impresses so well."

Changes in magazine content during the late fifties and the sixties contributed to the conceptualization of illustration. Whereas fiction had previously been the editorial illustrator's ghetto, increased and varied nonfiction subject matter required more abstract and symbolic illustrative solutions. As Weaver recalls, "Magazines like *Psychology Today* would ask for metaphorical imagery describing left-handedness—that was a pretty radical requirement to place on illustration." Also, the emergence in the marketplace of sophisticated men's magazines, curiously, fostered an illustration renaissance. Art Paul, former art director of *Playboy*, innovated a mode of conceptual illustration that not only became a striking counterpoint to the magazine's photography, but also highlighted its cultural nature. Other, less editorially ambitious imitators, such as *Cavalier, Dude,* and *Nugget,* also became wellsprings of young talent. As Barbara Nessim points out, "They were the few places that would publish my work and give me freedom."

There was also movement toward change in children's books. Maurice Sendak, though purposefully unencumbered by a single specific style, employed approaches that rejected commonplace, saccharine children's illustration. Again, as with the new forms of editorial illustration, change was fostered by an investment of self.

By the beginning of the sixties, a diversified modern art lexicon was unalterably wed to editorial, book, and advertising illustration. By then the "Push Pin Style" had become an institution. Moreover, rediscovered and reappreciated artists of the past, such as Max Beckmann, René Magritte, and Ben Shahn, became models for the *new* expressive illustration, exemplified by Alan E. Cober, Paul Davis, and James McMullan.

The early sixties was a time of extensive experimentation and derivation. Individuality was celebrated, and art directors hungered for new talent. As the innovators conjured up new directions, the less adventuresome practitioners followed their lead, borrowing and imitating whenever possible. The leading European illustrators, among them André Francois, Savignac, Ronald Searle, and later, the Alsatian transplant Tomi Ungerer, had demonstrative impacts on the practice of American illustration. Their sardonic, minimalist drawings were allusions rather than literalizations. Theirs was an art of mystery and surprise, cut by wit and humor and communicated in an abstract, often surreal, vocabulary.

Since many illustrators were committed to and participated in the social causes of the early sixties, politics was also a great motivator. *Monocle*, edited by Victor Navasky, was the first "graphically designed" satirical journal of the sixties and hence attracted many of the leading young illustrators. Edward Sorel evolved from a decorative illustrator to an acerbic commentator on *Monocle*'s pages. Robert Grossman began doing unconventional comic strips in pen and ink. Marshall Arisman worked in a lighthearted André Francois–like manner. Paul Davis honed his characteristic primitivism. In retrospect, much of the work published in *Monocle* appeared to be more style than content, but it was decidedly a timebomb of indignance, which exploded in the second half of the decade.

The turmoil of the sixties affected the content of illustrations; the most sought-after editorial illustrators were called upon to contribute points of view to the emerging sociopolitical magazines and newspapers. *Evergreen Review* and *Ramparts* were major outlets for nondecorative and polemical illustration. Sorel's regular feature in *Ramparts,* entitled "Sorel's Bestiary," ripped the façades off newsworthy Americans, while his covers for *Evergreen,* in the tradition of the political poster, served as rallying points for the disillusioned. Also working for *Evergreen,* Paul Davis created his highly visible and iconographic Chè Guevara cover, and Robert Grossman further fine-tuned his airbrushed caricatures. Limited-circulation magazines, such as *Fact* and *Avant-Garde,* encouraged self-motivated rather than "art-directed" illustration. Responses to growing political unrest— civil rights and Vietnam—resulted in a redefinition of the function of illustration that invariably had an effect on the way in which art directors used illustration in "commercial" outlets as well.

Many publications sprang up during the period from the mid-sixties to the early seventies, including underground papers and broadsheets, ushering in the psychedelic and underground comic-book styles. Brad Holland, who ironically began his career with Hallmark cards, somehow bridged the gap between anarchic comics and conventional illustration. He developed a mordant graphic commentary for the *East Village Other* and the *New York Ace,* which, once refined, was used by and became identified with the *New York Times* Op-Ed page. And it was the Op-Ed approach in general— a revival of a European Dada and surrealist vocabulary— as well as the proliferation of "designed" newspapers, that had a striking influence on the black-and-white line illustration of the seventies.

The Op-Ed page gave exposure to a worldwide community of illustrators and graphic commentators in the United States. Because its art director, J. C. Suarès, encouraged personal graphic vocabularies, the images took on a mysterious, poetic quality, ofttimes with symbols rooted in literature or mythology. Illustration in this context was not intended to be a slave to text; rather, it served to complement or even to counterpoint. In fact, most often, the art was done in advance of the stories and paired only after the writing was complete. Sometimes, as in the case of both Arisman and Holland, the editor gave story assignments based on the strength of a specific drawing. "It was the first time my work was being used the way I intended it," says Holland. Watergate further stimulated the creative impulse and enlivened the Op-Ed page with powerful, often witty, graphic commentaries. However, the success of this approach resulted in its inevitable demise, for the Op-Ed style became just that—a mimicked style, void of the passion that originally made it so striking. Among its original contributors, Arisman and Holland eventually changed their media from pen-and-ink to paint, moving on to the next expressive stage.

Beginning in the late sixties and reaching a peak during the Watergate era, *New York* magazine, designed and art-directed by Milton Glaser and Walter Bernard, continued the tradition of illustrator as journalist. James McMullan, who had remained true to watercolor through a period when it was considered retrograde, produced beautiful impressionistic series, including the one from which the film *Saturday*

Night Fever was modeled. Julian Allen, a British transplant, was employed to re-create unphotographable but newsworthy situations in the manner of the turn-of-the-century pictorial reporter. Moreover, *New York* provided an outlet to a kindred group of artists, including Sorel, Grossman, and David Levine. Barbara Nessim, another contributor, made her mark with the premier issue of *Ms.* magazine, launched between *New York*'s covers.

In contrast to the fifties, when there was virtually no similarity between fine and applied art, much magazine and newspaper illustration of the middle to late seventies was indistinguishable from gallery art. The demise of abstract expressionism in the late fifties caused a redefinition of modernism, which resulted in the revival and glorification of many approaches formerly considered to be retrograde. In the sixties, pop art was a celebration of commercial art as a cultural lynchpin. In the seventies, photorealism and superrealism were returns to methodologies employed by illustrators of the fifties. The embracing of narrative, symbolic, and representational easel art signaled an acceptance of a universal art vocabulary in illustration as well.

Reflecting the diversity in the art world at large, illustration today encompasses a multitude of trends and styles. English-born Sue Coe, whose mordant polemical art has inspired many young illustrators to explore their inner selves, suggests a daring combination of modern art influences. The language of Richard Lindner and David Hockney is wed to deeply felt political passion in her work. For Coe, a distinct style is the means to communicate a message. At the other end of the spectrum, John Collier, who initiated a pastel renaissance, also uses style to convey a message. But aesthetic concerns, which harken back to the Italian Renaissance as reaction against the modernist veneer, are predominant. While Coe's pictures disturb, Collier's soothe.

Illustration today may be at its most eclectic, with devout movements or schools being a thing of the past. Bascove's woodcuts build upon the German expressionist tradition; James Grashow's engravinglike cuts suggest a marriage of comic-book and fine-press traditions; Guy Billout's beguilingly elegant compositions beautifully blend the French cartoon look of "Tin Tin" and the simplicity of the Japanese woodcut; Elwood H. Smith's revival of the American comic-strip look of the 1930s gives new life to a vigorous style.

The term *new wave* has been ill advisedly applied to modes of contemporary illustration, as much of what is new today is rooted in the past. Some of the artists thought to be the newest New Wavers—many of whom are represented in this book—have produced consistently fine work for many years and have influenced a slew of up-and-comers. Moreover, they are the progenitors and the keepers of the flame of a mode of illustration not practiced by everyone. If one must tie them together, personal expression is their primary bond. This is the common trait that separates these twenty-one from the "slicker," more commercial narrative or decorative illustrators, for whom style, rather than content, is of utmost importance. It also isolates them from the so-called post-modern illustrators, many of whom rely on fashionable design conceits.

Illustration, however, is a broad field with coexisting methodologies and contrasting points of view. That the common trait of these illustrators is a very personal vocabulary reflects my own biases too. Exclusively decorative illustration is not as exciting or engaging to me. Many talented practitioners are not included herein because their work does not conform to this preference. Some have been regretfully left out of this volume, with the hope that a second volume will be published at a later date. And because this book is focusing on only three generations, it is hoped that the "newcomers" who have recently created a stir in the field will be covered at another time.

The interviews for *Innovators of American Illustration* were conducted from September 1984 to March 1985. Because the first question posed to each artist was, "How did you get into the business of illustration?" the interviews begin with the answer to this question. I have known many of the interviewees for a long time; some are good friends, others, acquaintances. I was happily surprised by many responses, because I learned how much I did not know about their processes and motivations. The act of interviewing was an enlightening experience for me, both as a procurer and an aficionado of illustration. I hope that this material will be equally instructive and entertaining for the reader.

Steven Heller, September, 1985

ROBERT WEAVER

Robert Weaver (born on July 5, 1924, in Pittsburgh, Pennsylvania) is the undisputed pioneer of contemporary expressive illustration. Having entered the field by chance, he has been one of its most ardent and loyal practitioners. Unhampered by the conventions of American illustrative realism, his representational painting borrowed from abstraction at a time when such work was decidedly taboo. He influenced the field by example, in the scores of publications that he appeared in regularly and through teaching at the School of Visual Arts in New York for over thirty years. Indeed, he has touched more artists in the fine and applied disciplines than can be counted. Moreover, his development of the unconventional multiple-image serial illustration continues to have an effect on the way illustration is practiced today.

I was an early draw-er back in Pittsburgh. I went to a private school that encouraged the artist in me. I then went to a public high school where, again, there was a very good art teacher. But things didn't really make any sense until after World War II. I had completed a year of study at Carnegie Tech and did not go back to it after the war, because I made two or three discoveries that I think were crucial.

Before this period, I had liked the picturesque painting school, painters like John Steuart Curry. They were the modern equivalent of Currier and Ives—picturesque prints showing farmhands coming home after a hard day's work for the big farm dinner. But after the war, Ben Shahn startled me with paintings of very ordinary people sitting on park benches—not heroic, but rather harsh. And he did postwar pictures about Europe showing Italian women within the rubble of bombed-out cities. I could see a story that I had not seen in American paintings. Next the postwar Italian movies came along, and I was very excited by Rossellini's *Open City* and DeSica's *Shoeshine.*

What excited you about them? They were not slick like Hollywood movies. They were exploring the real world and using the camera in a wonderfully interesting way. Moving the camera to examine the real details instead of the phony sunlit props all filmed at high noon on a Hollywood lot. But I didn't know what to do with this.

I went to Italy in 1949, and while there I studied under a well-known Venetian, Maestro Cadorin, who taught egg-tempera techniques. While I was there, I painted the gondoliers, the pigeon lady, and the man who sold postcards, and I continued to look at Italian movies. I was probably the only person in Venice who attended the premiere of

Illustration in Cosmopolitan *for a John D. McDonald mystery. 1961. Acrylic on canvas. Art director: Tony La Salla.*

From a work in progress entitled New York, New York, *a two-layered visual narrative: Jason Robards rehearsing for* Huey *and Times Square signage. 1982. Acrylic on paper.*

Bicycle Thief. Everybody else was dying to see American extravaganzas.

Were you in Italy with the intent of becoming an artist? I didn't have any grandiose ambitions. I had a chance to go to Italy because my uncle, who was a sea captain and lived in Venice, gave me free passage on his ship. I stayed with his wife and daughter, and I took two free classes there. I knew only that I wanted to get other experiences. The prevailing art of that time, the gallery art of the United States, did not interest me. This was the period of almost universal infatuation with abstract art. And there I was, painting real people and pigeons and boats and things, with no idea how I was going to put this to use or make a living when I came back.

Was your objection to abstract art intuitive or intellectual? I could, sort of, intellectually see its importance. But it bored me! I thought art required skill, and I had the skill. So, I came back to America after two years with a crazy idea of doing murals.

Murals in the WPA sense? Scenes of class struggle or idealistic scenes? It occurred to me that all public buildings,

with vast, empty walls everywhere, needed murals. So why not provide them, as the Italian artists had centuries before? You saw art everywhere in Italy. Why not put art into restaurants or into lobbies of apartment houses? I did a whole series of lengthy color sketches of numerous ideas. I had a whole book of these, which I showed when I went around. If I saw an empty wall, I would ask to see the manager of the establishment and would show these mural ideas—they all had stories of some sort to tell. Some of them fantastic, that is to say, stories of an unreal world; and some of them quite real. For example, I had one showing mandrills in the moonlight, or another of rooftops or of a forest of ship's rigging. Anyway, nobody was interested, except for a few low-class bars who from time to time had to be closed down by the police.

You actually completed some murals? Yeah, I did a few of them in bars. I thought one of them was very nice, but subsequently, after a police lockup, it was taken down. Anyway, with these sketches, I stumbled into the office of *Town and Country*, thinking I could get some kind of job as a color consultant. I did not know anything about illustration.

It had not interested or appealed to me at all because of the prevalence of the boy/girl pretty stuff in magazines. No serious artist would ever consider doing illustration!

Yet you did go to a magazine. What made you stoop so low? I thought I would just get some art-related job. I assumed they paid *very* well, you see, and all I would have to do would be to show up and advise on colors and say: "No, I don't think you need all that red there." Tony Mazzola, then the art director of *Town and Country,* set me straight. Apparently, he saw my drawings as so different from what anybody else was doing that he gave me a couple of manuscripts to illustrate.

So this was in the early fifties, a time when Steven Dohanos, Albert Dorn, and other realists were in their prime. Yes. But even more in their prime were the Cooper Studio people, the Joe Bowlers and the Coby Whitmores and the Jon Whitcombs. I remember liking Al Parker more than the others, although he certainly did that type of cutesy stuff. It was the ponytail period in American culture.

Did you also work for Leo Lionni at Fortune? I did quite a few things for him over six years . . . including single-

page illustrations and some covers.

Did you go out on journalistic assignments? Yes. I was strictly a sketcher. I used no cameras. I just made drawings and brought them back. Obviously, people noticed that quality in my work right away.

How long after that did other work start coming in? For the first few years, it was pretty sporadic. I had a part-time job as a drugstore fountainman, and I did some proofreading for a Wall Street firm. But I would also get some illustration jobs. Henry Wolf at *Esquire* gave me little black-and-white spots to do. People like Tom Allen and Andy Warhol were also working for *Esquire* at that time.

At that point, did you have the desire to do art that was not illustration? Or did you see illustration as an end in itself? Well, I saw illustration as an end in itself. I began to see it as a real calling and not just a way to make money. I was certainly lucky. There were some very good art directors around who would let me do it my way, Cipe Pineles and Bill Golden, for example. The realities began to sneak in, though, when I began working for Bernie Quint at *Life*. He had some very strong ideas of his own, and we

Sketches and finished drawings for "Long but Profitable Climb," a Fortune *article on climbing the corporate ladder at Woolworths. 1962. Pencil and acrylic on paper. Art director: Leo Lionni.*

used to really wrestle with each other. He had some rather dumb ideas about what was exciting. Like wanting everything to shoot across the page in big, thrusting surges. Most times that seemed to be inappropriate to me, because his whole concept was oriented toward *layout* rather than accuracy or credibility within the picture itself.

So the distinction you'd make between the art directors like Lionni and Quint is that Quint was being the designer and Lionni was being the art director. Lionni trusted the artist, and once he picked the right practitioner, he let him alone. One valuable lesson from Lionni was when he asked me to do a cover for *Fortune*. What I did was go to the library and look up all the preceding *Fortune* covers under his direction. I made up my mind that there was a certain kind of cover that he wanted, which I then proceeded to copy. Of course, I did an ersatz *Fortune* cover, which he quickly rejected, saying, "No, no, no, no, do it your way." He looked at my sketchbook and picked out a most unexpected drawing for a cover. I told him that it didn't look like a *Fortune* cover, and he said, "I don't want it to look like a *Fortune* cover."

Was Lionni the first one to commission you to work from life, or was that an idea that you came up with? That was *Fortune*'s policy, to send artists on stories. I was sent to Ohio and Alabama, just all over. *Sports Illustrated* later did the same thing.

Did you consider yourself a journalist? Or was this what you thought an illustrator should do? I saw it as journalism. It was not the kind of mythologizing illustration that you saw in *Cosmopolitan*. Theirs was not attached to the real world, and that's why I liked the journalistic side of it. I think most artists have the desire to reproduce the things they see. And I feel *that* is the job of an illustrator. I did do some *Cosmopolitan* work, a lot of detective stories, which I enjoyed doing, but even that kind of fictional illustration grew out of the real. I used *real* data.

How did you research the pictures? First, I had some kind of an image on my mind. I sort of knew what I wanted to get. But you see, I based my *Cosmo* work on a lot of sketches of real situations. I was telling a fictional story, but using real life people in the interest of credibility. I actually liked working for *Cosmo*, before Helen Gurley Brown took it over and ruined it.

What is the genesis of your sequential work? Did you have to fight for space for this unique approach? In the case of *Cosmo*, I almost always had two pages, sometimes three. That was the nice thing about working for them. The magazine was filled with illustrations. There were sometimes six or seven short stories in an issue, and six or seven different illustrators did them. Sequences allowed me to share more information with the viewer, rather than reducing a complex notion to a simplistic symbol.

How is it that the great masters were able to tell a story in a single picture while you seem to require eight or ten? Well, that's a good question. If, by some trick of history, the painters of the past routinely worked in sequences, then it would have been necessary to discover a way to tell stories within a single picture.

Your feelings about gallery versus magazine painting are very well known—you refuse to be a gallery painter. Did you find that illustration was the best way to express yourself? I don't feel that way now, but in the early days, yes. I felt that everything I needed to say could be said in illustrations. In other words, I would find within a manuscript some way of putting myself into an illustration—there was plenty of room for me to roam around. Now illustration has become very constricting.

Was it difficult to get your philosophy of illustration understood by the art directors or editors? I was known for the kind of work I did. I rarely had to defend it or argue for it. They came to me, and they knew what they were going to get. I worked for *Life, Sports Illustrated, Esquire, Look.* Those were my best outlets, as I recall. I never worked for *Holiday;* they were a little too well dressed, and the people that I drew were always kind of klunky.

You were working for Playboy *and doing a number of inventive pieces. Why were your paintings so collage looking?* It had to do with the specific story, but usually it's a means of telling a complex tale with many elements. It needs to be like a collage, because any one of the elements by itself would be meaningless.

Where did the idea of splitting a picture into halves come from? Probably the impulse to compress. Clearly, I wanted to get as much into a picture as possible. I think one of the triggers was seeing Andy Warhol's movie, *Chelsea Girls,* which used the vertical split-screen technique. The same scene was shown from two different cameras. Occasionally the arm of the girl in one picture appeared on the other side of the screen. For me it was an insightful way of working with two-dimensional space. After all, the sentence, "I thought of Zelda in Paris," is encompassing four thousand miles and fifty years in only a few words. Why can't I do that visually? Life is not a single snapshot; it is a series of events that are chain-linked and proceed frame by frame.

So did that method apply to many of the assignments you were doing and most themes you were covering? In some

Illustration about Vietnam for a special issue of Mother Jones *on remembering the war. 1983. Acrylic on paper. Art director: Louise Kollenbaum.*

cases the single image was sufficient.

Were you called upon to do what's called conceptual art? Yes. The kinds of stories that I illustrated back in those days were rather complicated. I had to find ways to draw or paint that would match the abstract complexities of the writing. Mine was no longer the era of Norman Rockwell, where everything was easy, obvious, and on the surface. How would Norman Rockwell illustrate the problem of left-handedness? Magazines like *Psychology Today* were publishing articles about complex ideas; they needed a conceptual artwork.

So, in a sense, your ascendancy paralleled a new era of magazine content. I suppose so. I don't remember ever reading anything in the *Saturday Evening Post*—I'd just look at the pictures—but I doubt the articles were very taxing on the brain.

Isolated from a text, do you feel that your images can stand up as art? I've always hoped that would be true. They're not so specific that they are meaningless without the caption or the text. The chief problem with most illustrations is that they're too specific. They're so specific that when you see them in the Society of Illustrators' *Annual* out of context, they make no sense whatsoever.

When did the camera become a tool? I adapted very easily to the camera because it is an extension of the eye. Many of the best photographers are painters manqué.

This leads us to a question about process. How do you do what you do? I can show you an example of a drawing and the finished painting that came out of the drawing [see accompanying illustration]. These are assignments for *Fortune,* where I am realistically and symbolically going up the corporate ladder at W. H. Woolworth's. It starts with the stockboy, and I use chairs as a metaphor for power. The chairs become more and more elaborate as we go to the top. The drawings were rendered from life. I asked the stockboy just to stand for a few minutes, and finally, I rendered the big-time lawyers. As for process, essentially there is not a hell of a lot of transformation between the sketches and the finishes. I've simplified the finish a little bit and added some color. I've actually made the pictures more decorative. My sketches are notes, and the color variations stay in the mind. I make the drawings without colors, and later I simply bathe the picture in what I remember to be the proper light.

What materials did you use? I abandoned egg tempera shortly after I came back to this country. Acrylics were just beginning to be used widely, and I was given a whole supply in return for an endorsement. It's a convenient

From a work in progress entitled
New York, New York, *a split image*
of the Thanksgiving day parade and
Park Avenue. *1982. Acrylic on paper.*

medium that dries fast. I can still be working on a painting an hour before it is due. I simply apply a hair dryer to it, and I'm on my way. Since I used to work with oils, I was familiar with paint.

Do you consistently maintain a sketchbook? I don't keep the book intact. I tear out the best drawings from the sketchbook and save them. These are essentially informational notes that I've never thought of as art. I find if the initial drawings are good, the painting comes easy.

And if the drawings are bad? I have to sweat, and I have to go to photographs or use whatever else I can find as reference.

All around your studio are found ephemeral materials. Do you work from these as well? Sometimes I tear posters down from telephone poles and paint them into pictures.

Have you used models? Yes. Usually friends or wives. Anybody who happens to be around to simulate a real situation—a hand holding a coffee cup or combing the hair— I can't make it up. I have learned that if you make it up, it's unconvincing.

Would the bottom line for you be to make a picture convincing? I'd say credible. In order for you to *feel* a picture, you have to be involved in it. So the more I can create the illusion of some reality going on, chances are that the viewer will be touched in some way—scared, angered, or whatever.

What kinds of emotions are you interested in provoking? I'm really not interested in provoking a lot of emotion, just in stating a case as clearly as possible. I don't believe in literally drawing conclusions. I like a line by the English actress, Dame Peggy Ashcroft, who said to John Gielgud, who was a notorious weeper on the stage, "John, if you cried less, maybe the audience would cry more." That's why I don't like symbolism. It's very hard to feel emotional about a symbol.

But you've said that your School of Visual Arts exhibition poster symbolizes "art." I am making that point, it's true. But I'm using real and appropriate symbols. The poster I worked from is *my* poster. That's *my* umbrella. The symbols are appropriate because they effectively represent *my* life.

I'm not using three-headed trumpet players like Brad Holland—not to mock him, but I don't do that kind of thing. He does it effectively, but it's not what I like to do.

We spoke before about magazines having been an effective outlet for your feelings, and now they aren't. Is that why you've done so many personal books? When illustration assignments provided an outlet, there was no need to do books. The books represent a way of controlling my flow of thoughts. But also, I have grown up, and illustration is a younger man's art form. I think one eventually gets tired of that kind of illustration where you have to make up solutions to stories that essentially are simplistic. If you really do have an interest in art or in ideas, you need some way of letting that come out, and you can't do it in illustration alone, unless you're given a lot of paper and a lot of time and freedom.

When did you begin to work on these narrative books? In 1976 or 1977. The first one I did is all drawings, using quotations and fragments and snippets from illustration. It was an attempt at some kind of autobiography, but very, very elusive. Very hard to follow, and very private. Almost unreadable to anybody who doesn't know me. You know, references to Venice and Pittsburgh. I had accumulated a lot of material on the city of Venice. And I happened to have scores of photographs showing both sides of the Grand Canal. There's no way you can understand that city unless you've been there, and no book of photographs has ever done it. Mine is an attempt to explain the strange city where the "streets are paved with sky."

I also do "two-story" (split-level) books. Doing in pictures what writers can do casually without having to defend it. Writers are able to suggest three or four things going on simultaneously. Short stories, which I like to compare to my sequences, are delayed pictures. You don't see the whole picture right away. I'm holding back something until the end. One part is like a musical accompaniment. The other part contrasts. I see no reason why the brain can't take both in. Probably you can take in a lot more than you think you can.

You also make use of signage typography as a contrast to the purely pictorial. Yes. For example, one of my stories shows Jason Robards rehearsing for a play in a Broadway rehearsal hall, amidst all this Forty-second Street sleaze. I love the idea of showing what's outside of the rehearsal hall through typography, and then portraying the thoughtful actor inside.

Obviously, you're working on both sides of the paper, as with any book. Aside from the physical composition, what is it about this that would prevent you from making an exhibition? The answer is that the experience you have in your life is one of moments that succeed and replace other moments. Each new moment destroys the preceding one. You cannot take it in simultaneously. Life is a series of moments that can be taken only one at a time. In the same way that music cannot be heard all at once, you have to remember how the music started if you want to enjoy how it ends. Writing does the same thing. It requires memory. So my work is simply a visual equivalent. If I had the separate pages stretched across a room, it would be artificial. Because that's not the way we experience life. You have to see it page by page.

Then, this notion goes contrary to your earlier method, which was to put as much information as possible into one picture. Well, you can still put a lot of information into one picture. Or you can have a lot of pictures. Whatever is the most effective way to say something.

How do you apportion your day or week? Do you have a regular working schedule? Daylight hours. I'm essentially a daylight artist. Colors are so different under artificial light.

Are there specific periods of time you allow to either an assignment or working on a personal work? Well, if the assignment is pressing, it must be done. I sometimes resent the time I have to spend on an assignment as taking away from the time I could spend on my own work. I work every day. Sundays. Holidays. Not always fruitfully or productively. But something always gets done.

TOM ALLEN

Tom Allen (born on January 23, 1928, in Nashville, Tennessee) was, in the mid-fifties, a pioneer of the new impressionistic illustration. Divorced from the characteristic sentimentalism of the period, he drew from life and the imagination in a distinct manner that would influence scores of others years afterward. His record album illustrations brought success, as did regular spot drawings for the jazz profiles in the New Yorker. Since 1983 he has been Hallmark Professor in the Department of Design at the University of Kansas.

I grew up in Nashville, Tennessee, where I was born in 1928. My childhood coincided with the Great Depression. Though we weren't as affected as were many, it was all around us. As a kid, I wasn't the scholarly type. I thought I was pretty smart, but I was more interested in playing; and drawing was a form of play. Living on the edge of town, I could play in the woods and fields and even ride my bicycle to my grandfather's farm. I could also ride the streetcar to town for art lessons, which I started when I was nine. I took those lessons from a wonderful man named John Richardson until the World War II draft called him to serve. By then, I was in high school and put art on the back burner in favor of athletics. I went to Vanderbilt University for two years on a football scholarship. At the end of that time, I realized that if I wanted to be an artist, I needed to have a good four years away from athletics and social life. So, I enrolled in the painting program at the school of the Art Institute of Chicago in the fall of 1948. It was an exciting time to be in art school. There was a lot of energy generated by the older students who had served in the war.

Did you begin your illustration career after graduation? Not exactly. I had joined the Marine Corps and didn't have to report right away, so I spent a few months in New York. I had no idea, really, that I would make a career as an illustrator. However, I met some illustrators, and they thought I should show my drawings to Henry Wolf, who had recently become art director at *Esquire.*

Was your work representational or realistic? I had developed my own vocabulary by sort of creating my own world, I guess. I don't know what any of it meant. But since I liked big shapes, I put whatever the information was into one big mass. I liked dramatic colors—red, black, and white. And I employed certain distortions, like showing a full-faced front view with the side view within it. In the beginning, I had a lot of big heads, painted in oil on paper. That was influenced by Leon Golub, who was at the Art Institute at the same time I was.

Illustration from series for Esquire *entitled "Country Music Goes to Town." 1959. Oil on canvas. Art director: Robert Benton.*

I did two illustrations for Henry and one for the *New York Times.* Then I reported to the Marine Corps. I was discharged in 1955 and that same year collected the twenty-five hundred dollars that I'd won in a fellowship competition for painting at the Art Institute in 1952.

From your military life, was it difficult to return to the rather undisciplined life of an artist? No. I figured I would come back to New York and settle into a walk-up apartment, which I did, and pursue my career as an artist. I didn't do very well at finding galleries, though.

I figured that I could always get seventy-five bucks a month out of Henry at *Esquire* and with that I could survive until I worked out what I was going to do. Slowly, I involved myself more and more in illustration. I worked for Marvin Israel at *Seventeen* magazine; I did a full-page drawing of Hitler for *Collier's*; I started doing trade ads for NBC; I worked for a pharmaceutical company, because I was good at drawing sick people.

In the mid-fifties the predominant style was Cooper Studio. How did you fare? Well, it always amuses me a little when people who have written histories of illustration categorically say that the fifties was about Cooper and those people. The fact is, the fifties was about the demise of that school of illustration. Many of the gold medals were won in the second half of the fifties by Bob Weaver, Robert Andrew Parker, and me. So it seems to me that the fifties was about the emergence of self-expression in illustration, and the interesting thing is that the three of us never studied illustration.

In the early stage, was it difficult to get ideas through? Were you meeting with resistance? It seemed pretty easy, but I was very naive. In the beginning, just about everybody I showed my work to gave me a job.

Do you remember some of the comments? The one that I will never forget was a noncomment from Henry Wolf. I had my work stuffed in a book with plastic sleeves. He put it on his desk and flipped through very rapidly. After about a third of the way through he stopped, slammed it shut, turned his back, and walked away. I thought I had been dismissed. Surprisingly, he caught me at the elevator and gave me a manuscript.

I don't remember anybody saying anything, but I could sense some enthusiasm for something new. People like Cipe Pineles, art director of *Seventeen,* and Neil Fujita, art director at CBS, were very important to me also.

Did they give you freedom, direction, or both? The first assignment Fujita gave me was an album cover for a jazz singer. The record was called *The Jazz Odyssey of James*

Sketches for the article "Alex: The Life of a Child" by Frank Deford. 1983. Pencil on paper.

Rushing, Esquire. Rushing started in New Orleans, came to Kansas City, then up to Chicago and over to New York; so this record album was covering that whole trek. Fujita had liked some things that I had done for NBC. When he gave me this assignment, he arranged for me to go to the recording session, so I could hear the music. Then I could meet Rushing, touch him, talk to him, and take pictures of him. He was the original Mr. Five-by-Five—five feet tall, five feet wide, and a line of jive, or something like that. So he was the perfect shape for me to work with, since I enjoyed big, round masses. Anyway, the cover won a gold medal in the 1957 art directors' show. After that, as long as Fujita was at CBS, he would give me work and sort of served as my mentor as well.

He also included me in dinner parties with people like Ben Shahn and Lotte Lenya. It gave me a sense of belonging in New York.

Did knowing the subjects help the picture-making process? Oh, yes. The more you can experience something, the more authentic the image is going to be.

So you would do portraits from life rather than from photographs? I've done them both ways. Very often, you just don't have the opportunity to see the person in life. With the Rushing job, I had a concept that could not be drawn from life. So I took a set of pictures of him and then painted the concept; he was running, holding his hat on his head with one hand and his suitcase in the other, with a road sign behind him that had arrows pointing to the different cities. Nevertheless, getting to meet him, hear his music, and talk to him gave me a sense that I knew this *person.* Even if I work from photos, I try to meet the subject of my drawing. By the way, many of the drawings that I've done for *The New Yorker* are done from life—dimly lit bistros, you know.

You do all the jazz profiles for The New Yorker? Right. Since 1966. Whitney Balliett writes them, and the artist who did the drawings before me had died. Whitney took my Jimmy Rushing album to show William Shawn, the editor, and he gave me a tryout. I had to draw Red Allen, who played the cornet. Allen was a great tease. He introduced me to the audience as his cousin—of course, he was black and I'm white. I did several drawings of him that night, and I sent them all in with a note saying which one I liked the best. A couple of days later Mr. Shawn's assistant called me and said, "Welcome to the club."

Were you involved in music before doing album covers? Does music play a role in your art? The only involvement I've had in music came out of a friendship with Earl Scruggs,

Finished illustration for the People article "Alex: The Life of a Child." 1983. Watercolor and ink on paper. Art director: Sanae Yamazaki.

which came out of an assignment that Robert Benton gave me to do a series of paintings on country music for *Esquire*. That was in 1959. The title was "Country Music Goes To Town," in which country came to New York. Those days, every picker and grinner within a hundred miles would come to Washington Square Park every Sunday to play and sing. So that's just the image I used. One of the paintings I did was of Lester Flatt and Earl Scruggs. Earl traded me a banjo for it, and we became close friends. Later, I kind of taught myself a three-finger roll. And much later, in Putnam County, John Cohen, who played with the New Lost City Ramblers, and I formed the Putnam String County Band with a few other local pickers. We played for square dances, fundraisers for good political people, the Hudson River Sloop, things like that. So that's the only real music that I've been involved with.

You were once involved in an environmental action group. Was any of your work politically motivated? My work in the sixties was not overtly political, but it took several paths. When Dick Gangel became art director of *Sports Illustrated*

James Whitmore IN

WILL ROGERS'
U.   S.   A.

in 1960, he picked up what Benton had started at *Esquire* by using illustrators as journalists. So I started doing all kinds of things for him and traveled all over on assignments.

Such as? The first one he gave me was a story on fishing within a hundred-mile radius of San Francisco. That led to fishing in the Yucatán, Nicaragua, Costa Rica, Panama, the Bahamas, Nova Scotia. I also played and drew all the golf courses in Scotland.

Dick is a bit romantic. He wanted to revive this old tradition of sending out Winslow Homer or Frederic Remington. In fact, one of the best assignments he gave me was to retrace the tracks of Frederic Remington. I didn't know much about Remington, except from seeing his Western paintings. So I went to the New York Public Library, discovered he had written and illustrated many articles for *Harper's* magazine and others. I found out that he was from upper New York State, went to Yale, played on the football team, and only became an artist after he had failed at seeking his fortune. He went out to look for silver in the mountains of Arizona and failed miserably. When he came out of those mountains, he met a troop of cavalry that took him into Geronimo's reservation, and he started drawing the Indians and cavalrymen. By the time he got back to New York, he had a whole bunch of these drawings. He took them to an outdoor magazine, where it turned out the editor was another guy from the Yale art class.

I rendered a pictorial history of Remington. The statement I made through that story was environmental and sociological, not political. I went out West with the thought that I could find Remington's West, but no matter how high up in the mountains and in the reservations I would get, there was still a Coors beer can two feet off the road.

Is that what you portrayed in your pictures? In essence, yes. So that was one direction that my work took, but I still did album covers. And Otto Storch, the art director at *McCall's*, used me a lot for fiction and various other things. He saw in me the Americana that I was trying to stifle. It took me a long time to give in to the fact that I am an American illustrator and that the best stuff I do comes out of my childhood experiences and so forth. I always wanted to do sophisticated artwork like Etienne Delessert or someone like that. But I'm not that kind of artist.

So the drawings that please you the least are ones where you have to grab for symbols? Weaver brought it home to me that I could really draw. He said, "Not many people can really draw, and you're crazy if you make something else out of it."

So how did that affect your work? Well, it allowed me

Top: *Illustration, which appeared in the final issue of* Life, *for an article on the life of Harry S. Truman, showing the meeting with General Douglas MacArthur. 1972. Watercolor on paper. Art director: Irwin Glusker.*
Bottom: *Illustration for "An Encounter to Last an Eternity," a* Sports Illustrated *article about the death of an Indian boxer. 1983. Watercolor on paper. Art director: Harvey Grut.*

to drop some of the symbolism and some of the contrived forms and shapes, and I got more interested in the quality of light and drama. I got more natural.

You do a lot of sketching. How does that affect your work habits? I don't start an assignment until I've explored many ways of approaching it. Sometimes it only takes two or three sketches, and sometimes fifteen. For instance, I did a picture that was about a boxing death in New Mexico. A Navajo kid died in the Golden Gloves competition in Albuquerque. So I had the Navajo boxing team coming down from the mountains, out of the reservation, to Albuquerque, in a mud-splattered pickup. The idea first came to me when I was driving up into that reservation; it was in February, and there was no snow ahead of me, because I was driving north, and the sun was hitting the south side of the mountain. I looked in the rear view mirror, and there was a big snow scene behind me. I fooled around with that, trying to find a way of showing Albuquerque through the windshield and the reservation in the rearview mirror. I fooled around with it on paper and in my mind, and it just wasn't working well. When I gave up that idea, a new solution jumped out at me and I sat down and I did the one shown here. One band of black has the pickup in it. The black was the symbol of death. It was a story that I could not totally divulge: I couldn't show the action in the ring; I couldn't show anything really happening. When I showed the funeral at the end, I only suggested it with a faded pressed rose and through the caption, "Tis Grace hath brought me safe thus far, Tis grace will see me home," which they sang at the funeral.

Have you done your own stories—where word and picture have been wed? Or where pictures tell the entire story? I've done a children's book called *Where Children Live.* The main part of that was the research, and then I came up with the image of the child for each country, thirteen in all. The writing came last, more or less describing the child and his or her life-style.

How much research do you do on a given assignment? Probably ten times as much as I need to do. For that book, I had a whole roomful of stuff, thanks to my wife's exhaustive research. I think identifying your problem is the first thing, and then understanding it. If it's something that I haven't had direct experience with and I can't re-create out of my own experience, then I've got to research it to the point where I can empathize with it enough to make the situation believable.

Does the medium play a role in that believability? When I first started illustration, I knew those illustrators at Cooper Studio, and I would go up there once in a while. They all

worked with tempera. So I thought, well, if they're illustrators and if I'm going to illustrate, maybe I should try this stuff out. Total disaster! In art school, I painted in oil and in watercolor, and drew in charcoal and pencil and pen-and-ink—and that was about it. I did have a brief flirtation with egg tempera because Bob Weaver was using egg tempera, and he did it so beautifully. I abandoned that after a while because it was such a tedious process separating the yolk from the egg and mixing it with little bits of powdered pigment. When acrylics came out, Bob abandoned it too. But still, the basic materials I once used are the things that I use now. I did develop something with that children's book of drawing with conté pencil and then applying oil washes, and going back in with oil pastel and pencil.

Do different media evoke different emotions? It depends on the subject. I think I got more emotion out of the watercolor I used for a *People* magazine project than I could have with oil.

What was the project? Frank Deford, a senior writer for *Sports Illustrated* and a friend of mine, had a daughter named Alex who was born with fatal cystic fibrosis. She lived for eight years. Frank wrote a book about her—*Alex: The Life of a Child*—about her life, and their life with her, and about her rather spiritual death. *People* ran it in two issues, and Frank requested me as the illustrator. It was one of those things where I couldn't be literal; I had to be symbolic. The rosebud is the symbol for Alex. There were certain things expressed. . . . The day Alex died—she died in the afternoon—Frank came down in the morning, one of those cold January mornings, and looked out the back window at the backyard, and there was this huge raven very close to their house. He said out loud, "So this is what the day your child dies looks like." Man, I had a hard time dealing with that story. Knowing Frank and having met Alex made it harder, because I was not only having to please the art director and editor for *People*, I was doing it for Frank. I'd never had that experience—doing something for a magazine but knowing the author well enough for him to have his confidence in me be justified.

You avoided morbid imagery too? Completely. One page I read over and over and over, and finally found one little thing. During the last autumn of her life she wanted to go back to school, but it wasn't possible because she had to keep going to the hospital. Frank wrote something like, "Here we are talking about grades and schoolbuses and so forth, when surely she would never see another spring." So finally, I picked that out and I did a little watercolor of a dogwood blossom.

What kind of work do you do for yourself? It depends on where I am, in a personal sense, at the time. When I got divorced—after twenty years of marriage—I moved into a little cabin. I had to stuff old socks in the cracks to keep the winter out, and I lived there for almost four years. It was really a getting-it-back-together period. I wasn't very successful at all, but what I did was, I had salvaged all these old Mason jars out of a barn, and while I was researching the Remington project, I got interested in the paint quality that he was getting into at a certain point. So I made a series of paintings of these Mason jars. Just sitting and looking at them and painting as accurately as I could. That was very good for me, at the time. Now, I'm into more autobiographical kinds of things. I'm giving up significant thoughts about painting and just enjoying it. The inspiration for that comes from Red Grooms, who is a friend of mine and also grew up in Nashville. Anything goes with him. So that's the inspiration for my new rebelliousness. If I think of a color that should be in a picture, I'll use the opposite color.

What autobiographical explorations are you involved in? I'm doing a painting about a Cuban experience I had when I was twelve years old. I spent some time there with my parents. I played baseball every day with a lot of Cuban kids, and it shocked me, because there was so much poverty. The man who cooked for us invited my brother and me to his house. It had banana-leaf sides and a palm-thatch roof. Inside was a dirt floor and walls made of crates with lettering saying, "Caution: Handle With Care." And in a corner, dug out of the dirt floor, was a hole with mud in it and a huge hog. That was his wealth, that hog. So the hog occupied a most important spot in his house. That really hit me. I left my Cuban friends my baseball glove, my shoes, anything I didn't need for the trip back to Tennessee.

When I went back to Central America for *Sports Illustrated,* years later, I didn't expect to see that again. But I did. Everywhere. Nothing had changed. I made three trips in the late sixties to remote areas of Nicaragua. I knew then that there would be a revolution, because they were all talking about it. It wasn't something dreamed up in Moscow. But the first time I saw the world from a different perspective was as a kid in Cuba. And that's why I'm working on paintings from that period.

You've taught for a long time at Syracuse and the School of Visual Arts and now at the University of Kansas. In what way does teaching help you in your own work? When I hear myself talking to them, critiquing their work, I'm talking to myself as well.

ROBERT ANDREW PARKER

Robert Andrew Parker (born on May 14, 1927, in Norfolk, Virginia) has raised the simple, childlike scribble to a high form of illustration. An unconventional expressionist, using shrimp pink and banana yellow, he imbued illustration with a painterly whimsy. His first major exposure, in Esquire magazine in the early sixties, was a flight of fancy titled "The Imaginary War," a series of battle pictures originally made for his son. Parker has also traveled around the world on journalistic assignments. Hence, he walks a tightrope between the real and the imagined.

I used to buy paperbacks that had ugly covers, and I would make my own. This was during school days, at the Art Institute of Chicago. In addition to painting and print-making by day, I would make covers by night, just as an exercise for myself, not with the intention of being an illustrator. Then, after graduating, I came to New York and taught at the New York School for the Deaf.

What were you teaching? I guess they called it "art." I had deaf children from ages seven to twenty-one. I did that for three years, and then in 1953, I had a show at the Roko Gallery in New York. I was lucky; the Museum of Modern Art bought several pieces, and at the same time, Cipe Pineles came to that show, she liked the work, and asked me to do an illustration for *Seventeen* magazine.

What kind of work was in the show? Was there a theme? They were imaginary portraits of writers. My interests were always literary—in fact, I know a lot more about writing than I do about painting. The title, *Triple Thinkers,* was from an Edmund Wilson essay.

It sounds as though you were illustrating, though. Well, I guess I was. I never thought of them as such. In any case, Cipe Pineles asked me to illustrate a story for *Seventeen,* which went across two pages. I treated it just like a painting. I must have given her thirty versions of it.

I remember seeing something very exciting by you many years ago in Esquire—*scenes of an imaginary war.* I had done battle pictures for my son's bedroom. We were living in Brewster, New York, then, and a friend who used to come up and spend weekends with the family saw those pictures and showed them to Bob Benton, the art director of *Esquire.* Much to our surprise, Benton printed them. It really wasn't a conventional illustration job, they were pictures that I'd already done and boys being what they are, my son liked a lot of detailed stuff. So all the guns, ships, and uniforms were accurate, and there were thousands of soldiers all running across great battlefields amid bombshell bursts.

Illustration of The Bride of Frankenstein *for a series of articles in* The Lamp *on old films bought by Exxon and given to public television. 1978. Etching/aquatint, handcolored with watercolor. Art director: Harry Diamond.*

Illustration of Grand Illusion, *for the same series in* The Lamp. *1978. Art director: Harry Diamond.*

GRAND ILLUSION

Why did you pick the war theme? I always liked the subject. I had collected toy soldiers and so had ready-made models on hand. At that time, my oldest sons and I were casting soldiers and re-creating big battles outside.

With that particular issue of *Esquire*, I got a lot of attention. And oddly enough, it led to a lot of other jobs.

In what manner were you drawing? I don't think it changed that much from my earliest drawings. As a kid, I was sick with TB and in those years there wasn't television, and where we lived in the New Mexico mountains there wasn't even a radio. I entertained myself by making pictographs and big battle scenes. Usually they were done in pencil because I would erase them as the action went by. I still have those sketchbooks: pirates, airplanes, land and sea battles, knights in armor. In 1936, before we moved to New Mexico, we were living in Detroit and had an Italian woman working for us, who'd come in every morning with the latest news of the Ethiopian War—she was a great fan of the fascist legions. I had a very weird view of that war, because she always described the Ethiopians as being cannibals, eating up the brave Italian soldiers. One morning she dictated a picture to me and I drew it. I guess, in a way, that was really my first illustration.

Were you aware of current painting and illustration trends when you were at the Art Institute? I never looked at illustrations then. I never learned any names, even. Although, as I said, I would be aware of it in terms of those paperback covers. However, to get to school I walked through the museum and looked at the pictures every day. I walked through the French impressionist section, and in the morning I'd pass Van Gogh's *Sunny Midi* and a big Chagall, *The Rabbi*. I don't usually like him, but this one was terrific, all black and white, just a bit of red in it. The Art Institute had a Max Beckmann painting I liked very much. And I'd pass a couple of Vlamincks that I liked very much. Also in Chicago, there was a show of Alfred Stieglitz's circle. I got to see Charles Demuth, Marsden Hartley, Arthur Dove, and Georgia O'Keeffe. I loved Demuth's watercolors, which were a big influence on my work.

Did you try to reconcile or combine Demuth and Beckmann into your own work? Yes, and of course, George Grosz enters in too. I also admired Otto Dix's etchings of World War I.

Did the savage content of Grosz and Dix appeal to you, or was it their expressionist style? I think it was both. In Chicago there was an interesting atmosphere, because there were a lot of German immigrants. It's where the proponents of the New Bauhaus settled. The Institute of Design was

there, of course, but not only that, there was something in the Chicago air that was very original. My class included Robert Indiana, Claes Oldenburg, and Leon Golub. We were learning from each other.

You play music now; were you playing then? No, not much. But in high school I didn't do any art at all—I just played jazz. I was playing reeds, clarinet, and soprano sax. In fact, I was in the army's squadron band. Now I play drums.

Does music fuel the painting in any way? I don't think so. There are moments when I use musical themes. For instance, I did a lot of paintings of Thelonious Monk and other players. But generally, one doesn't feed the other. Music is something from which I get tremendous pleasure, and it's something I really miss if I don't play for a while.

How did you get recognized in the illustration world, and what kinds of jobs did you get? Well, in the late fifties I had an agent named Eugenia Lewis, who got me a lot of jobs very quickly. I was amazed when people would use me. I didn't dream that what I did would interest a mass audience. I didn't think my paintings would be accepted as illustrations. So Eugenia Lewis began to get me a lot of little jobs for pharmaceutical companies. They were embarrassingly easy. In fact, what I did was complete them in a few minutes and then hold onto them for a few weeks so it didn't look like I rushed through.

Were those conceptual drawings? Drug companies usually require a certain kind of "poetry." I drew metaphoric people in bed with crippling arthritis. I did allusions for pills like Valium. Then, Leo Lionni at *Fortune*—I guess he saw an early show, too—began to give me some terrific jobs. He sent me to Atlanta, which was the first major reportage job I ever had. The piece was called "The Economic Progress of the Negro," and I got acquainted with the black editor of a newspaper there and met a lot of black workers in the Lockheed plant. At that Lockheed plant in Marietta, Georgia, I was offered a classic line by the P.R. man. He said, "You're not going to come down here and stir up our *nigras*, are you?" Right out of a Karl Malden movie, you know. I didn't write the story, I just did the pictures. After that, Lionni sent me to Guatemala to live with the United Fruit Company in Honduras. My politics have always been leftist, but to see these company people in action is very sobering. United Fruit Company didn't hide how they *ran* that government.

Were you able to convey your feelings through your pictures? I didn't even attempt to do that. It was hard enough just doing the assignment. For one thing, because I was from

*Illustration for the Franklin Library
edition of Joseph Heller's* Catch 22.
1977. Etching/aquatint.

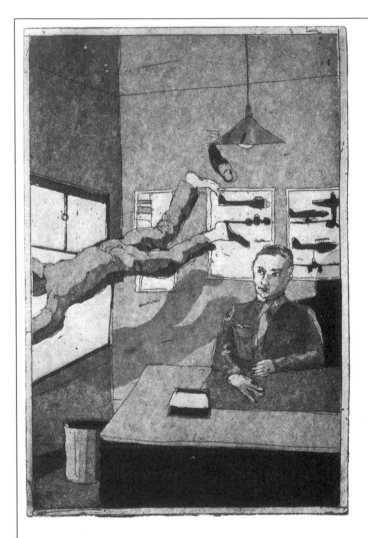

New York and an *artiste,* the attitude of the United Fruit
employees toward me was really unpleasant. I was assigned
to other interesting places, though. Lionni sent me down
in a coal mine, in Pennsylvania; then around the world on
a fact-finding trip for an article called "New Sources of Oil."
I went to North Africa, West Africa, South America, and
Europe. I was gone for months. It was a terrific year to
be in Africa, especially in West Africa, because in 1960
they were all within a few months of independence. West
Africa was really filled with good feelings and hope. It all
came to naught, but in 1960 it looked terrific.

*Did you draw in a sketchbook or did you finish pictures
on the spot?* On the Nigerian job I moved so often that I
kept sketchbooks. They were small ones. I had a camera
then but never used it for the job. I had a funny method—
I was photographing things that I knew I'd use for paintings
when I came home, and in my sketchbook I was drawing
people working on wells or cutting bananas, which I knew
I would probably never use in paintings, for myself. I used
the photographs for years and years afterward. I didn't
work from them very directly, but would go through them
occasionally and be reminded of things. I remember finding
an abandoned truck in Cameroon with a skeleton in the
driver's seat, which was the source for many monoprints
later on.

*You do so many different versions of the same image;
do you know what constitutes a good one?* Well, I think I do.
But I certainly have disagreements with other people. In
the old days, my wife had a terrific eye, and she was a
very good critic. At the end of a day, I would ask her to
look at the day's work. I would already have decided which
one I liked the best, and it was often not the one she chose.

Can you say what makes a good picture? I know there
are some things that I've done that continue to please me.
I rely on accidents, which is probably the other reason why
I do so many in a series.

I'm interested in visual subjects. I'm interested in subjects
of books too. I'm not just reading stories because of the
craft of writing; I'll find myself reading because of a particular
setting or time of day or a place even. I remember taking
Anna Karenina with me when I was in Cameroon, taking
great pleasure in reading it while sitting smack on the
equator. Each page would get wet with sweat, and I would
be reading about steam in a train station in Leningrad or
Moscow. I did it deliberately; I took that book with me
until I was at the very hottest part of that trip.

What kinds of jobs do you prefer? I don't like the idea
of drawing a whole roomful of people typing. I had to do

that recently for some annual report. Occasionally, I'll get something that's absolutely wrong for me. But mostly I get well-thought-out jobs. I did some etchings for Mobil of classic movies—*Metropolis, Dr. Caligari,* and *Potemkin*—and that was truly fun, because it was exactly what I was doing for myself, anyway.

What is the difference for you emotionally between illustration and the work that you do for yourself? When I work for myself, I have to get in a particular frame of mind, which is to get rid of all the other baggage. That's one of the reasons why, I must confess, I do illustrations in a great hurry. I work fast anyway, but I want to get them in and out, and literally cover them up. I would finish them in the studio, then I would put them under the sofa or something, under the chair, so I wouldn't have the image in my mind anymore. Then I would get to the other work. That is what I love, when I can start messing around and do whatever I want to do.

A guy once gave me a huge box of cheesecake photos from the thirties and forties. A great joy of mine is to have no work to do and go through my photos and decide to do some scene from one of them. The freedom to look at something and decide to spend a day or a week or a month making pictures is heaven. I had an illustrated dictionary, and I'd often flip to a page at random; whatever that image was, I would draw. I did one about the word *X-ray,* one about swimmers, one about magic lanterns. Oh, and one about a château; there was a nice picture of a château. Also I flipped it, and there was an image of death, a skeleton which I put over the château; I worked on that for months. I did it over and over as etchings, watercolors, some big oil paintings even.

With what goal? Simply as the ultimate luxury—to learn. I saw a David Hockney show recently, and he's in that enviable position where whatever he does will be hung. A friend said, "I don't know why we're paying to watch him learn how to paint." But on the other hand, I like that about Hockney—he's not afraid to show these things. In this show, there are a couple like Francis Bacon, one like Léger, and some like early Hockney. For the artist to get in a position that whatever he does is interesting to people is terrific. The classic is Picasso—everything he touched turned into art, and he didn't give a damn if it looked like this or that, or who influenced him or anything!

Is that what you try to do? I think that's the ideal. There were years when I really lived like that. I was lucky, because the illustration jobs didn't take much time and they paid well.

Have your illustration assignments influenced or fed other work? Or vice versa? The latter, probably. My personal etchings affected the way I illustrated. Occasionally I get jobs, and I do etchings for them, which is terrific because it makes the jobs interesting again. I'm at a point where I probably do more jobs as etchings than I do in watercolor. I usually hand-color the etchings, so they are rarely just black and white.

What other methods do you use? Watercolors and acrylics, and acrylics used as watercolor, whereby I use them thin. Leonard Bocour (owner of Bocour Paints) and I made a trade years ago, which left me with so many acrylics, I had to use them for everything. I even used them for painting cabinets. So naturally, I use acrylics for watercolors. I feel less cautious with them, since I'm not squeezing out a six-dollar tube. Another reason I use them is that I always use cheap paper. It makes me relax, so I don't feel like I've wasted a six-dollar sheet of paper. I use backs of paper too. Once in England, I bought some books that the store-keeper wrapped in brown paper. When I returned to the hotel I made pictures on the wrapping. Cheap paper is important to me, because it's the only way I can be myself when working. One of the pleasures of being a successful artist like Picasso would be to buy ten thousand sheets of the best paper in the world and use it like garbage.

You once described yourself as being an expressionist with banana yellow and shrimp pink. Where does this come from? My colors and Demuth's watercolors are very similar. I like the transparency of his color.

Is there something that you're trying to convey to the viewer through your art? You've done antiwar imagery, there must be a message in some of your work. It's a paradox. War is disgusting, yet I've enjoyed drawing the details of war—uniforms, equipment, badges, company colors that really interest me as objects. During the Vietnam War, I would be arrested for demonstrating outside of the Pentagon and then I'd come home to my collection of toy soldiers.

Do you have a daily working routine? Ordinarily, I spend

Top: *Album cover for Berlioz, produced by Odyssey Records. 1973. Watercolor on paper. Art director: Henrietta Condak.* Bottom: *Illustration for an article in* The Lamp *on the uses of peat moss. During World War I, the Scottish highlanders used peat as a bandage and in the curing of whisky. 1974. Etching/aquatint, handcolored with watercolor. Art director: Harry Diamond.*

all day in the studio. I work on commercial projects until they're done and then start my other work.

You've initiated many children's books. One about flying, one about fishing in Ireland, and one an update of *Frankenstein.* For a long time, I'd get books about preteen girls and how they learned about nature—the wonder of weeds and grasshoppers and all that. I prefer to illustrate books that are *not* about contemporary life. I enjoyed doing one about an American Indian poet, and I did an anthology of nature poems by William Cole. Speaking of poetry, I made a couple of movies about poets, one about Wilfred Owen and another about Keith Douglas. I did watercolors that were photographed and used as a background for a narration.

You also worked on the film Lust For Life. *What did you do for that?* I made facsimiles of Van Gogh drawings and paintings. Van Gogh's great-grandson objected to Irving Stone's book *Lust for Life* and was instrumental in preventing MGM from photographing any of the paintings. MGM had this martinet, Vincente Minelli, who because there was an obstacle in his path decided, in his petulant way, that he had to have these particular pictures. Actually, he could have done very well with the pictures that had already been photographed. I was asked to make the facsimile drawings that would appear in the film. I'd go with John Rewald to museums, and we would take secret photos and buy catalogs. The studio spared no expense to duplicate the paper and materials, and I made absolutely faithful copies. It's a terrific way to learn an artist's work.

Can you define the role of the illustrator in relation to your own work? An illustrator is somebody who is willing to use what talent he has to illustrate someone else's ideas— a notion that a lot of painters would find objectionable. So I guess that being an illustrator is being willing to submerge your own ego, at least temporarily, and do something that is not of the most immediate personal importance.

How do you think illustration is faring today? Teaching as I do, at Parsons, I realize that for many students the work that I do is not something they're interested in. I think they're interested in things that are so immediate, so new that we can't keep up with the change. When someone like Keith Haring is an influence already, it's mind boggling. He's only been alive a few years. It's like having Mr. T as an influence. So I sort of resent them in a way, and I feel sorry for them in another. I mean, when you can say John Graham to students and they say, "How do you spell his name?" It's depressing. And you could say Max Beckmann, and I have a feeling you could say Degas, and they still would look bored.

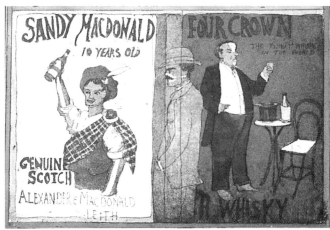

What are some of your current projects? I've been doing a series about Mr. Jiggs, a monkey that entertains in nightclubs. It was done for a summer show at the Terry Dintenfass Gallery. I often create my own fictional situations that I then illustrate. Mr. Jiggs stems from a flyer somebody gave me, showing a monkey who shoots a gun, takes Polaroid photos, sings into a microphone, and drives a motorcycle.

So you're still drawing the way you were drawing as a kid. You're making up stories and playing them out. Yes, we never grow up.

SEYMOUR CHWAST

Seymour Chwast (born August 18, 1931, in the Bronx, New York) was a cofounder of Push Pin Studios. His talent has been augmented by a devout fascination and keen understanding of the history of design and style. Though he works in many media, in seemingly various styles, the work is always distinctive. Chwast is an accomplished editorial, poster, book jacket, and children's book illustrator, whose sense of humor and affinity for the absurd is always present. In 1970 the Louvre mounted a Push Pin retrospective, and in 1985 his own retrospective volume, Seymour Chwast: The Left Handed Designer, was published. He is best characterized as a designer who illustrates. Chwast is a director of The Pushpin Group.

I thought that I was destined to be a cartoonist. I drew funny air battles between the Allies and the Axis and made my own comic books filled with characters I created.

When did you become interested in graphic design? I entered an art class at Abraham Lincoln High School in Brooklyn taught by Leon Friend, a charismatic father figure who gave me an appreciation of typography and graphic design and equated success in these areas with achieving nirvana. Friend introduced me to the great poster designers, and to the work of some of his own students who became accomplished themselves.

Of course, this interest followed you. What did you do when you graduated? I went to Cooper Union in Manhattan. I owe my life and career to that experience. I learned as much from some of my fellow students as I did from the teachers—Milton Glaser, Ed Sorel, and Reynold Ruffins were in my class. I also learned by looking at paintings by artists such as Rouault and Paul Klee. And, perhaps the most significant event at that time was a Ben Shahn exhibition at the Museum of Modern Art—his work proved to be a major influence. The power of his work emerged from the immediacy and directness of his style. It was awkward and somewhat decorative, like primitive art, but the depth of his feeling and his humanity was always evident.

In addition to graphics, were you also studying painting at Cooper Union? I took painting courses, but my paintings ultimately became cartoons. My first woodcut in printmaking class, and my one and only lithograph, were both funny. I couldn't help it. I was very serious about what I was doing, but my work was different from that of most of the other students, who always seemed to be painting onion shapes.

Did you have a distinct style at that time? No. Jan Balet and Roy Doty made decorative figures with rubbery elbows. I did that, too.

Poster advertising Happy Birthday,
Bach, *a book by the artist and Peter
Schickele, published by Doubleday.
1985. Acrylic on chipboard. Editor:
Jim Fitzgerald.*

Top: *Illustration from* A Book of Battles, *a privately printed volume. 1957. Woodcuts handcolored with watercolor.* Bottom: *Illustration from a brochure on country bluegrass music. 1963. Linoleum cut. Produced and handprinted by Mo Leibowitz.*

You once told me that Goya and Daumier affected your work. How did you incorporate them, if at all? Theirs was a passion motivated by their beliefs about politics and society. Their work had bite. They expressed *feeling* you could only get through a print, and that approach conformed to the way I was thinking in those days. I was active politically, and I was sympathetic to radical and pacifist causes.

I could only be good as a nonconformist. Art has to establish its own order and authority while attacking the existing one. Therefore I try to use my assignments as platforms for whatever I have to say, while the client, in turn, uses me.

Who or what were you rebelling against? Around 1950 we were coming to the end of the era of the glorious illustrator—the people who worked for the *Saturday Evening Post* and various women's magazines. Norman Rockwell and the realistic illustrators were, in a sense, the enemy, because their work was too sentimental. Those story-telling renderings were pedestrian compared to the work of George Grosz and Saul Steinberg. Interest was shifting to our interior psyche rather than our exterior surroundings. On another level, I was also concerned with the process of reproduction, how the type looked, how the spread looked, how the work was being used. Design was much more important to me than the illustration alone.

What did you do after leaving college? I worked for George Krikorian at the *New York Times* promotion department as a junior designer. I was able to create my own designs and illustrations, which included woodcuts—rather innovative for that time. I left to work for *Esquire,* my first job failure in a string of failures that included jobs at a design studio and an advertising agency. Herb Lubalin fired me at Sudler and Hennessey because I couldn't do comprehensive sketches. Then I worked for the *House & Garden* and *Glamour* promotion departments for about a year, and around that time Ed Sorel, Reynold Ruffins, and I developed something called the *Push Pin Almanack,* which we mailed out as a bimonthly personal promotion piece. Happily it resulted in a great many freelance assignments. Other illustrators were doing blotters. The almanac format was convenient and novel. While it had its own conventions, we applied our personal typographic sense and did quaint drawings, consistent not only with almanacs but with the style of the time. Each issue was based on a different theme which we edited and designed.

Then you started your own studio? Yes. With Milton and Ed. In those low-tech days of 1954, it took very little capital to go into business. We used the name Push Pin

Studios because the *Almanack* was helping us to gain a reputation.

Did each of you come to Push Pin with an individual style? Was style important to you then? Yes. I made woodcuts, monoprints, and drawings with a Speedball pen, which gave me a bold line. Ed worked with abstract shapes completely different from the way he works now. Milton used a fine pen, resulting in beautiful engraving-style drawings. All of this was in the spirit of decorative illustration.

How did you get interested in woodcuts? I was attracted to the graphic quality of prints while at Cooper. My first woodcut was a depiction of Susanna and the Elders. A little later, when I got involved with typography, I learned how to print type and a woodcut together. I had printed seventy-five copies of a book of woodcuts and antiwar quotations called *A Book of Battles.* I also used it as a style for a number of commercial illustrations.

You were bringing techniques to illustration that were not frequently used. It seems to me that illustration in America, then, was mostly painting and a little drawing. Through the *Push Pin Graphic,* which succeeded the *Almanack,* we were doing illustration that technically and stylistically wasn't being done. Moreover, our typographic style, which was based on traditional approaches, was unique to that period.

Push Pin revived past styles, making them viable again. Would you say that is your most significant contribution to graphic design? It seemed to be. I found that around 1950 designers had come to the end of a period of evolving style. We came to that point because extensive publishing allowed us to observe and digest everything that had been done before. We started borrowing from the past, and that seemed to progress chronologically. First, we were interested in Victoriana, which had a vigor and charm and directness derived from the limitations of the printing methods of the period. Then we discovered art nouveau and art deco. Psychedelia was somewhat original, but it had Jugendstil roots. Now New Wave is a recycling of constructivism with variations. If any original styles have been developed in the last three decades, more time will be needed to provide perspective.

What was it about each of those styles that appealed to you? You still bring them to the fore in certain illustrations. Style in general provides immediate clues to the message. It might signal "elegance" or "modernity," for instance. Putting an old style in a new context is surprising, because certain relationships may be ironic; others may fit perfectly well. But they allow me to make very graphic statements.

In the sixties you contributed to substantive trends in

design and illustration. Were you terribly excited? Well, I had no idea that Push Pin was going to be as influential as it was. I had no overview of how the studio work was evolving or what we were contributing to the fields of illustration or graphic design. I was just doing jobs and allowing everything around to influence my work. For example, surrealism had a marked effect—misplaced objects, the idea of doing fairly realistic situations that are confounded by odd relationships and strangely connected elements.

Essentially, as you were introduced to different approaches, you assimilated and reworked them as part of your own style. Yes, and I was able to do it freely in the *Push Pin Graphic.* The art directors responded to that. They might not have been able to sell our approach to their clients, but us selling it to *them* was half the battle. It proved that we as a studio and individually could think, organize, and translate literary materials into visual statements. But more importantly, I think our work has always been accessible. It used to be called "far out," but if our interpretation was right, the style was unimportant to the client.

In going through those art historical stages, you were definitely educating others to different forms. Were you educating yourself at each stage? I hope we were *inventing* things. That's the joy of it. It's great when a discovery is made and applied to something previously commonplace. One such seemingly unimportant breakthrough was when I did my first drawing with a broken line. Other broken-line artists popped up almost immediately.

You call yourself a designer. But many of your assignments involve illustration with little or no design. I'm a designer who illustrates. I observe the formal principles of design—proportion, harmony, dynamics, symmetry, line, mass, texture—while I am manipulating elements to suit my purposes. The way I articulate the solution is most often with an illustration (which is most often the client's expectation).

You have so many styles. Did you change your approach over the years as much to grow as to get away from imitators? Growth comes out of a creative curiosity to explore and invent. On a banal level, it also satisfies a need to compete with our peers and keep one step ahead of imitators. Drawing and concept cannot be imitated but style *can* and when that occurs vitality is soon gone.

How do you technically approach your drawing? I often battle with the paper. I could never work with a crow quill, but a Speedball or Rapidograph pen enables me to bear down on the paper. My drawing is weak. But I am not as interested in that as I am in making a graphic idea work. That's why I'm less concerned with *finish.* The concept

has always been most important; therefore I look for the style most appropriate to express the idea. Surface, neatness, rendering, and craft interest me less.

Tell me something about your use of typography. Are you more conservative than with illustration? Choice of type style is an aesthetic judgment. My sense of typography is rooted in tradition, so it tends to be conservative. For instance, typographic letterforms were originally designed to fit the limitations of the metal—I disavow ligatures and tend to print my type in black. Understanding the rules means knowing what you can't do. I generally don't illustrate with typography, but rather use it to integrate with or counterbalance the image. That's why I don't use freehand lettering, which competes with it. Sometimes my type may be elegant to go along with a very inelegant drawing.

So with typography, you follow the law, and with the drawing, you follow your intuition? I play with type since it is a design element, but I respect its rules. The rules

First submission and final illustration for an article in The Atlantic *entitled "Living with the Bomb." 1984.* Left: *acrylic on chipboard;* right: *pen and ink with Cellotak. Art director: Judy Garlan.*

Illustration originally created for an IBM calendar but rejected; published in a German newspaper supplement, Die Frankfurter Allgemeine Zeitung. 1984. Pen and ink with Cellotak. Art director: Hans-Georg Pospischil.

of drawing and basic design are also supreme, but they can be stretched and expanded.

How far do you compromise to serve your clients? The client's message must be presented in the clearest manner possible. As long as I take care of the client's needs, I can be as outrageous or as unexpected as I want. My reputation doesn't matter if I don't communicate the message, or if the client has no understanding of what I'm trying to do. After all, my graphic idea and the client's story have to work harmoniously.

How flexible are you when coming up with ideas? Do you struggle? You have to know how far to go. If the idea doesn't gel after a certain amount of struggle, you have to give up. I read once about lateral and vertical ideas. If you dig a hole and it's in the wrong place, digging it deeper isn't going to help. With the lateral idea, you skip over and dig someplace else. Joy, of course, comes with final success.

Where do you get your ideas? Sometimes in the morning, in bed just after the alarm goes off. Other times I use references. Occasionally a photograph or an old poster may spark off a notion. If I'm parodying a style of the past, I will use all the source material necessary to replicate the gestalt of the style.

Do you ever get to a point of frustration or fear that what you are doing is tired? Is there ever the compulsion to do something different for the sake of doing it? It's a prizefight. The creative urge versus constraints either of time or the client or my own laziness or lack of patience.

What are some of your significant jobs? What drawings have indicated specific directions in your work? My book *Happy Birthday, Bach* was a project suited to my interest in styles. It had one likeness of J. S. Bach for every year since his birth, done in a style that related to the locale and events of each year. My cleverness was constantly being tested, and unlike most illustration projects, this book stands completely on its own.

"Whatever Happened to Father?" was a Father's Day story in the *New York Times Magazine*. The focus of the article was the disappearing role of the father in the family household. My interest in the German poster design of Lucien Bernhard and Ludwig Hohlwein was employed. My drawing was of a decorative chair with only a suggestion of the "father." The viewer knows he is distant and uninvolved because he is reading a newspaper. It was uncharacteristic of my work because I had to do without the outline to define form.

With the *My Best Work* poster, I developed a new design style—a subtle broken line that was inspired by an early twentieth-century German comic strip I once saw.

How many assignments do you work on in a year? I'm always working on half a dozen things simultaneously. While I'm working on drawings, I might be conceptualizing and designing in collaboration with other members of my studio.

How can you work on so many things at once? Isn't it hard on your concentration? It's the way I've trained myself—I need deadlines. The worst for me is being down to the last job, because what motivates me is getting on to the next thing.

Do you have taboos? Are there assignments that you wouldn't touch? I wouldn't work for a politician whose philosophy is radically different from mine. And I wouldn't work for the armed forces of any country. Sometimes I take a cigarette assignment and sometimes I don't. It's difficult for me to inject my own biases in deciding when not to take an assignment since, as principal of a studio, people depend on me for their livelihood.

Are there techniques that you wouldn't try? Watercolor and delicate pen work require craftsmanship and a drawing ability I do not have. I haven't done an airbrush illustration since I lost a poster contest in high school. However, there

Top: *Illustration for a poster promoting the Simpson Paper company, showing connections in one's personal or professional life. 1984. Acrylic on chipboard. Art director: James Cross.*
Bottom: *Illustration for a poster promoting* Forbes *magazine. 1985. Pen and ink with Cellotak. Doremus & Company; art director: Paul Shields.*

are aspects in all styles that I can respond to.

What does your drawing table look like when you're working? I make a lot of preparation sketches, but I throw them away as soon as the work is complete. I seem to be constantly surrounded by paper. Generally, unless it's a poster, I work full size, and about four minutes into the assignment, when I realize I'll never draw again, I start making thumbnails, and generally an idea forms. Then it becomes necessary for me to go back to full size again and hope that I can keep some of the energy that was in the thumbnail. As soon as I have a finished drawing, I get rid of all my sketches as quickly as possible.

Are you insecure about losing the gift? Even though there's a history of achieving the right solution most of the time? But that's it. With the *last* drawing, I've done my *last* good idea. It's a struggle, since everything's been done. I imagine for younger artists it's going to be harder. They have to invent something completely different.

Do you feel you've grown up as an artist? I hope not. You should never lose the urge to be playful. I mean using ideas that may seem arbitrary to carry you from one place to another for no apparent reason. Keeping that "youthful" open mind is the only way to make discoveries.

Do you feel you're communicating a point of view? What I do *is* my point of view. It pleases me that my work, including my idiosyncrasies, is understood and that it creates a bond with others.

Does graphic design serve you in that way? I love working with media, working with printing papers, finding new methods of printing. I am still amazed and get great satisfaction in seeing a drawing that I had done the day before printed in the *New York Times.* My work, as a commercial artist, seen by millions, gives me satisfaction that "fine" art cannot supply. Besides, since the sixties there have been so many crossovers that the line between fine and applied art has become blurred. The only real difference between them is the intent.

Did you ever want to be a gallery artist? Oh, no. I found that I needed a message or literary reference to react to. Solving aesthetic problems was either beyond me or else seemed self-indulgent, considering my working class background.

What is different with your work today vis-à-vis the past? What have you learned? What would you still like to accomplish? What I had in the past that I no longer have is innocence. I've been to too many shows and seen too many annuals. I've exchanged that innocence for professionalism. I would like to have both.

Poster for the artist's exhibition at Galerie Bartsch et Chariau in Munich. 1984. Colored pencil on chipboard.

MILTON GLASER

Milton Glaser (born on June 26, 1929, in the Bronx, New York) was a cofounder of Push Pin Studios. While in Italy as a student of Morandi, he learned the techniques of the master printmakers, which influenced his own historically rooted drawings. In the mid-fifties, a period when design and illustration were poles apart, he wed the two forms. Glaser is indeed a Renaissance man, practicing all aspects of applied art. His numerous typeface designs derive from the playful spirit exercised in his illustration. Now the proprietor of his own design firm, Milton Glaser, Inc., he has blazed new paths for the illustrator/designer through the complete design of supermarkets and restaurants, products and textiles.

I have a precise picture of the moment I wanted to become an artist. I may have had some inclination before that, but the crystallization of it happened when I was five and my cousin, who probably was ten or fifteen years older than I was, came into the house with a brown paper bag, and he said, "Do you want to see a pigeon?" I thought he had a pigeon in the bag, and said, "Yes." He took a pencil out of his pocket, and he drew a pigeon on the side of the bag. Two things occurred. One was the expectation of seeing somebody draw a pigeon; and two, it was the first time I had actually ever observed someone make a drawing that looked like the actual object—as opposed to my own rudimentary drawing. I was literally struck speechless. It seemed a miraculous occurrence, the creation of life, and I have never recovered from that experience. I am still astonished when miracles occur in the process of creating form. At that moment, I knew that my entire life would be involved in the question of trying to create magic, although I didn't know exactly what that meant.

How did you build upon that? That interest developed into sort of an incessant pattern of drawing, which was reinforced in school when I became the class artist in kindergarten. You always could get out of the less interesting assignments by being the class artist. It was a position of privilege. So, early on I made an internal decision, and then the world confirmed and encouraged that decision. I basically never deviated from that.

Were you looking at art? I was looking at Walt Disney and the comics. By the time I was thirteen, I had already done life drawing in a class that was conducted by Moses and Raphael Soyer.

Was that a private class? They had a life drawing class on the weekends, and when I was thirteen I started going. Then I went to the High School of Music and Art, which

Page that features Gustav Klimt from Zanders feinpapier *calendar entitled* Masters of Color. *1984. Pencil and watercolor. Art director: Milton Glaser.*

ALBERT KING MASTERWORKS

(or, The Velvet Bulldozer)

When Albert King hooked up with Memphis, Tennessee's super-hot Stax label in 1966 and began making singles with backing by Booker T. and the MG's and the Memphis Horns, fortune began to smile on him. He was not a youngster. He was born near Indianola, Mississippi, which is the heart of the Delta, blues country, in either 1923 or 1924, and he made his first records in Chicago in 1953, thirteen years before the beginning of his fortuitous association with Stax. But it was at Stax that his mature playing and singing and the definitive soul rhythm section of the sixties clicked together to produce music that would fundamentally alter the mainstream of white rock as well as the sound of commercial blues within a few years' time. In 1968, Stax collected King's best singles of the preceding two years on an album, *Born Under A Bad Sign.* It was the most influential blues album of its era. Within months, Eric Clapton and Cream were regurgitating chunks of it whole (e.g. "Strange Brew" and their own "Born Under A Bad Sign") and rockers everywhere were scurrying into their woodsheds to learn King's songs and his signature guitar licks.

Seven selections from the *Born Under A Bad Sign* album are reissued in this collection: "Personal Manager," "The Very Thought of You," "Born Under A Bad Sign" itself, "Laundromat Blues," "Kansas City," "Crosscut Saw," and "As The Years Go Passing By." Since *Born Under A Bad Sign* hasn't been available in this country for a number of years, these tracks, the backbone of any good modern blues collection, are worth the price of admission all by themselves. But there is more here, lots more— Albert King with the great Allen Toussaint's New Orleans band ("Angel of Mercy" and Toussaint's "We All Wanna Boogie,") King with several other groupings of musicians, updating his backdrops, as he always has, while playing the natural blues.

The development of King Albert's music, and especially of his recordings, is the ultimate case study in the continuing relevance of the blues, which keeps hanging in there with an almost uncanny tenacity as changing fashions swirl around it. To begin with,

(Continued on inside)

was terrific. I remember the first art class I went to. The instructor introduced us to the ideas behind Cézanne's com-positions. For a fifteen-year-old, that was pretty heady stuff. But it was a very sophisticated school. It provided a place for gifted young people to be brought together by virtue of talent. You really had an extraordinary cross-section of economic groups. It was the sort of image that you got in 1940s movies: the blacks, the Puerto Ricans, the Jewish kids, the rich, the poor, all living together in perfect harmony united by a love of art. And there it really happened. It was a fantastic opportunity for cross-fertilization. Also it was one of the reasons that I developed my lifelong interest in music. It was just a wonderful preparation for any future. I found that as a result of that preparation, I had an advantage going into Cooper Union afterward.

Was it a direct line to Cooper? What actually happened at Music and Art was that the dean of Pratt Institute came to look for possible scholarship candidates. He saw my portfolio and said, "Young man, I'd like to give you a four-year scholarship to Pratt Institute." And I said, "Fine," and didn't apply anywhere else. Then I took the entrance examination and failed. I went to the dean and reminded him that he gave me a scholarship. To which he said, "I'm not going to let you in the school if you can't even pass the entrance exam." I took the night school entrance exam and I failed that too. My understanding is that I am the only person in history who has ever failed the Pratt Night School entrance exam. As a result I went to Brooklyn College for about two months, which meant traveling four hours a day on the subway back and forth. I was spending a quarter of my life underground. I decided that I would take a year off, get a job, and take the Cooper Union test. I found a job in a small packaging outfit where I worked as an apprentice. By the end of the year they made me the art director, although as the art director I was still doing everything the apprentice had to do; it was just me and two bosses. There was some great benefit, actually, in not going directly to Cooper Union, and having a little job that began orienting me toward what I might be doing in the future. Moreover, that year I went to night class at the Art Students League.

Did you know what was going on in illustration at that time? I was looking at the same sort of things that young people look at now, such as the *Art Directors' Annual.* I was interested in illustration and studied with Howard Trafton at the league.

Did you want to be an illustrator rather than a painter? In those days I basically wanted to be an illustrator. I was

always very interested in comic art of various kinds.

What about the comics interested you? I loved, and still do, storytelling and narration through pictures. My interest was always in that and in wanting to pictorialize literature.

I wanted to be a comic-strip artist. I remember even going to see a guy named Shepherd, who was an illustrator, who worked on Forty-Sixth Street in a really dingy walk-up studio, one of those filthy places with a window looking out over Times Square. However, I thought it was the most glamorous place on earth. I brought a strip that I had prepared for him. He looked at it and he said, "Good work, kid. You'd better use a ruler to rule those panels." That was the end of my comics career.

So the next step was higher education? Actually, that

53

Poster for the School of Visual Arts entitled Surface. Texture. Form. Line. Color. Only Words until an Artist Uses Them. *1985. Cut paper and masking tape. Photograph by Mathew Klein. Art director: Milton Glaser.*

Surface. Texture. Form. Line. Color.

Only Words, Until an Artist Uses Them.

School of Visual Arts

was probably when I was a teenager and still in high school. But by the time I was ready to enter Cooper, I had gained some skills. Between working for a year and the very good education I got at Music and Art, I found that when I entered Cooper I had an advantage over many of the entering students, because they had not been as well trained, particularly not in art history.

How did your art history background help you? I was always interested in it, one way or another. They taught it at Music and Art, and they continued to teach it at Cooper. But my interest in art history, I must say, really emerged after I had left Cooper Union, probably when I began living in Italy. In any case, my education at Cooper Union broadened my point of view about the relationship between design and illustration, and I realized that in some ways I was more interested in some reconciliation between those two than I was in either one as a pure form.

Was this reconciliation of illustration and design something new at the time? I think so, because both activities were highly parochialized. Illustrators, as you know, did illustration; designers did design. I was never quite happy with that, partially because my interest was in both areas, and partially because I didn't understand the separation very well, particularly since illustrators were always faced with the problem of putting their work in context. When the context wasn't right, it could really damage the work. In fact, one of the things that gave me my start was designing book jackets, where the necessity for putting illustration and design together was the main issue. One of the people at Cooper who encouraged me in that path was George Salter, the great book designer. I wasn't attracted by his illustration at the time, but his integrity and intelligence were inspiring. His work was a demonstration of how one could integrate illustrative and lettering ideas.

Did you understand the rules of typography at that time? Some of them. Cooper taught typography, and I had developed an interest in that earlier, while I was still in high school. Typography is one of the things that takes longest to learn— it's really a lifetime's work. But the beginnings certainly were there. At that time my fellow students Reynold Ruffins, Ed Sorel, Seymour Chwast, and others shared the same interest.

You studied with Giorgio Morandi, didn't you? For almost two years. I lived in Bologna and during that period traveled all through Europe. I did a tremendous amount of drawing from observation in sketchbooks, some of which served as preparation for etchings.

I understand that it was sketching, but did you draw with a style or a personality? I don't think I had any particular style. It was the kind of drawing that you do when you want to make notes on what something looked like. My approach to style was influenced by my etching. I always cross-hatched. One of my early models was Rembrandt. The truth of the matter is, when I was at Cooper, even though I had the reputation of being a good draftsman, I knew I couldn't draw, and I realized I was going to have to do something very fundamental about understanding how forms are created in space through light and shade. During my time in Bologna I went to the academy and did academic drawing from Roman plaster casts.

It's the kind of experience that might have led away from commercial art, but it didn't have that effect. I never had

Peace poster, HEIWA, *published by the Shoshin Society. 1985. Marker, colored inks and dyes, watercolor, and crayon. Art director: Milton Glaser.*

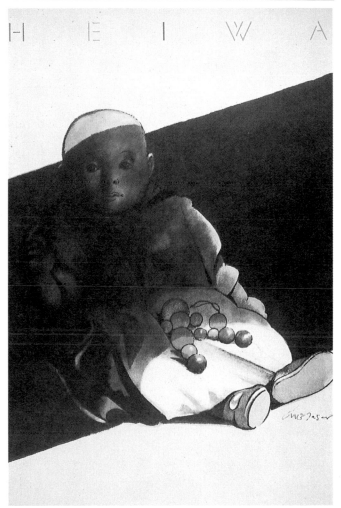

any idea of doing anything except applied arts. I never had any idea of being a painter or fine artist. While I didn't do any jobs when I lived in Europe, I always knew I was accumulating material for some future applied usage. I never thought of it as work independent of some other kind of application. So it didn't lead me anywhere except back here.

When you came back, the others had already started the Almanack? Reynold, Seymour, and Eddie had started the *Push Pin Almanack.* The *Graphic* we started together.

Did you join forces right away upon returning? Yes. They invited me to come back and work with them on the *Almanack.* I also did some work freelance for the same packaging people, who then agreed to represent us as a studio. We worked at night for a while, then we were able to switch to a daytime operation.

Did you have a graphic personality then? It was beginning. There was a certain way of drawing that was personal. But it really began to materialize early in the fifties, when I became interested in the work of Felix Vallotton. My earliest graphic work showed the obvious influence of art nouveau. A lot of my work is historically referential, as you know.

Picasso was a big influence, particularly his use of metamorphosis as an idea. The thing that really impressed me more than anything else was a single work of Picasso's, a cycle of twelve etchings of bulls done as an illustration for Balzac's *Hidden Masterpiece.* That work got me on a lifelong track. It was the idea that as a way of working there was no distinction between naturalism and abstraction except the issue of quality. One could do a great naturalistic piece or a great abstract piece, without having to take sides. There wasn't a question of loyalty to style. Early on, I didn't feel that there was any singular stylistic truth.

There was emotional truth, though. And there was a truth of quality. You look at something and say it's good or it's not good. You have to remember at that time, the fifties, the power of the Bauhaus and the idea of reductive form and clarity was the prevailing idiom. Truth resided in "honest" simplification. I disagreed with that, intuitively, and actually felt there was no single system under which either life or art could be subsumed. In retrospect, it was unusual at the time, because the ideology of the moment was extremely powerful.

Did that also reinforce your historicism? I'm not sure. I had always liked to read about design issues, and I've always been interested in how far you could push the idiom. It seemed to me that the entire history of the world could be used as a resource for visual material. I couldn't understand why people thought that they could only use what was

available over a fifteen-year period. I guess I have always groped toward solutions in direct response to the special nature of the given literary material. I know that you can't speak the same language to every audience. You basically have to respond to the peculiarity of that audience in relationship to the message you wish to convey. If your form is ideologically inflexible and you don't moderate it, something usually gets lost in the process. Design is fundamentally a dialectic; it's not a channel. And that has very much affected the way I work and what I do. Throughout my life, I have never believed that anything I've done is the truth, but rather a way of doing a job.

Did you have problems in conveying this point of view to the client? You mean changing my approach to work? No. Because I started that way. In the beginning, I didn't have

much skill, so I was doing what I could do. But I found that as I changed what I was doing, I generally didn't meet any resistance. Occasionally, as you know, particularly in terms of the kind of work that goes on at agencies, they say, "Well, here's a sample of what you did twelve years ago; do it," which I think is a problem for everybody. But I have found that I've been able to work around that problem and surprise people.

So you are always in a transitional state? Sometimes more than other times. But your themes tend to return, and your hand and eye are still the same, and your color preferences remain fairly fixed, and your neurological system is the same. Things do recur; there's no question about that.

Do you have a recurring vocabulary? I once did a content analysis of my imagery. There were only ten or twelve things that turn up over and over again. But you can make a lot of combinations of those things.

As you grew, Push Pin grew as well. Were you aware of its influence? After we had the show at the Louvre, people began to refer to the "Push Pin Style," things were described as "Push-Pinny." At that time I realized we were having an effect.

Could you define what that style was? Well, it wasn't a simple thing. Perhaps what people were beginning to identify out of our collective work was a heightened sense of color and the use of flat shapes. That, by the way, was a means of increasing our productivity, because we would do a drawing and then have somebody else fill it in, or do five drawings and have five people fill them in. It was the same reason that the same method was used in the comics or in animation.

You didn't feel compromised by the fact that someone else would be filling in the blanks. Not at all. No more than you'd feel compromised by using color-aid paper instead of paint, or having someone else paste the type into a layout. Because you're still making all the judgments of what the fill-in, the shape, or the form will be. Instead of a mechanical instrument, you're using another person to do it. If there weren't those personal judgments, I might have been compromised.

Were you entering more into other forms of design, such as typography? All during those years, we were really working between design and illustration, to differing degrees. Seymour and I both designed a number of alphabets, and we began to use type in a characteristic way, sort of Victorian at first and then with more variety. Also, in the same way that we began to challenge some of the assumptions about illustration, we began to challenge some of the assumptions

Finished poster, A View from an English Cottage into a French Garden with Japanese Objects through American Eyes, *for Conran's Mothercare. 1984. Pen and ink and Cellotak. Art director: Milton Glaser.*

about the different uses of typography.

What were some of those assumptions? The elastic nature of letterforms. What could be combined with what. How much they could be transformed. How much old material you could use with new material. Pushing the bounds of legibility.

Were you wed to the strict, classical rules of typography? I don't think so. There were certain things that you basically had to know, such as how long a line of type could be before you stopped reading it, and how to make a stagger look right. Mainly we were interested in typography as an expressive tool.

Was it an exciting time for you? It was a great time for all of us. It was a great learning time. It was also a time of tremendous graphic art activity in general. Psychedelia was being invented in San Francisco, and there was a tremendous vitality in illustration and design, perhaps more than there is today, in the sense that the barriers were being broken.

Your Life *magazine cover heralding the sixties youth culture was a benchmark in visual experience for the mass of America. What were the other things that you did then that were breakthroughs?* That's a hard question. The Dylan poster, by virtue of the fact that it was Bob Dylan, I think, as much as anything else, had a strong effect. John van Hammersveld wrote at the beginning of his airbrush book that the Dylan poster opened a new direction for him. It wasn't uncharacteristic of what I was doing at the time, but for some reason, that piece seemed to extend the language a bit.

Well, you took an icon and you made it a totem. I must say that while I was doing it, it seemed like everything else I was doing. There was a little something that made me like it. But its effect was cumulative. It took a while for it to mean anything. It wasn't for a year or two after I had done it that I began to get some feedback about it being significant. But I don't know how conscious anyone is that what they're doing is later going to have some impact or effect.

What were the directions in which you were going? The watercolors, for instance, are soft and friendly. The crosshatch had more graphic power, let's say. What were the changes in mood that came out as graphic changes? Well, I don't know if that's easily answered. Some of it is just the change of material, black-and-white, ink and a pen just produces different emotional and textural qualities than watercolors. Some of the work was simply done in response to the peculiarity of the material. Sometimes it's the nature of the

material, but sometimes you choose that material—I'm talking about a medium. You choose it because it seems more appropriate than one thing or another. Sometimes you change because the other doesn't work.

Do you try to choose your assignment material as well, or do you take assignments as they come? I don't take assignments that don't make sense to me anymore. I don't take assignments where the job is already done before I get it, which is really what most advertising is about.

And, you won't repeat yourself. Well, I have repeated myself, for sure. But I try to avoid doing it too frequently. I just did a piece for a store, for Conran's, which is done in the manner that I worked in twenty years ago. That's what I meant about we're all victims of our neurological system. I don't have any problems about redoing things if I can keep it alive for myself.

The Conran's piece is an Indian motif. What are some other influences? Islamic and Indian painting—Tantric painting in particular—with regard to the sense of form and color. Certainly Japanese woodcuts and Chinese brush painting. In terms of an attitude toward drawing, certainly Rembrandt as a draftsman. The work of Tiepolo and Canaletto. They're all slices of different kinds of work that engage my interest.

I understand you to say that each influence is a step along the way. Well, they are, but there isn't a sense of progression. They are just different things that influenced me at different times and continue to influence me. Also, I've always had this instinct to feel that when my work was thoroughly understood, it was time to move on to something else.

What do you mean, "thoroughly understood"? When

Personal painting entitled Shirley, Annie, *and* Mr. Hoffman, *used for a benefit. 1982. Watercolor, Craypas, colored pencil, and pen and ink.*

everything about it is predictable to me and to others. I left Push Pin basically because I felt trapped by Push Pin's history, and I felt there was too much understanding of what Push Pin knew and how they worked. And I felt very much that when people approached me there, the expectation was too fixed about what they would get. Push Pin was so publicized during the seventies, and the work that we produced was so well known, that I felt it was a burden.

Did you change radically after leaving Push Pin? My work is very different than it was. Partly because the nature of the work has changed; it's totally out of illustration, in many cases, sometimes even out of the usual definition of design. I'm doing some industrial design, I'm designing some furniture, I'm doing graphic design as a part of designing supermarkets. So, from Push Pin I moved on to other subjects, as well as other techniques. Certainly, a lot of the things that I do still refer back to the same idiom

because I'm obviously the same person.

Have you, through the work, tried to convey any message? I think there is, in the best work, a spiritual message. That has to do, in a general sense, with the meaning of a well-made object. I don't know what that meaning is, and it's like saying, "Well, what's the purpose of life?" There is some meaning in an object that is well made, whatever "well made" means. But it is not a meaning that is easy to describe.

There is so much work that you do, would you pinpoint one area as being more satisfying than other areas? Well, I like everything for a short time.

How short? Sometimes it's a week. Sometimes a year. But the thing I've discovered about myself is that what keeps me alive is variety and change and doing things that I'm not very good at as well as things that I'm accomplished at. So I like stumbling around in areas where I'm not terribly

Call for entries for the AIGA Book Show. 1983. India ink, marker, and torn paper. Art director: Milton Glaser.

knowledgeable. I just finished designing a lamp; I've never done it before, so I don't know whether it's a very good lamp, but I loved the act of doing it.

Are there other projects like this? Well, for Aurora, a restaurant that we're working on, I'm designing the rug, the lighting fixtures, and the plates—as well as the graphics.

What is the process of doing that? A lot of the things that I do have started with the word, in this case, *Aurora,* and once that was set, it became a question of dealing with the idea of light.

Could one say that you're illustrating *this restaurant?* Yes, you'd say that, if people didn't think that in illustration you meant naturalistic forms. People don't understand that you can illustrate in an abstract way. I am illustrating the idea of Aurora as the dawn.

Are there things that you do just for play? I'm always drawing something. But I've never thought of those as sort of independent works; I always think of them as preliminary for something that I'm going to use some day.

Do you keep a reference? I have loads of notebooks and sketches. Hundreds of drawings I've done while traveling.

Is there a desire to do something now that you haven't done? Yeah. I really would like to do a Mozart opera, do the sets and costumes.

Has music influenced your work? I think so. When I look at my posters, about 80 percent of them are about music. It's not so much that I'd like to do any specific sort of work, but I would like to keep working in areas where the possibility for breadth of activity is intriguing. Like the idea of, say, the restaurant thing, where you do the logo and the menus and the tabletop and the rugs and the lighting. I like that unifying vision brought to a complex issue. That's why the work on the supermarkets has been so interesting.

Is there an element of power in that kind of overall design? Power is an interesting word, because if you reduce its pejorative qualities and try to find out what it means, you'll discover it means the ability to carry out a plan. If you want to define the word *design,* you discover it is identical. Design and power, in fact, have exactly the same description. So I think if you're interested in design, you're interested in power, at least in terms of design. I'm not interested in power over others, but I am interested in having the ability to carry out my plans. And I don't think you can do that without recognizing the relationship between power and design.

Do you feel that what you are doing in graphic design, illustration, and industrial design is art? It most assuredly isn't. But since art is basically a historical agreement, whether

it is or not is an irrelevancy. If somebody in a hundred years says, "You know, that wasn't design, that was art," and gets enough people to agree, then that's fine. I don't know why people get themselves crazy about that issue. I mean, what it is at the moment is work. And if we leave it at that and just say it's good work or bad work or extraordinary work or mediocre work, that seems to be enough. But there's some impulse in people, and it's very mischievous, to want to characterize the work either as being art or not being art. Which is a nonsensical and useless activity. That definition doesn't serve anybody. It's also an illusion. But there's a social meaning behind it, and ultimately there is something about the nature of art that people need in their lives. I say that there should be an art exam for people, just for the right to call themselves artists—it wouldn't give you any other guarantee—if you're a brain surgeon, you have to pass a test. If you're an artist, you should be able to pass a test, too, at least something rudimentary and simple, but nobody seems to want to.

EDWARD SOREL

Edward Sorel (born on March 26, 1929 in the Bronx, New York) was a cofounder of Push Pin Studios. Unable to "work and play well with others," he was peripatetic, leaving one job after another until settling down as a freelance illustrator. When illustration rather than design became a focus, his conceptual approach changed, his caricatural skills emerged, and he became one of the most acerbic graphic commentators in America—one of the critical triumverate, including David Levine and Jules Feiffer. He has published two collections of political cartoons, Making the World Safe for Hypocrisy *in 1972 and* Superpen *in 1978. During the Vietnam and Watergate crises, Sorel's drawings were rallying points for a disillusioned constituency. Currently, he employs his finely tuned writing and drawing skills in the creation of visual essays on subjects as diverse as vintage movies and famous first encounters.*

My first memories of creativity are drawing with crayon on shirt cardboard.

Did you decide then to pursue art into adult life? No. My ambition in life was simply to leave home. All my waking moments were devoted to planning for that moment. I had no interest in anything else.

So art was a means to an end. I didn't realize it at the time. If I had realized that one could make money with art, I certainly would have taken it more seriously.

Since you went to the High School of Music and Art in New York, you must have had some idea that you wanted to do something in the field. I had four aunts, one of whom made it into the outside world. She had heard of Music and Art and brought the word back to our *shtetl* in the Bronx. So I took the test and passed. The very first day of my very first art course, I was instructed to do a full face, divide it in half, then divide all the planes in the face, and then color each plane of the face a different color. In other words, turn a face into an abstraction. For the next four years at Music and Art I was untaught how to draw.

Were you aware of illustration? What you have to remember is that in the late forties and early fifties, illustration was the lowest form of graphic art. When you said to somebody that you were an illustrator, it conjured up visions of Coby Whitmore, Steve Dohanos, and Norman Rockwell. Illustration was what was done in the *Saturday Evening Post* and *Colliers*. It was unsophisticated. The elite of the field were the designers. And Cooper Union, which I also attended, considered drawing very old-fashioned. So after four years at Music and Art and three years at Cooper

Illustration entitled The Twentieth Century Limited *for the* American Heritage *essay "Lost Pleasures," text and pictures by Edward Sorel. 1984. Ink and watercolor on board. Art director: Murray Belsky.*

Top: *Drawing of Nicholas Chauvin (whence the word* chauvinism *derives) from Nancy Caldwell Sorel's* Word People, *published by American Heritage Press. 1970. Pen and ink.*
Bottom: *Illustration from an essay entitled "Remainder Bound," a parody of current best-sellers, which appeared in* New York *magazine. 1980. Pen and ink and watercolor on illustration board. Art director: Walter Bernard.*

Union, I no longer knew how to draw.

Before going to school, what art inspired you? Well, there was "Dick Tracy" and other newspaper comics. I was also fascinated by New York genre painting: Reginald Marsh, Edward Hopper.

Once in Cooper, did anything stimulate you? From what you're saying, it seems your memory is mostly based on resentment. The greatest value of an art school is that it keeps you looking at art. It puts you close to talented contemporaries. I learned more from Seymour Chwast and Milton Glaser, who were in my class, than I did from any of my teachers. Late teens and early twenties is a painful age for most people, so I don't want to blame too much of my unhappiness at the time on Cooper Union.

If being an illustrator was the bottom of the barrel, what made you become one? I had no intention of becoming an illustrator. During college, I was still operating on my life's ambition to leave home. I went to school because afterward I would get a job and be able to have my own apartment. I assumed that I would be able to get a job doing mechanicals and someday make $85 a week. You can't always do what you want. I was incapable of doing mechanicals. I remember vividly cutting type on an illustration board and actually cutting into the table. This suggested I had a rather heavy hand for mechanicals. I got fired from eleven jobs my first year out of school. But, interestingly, it was a time when very talented people didn't stay at one job very long. So when I'd go for a job and said that I'd had eleven jobs in one year, they assumed I was one of the talented "hotshots." Every time I'd get fired, I'd get a higher paying job.

What were some of the jobs? I did mechanicals at William D. McAdam's agency; that was my first job, and I made $45 a week. I got fired because one of their direct-mail pieces was printed with my thumbprint over the type. Then I worked at a printing plant in New Jersey, and they had me designing annual reports. It took me two weeks to design an annual report that they usually did in three hours. I got fired after that. Job number eleven was working as an assistant art director at *Esquire* magazine doing editorial layout. After I had been working at *Esquire* for a couple of weeks, my old classmate Seymour Chwast was hired. Bored by the work there, he and I attempted to get some freelance work by sending out a promotion piece.

That means at this point you knew you wanted to do illustration? I knew I wanted to do illustration, which is ironic since I could no longer draw. All I could do after three years at Cooper Union was a two-dimensional kind

Sketch entitled The Watergate Shoot-out, *for* Ramparts. *1973. Pen and ink and watercolor on board. Art director: Dugald Stermer.*

of illustration. The closest thing to it would be Stuart Davis. Essentially it was a Bauhaus style. Cooper Union, like every other art school in the world, was at least twenty years behind the times. They were still teaching Bauhaus in 1951. My "style" was completely decorative, having absolutely nothing to do with drawing. Basically, art school had taken a kid who loved to draw detail and gesture and had turned him into a designer. For the first *Push Pin Almanack,* which is the mailer Seymour and I did, I used that Bauhaus technique. Aside from not being particularly amusing, this technique was also incredibly time consuming. I have a theory about people who do art that takes a long time: they really don't want to have time for personal relationships. My guess is, that at the age of twenty-four, I just wanted to be alone, and I had chosen for myself a style that was extremely time consuming and mechanical, because I wanted to have nothing to do with people. It seems to me that there is a perfect correlation between my art getting warmer, spontaneous, and less time consuming and my better relations with people.

What was the response to the Almanack? It was fairly good. It would not have been good enough to make us leave our jobs and start freelancing, except that Seymour and I got fired on the same day. Thanks to unemployment insurance, we were able to start a studio. Since my style was extremely uncommercial, I was the salesman for Push Pin during the first year. We all divided whatever income came in. Working next to Seymour and Milton, I gradually went back to drawing with pen and ink. It frightens me to think of what would have happened if I hadn't had the opportunity of working with them. I suspect I would have remained a designer, would have spent the rest of my life in an advertising agency.

At what point did your own drawings begin to form? I stayed at Push Pin for two years and quit on the day the studio moved from a cold-water flat on Seventeenth Street to lovely quarters on fashionable East Fifty-seventh Street. My accountant said it was a poverty wish. There were a lot of personal reasons, but probably the simplest explanation is that I do not work and play well with others. I've always

Finished comic strip for a regular feature in Penthouse *entitled "Parting Shot." 1985. Pen and ink on paper. Art director: Frank Devino.*

been a solitary person. Moreover, I felt that I wasn't contributing a third of the income, or a third of the inspiration, or a third of anything to Push Pin Studios. Clearly, it was Milton and Seymour's ingenuity that was responsible for its immense success. So I decided I would just cut out. I went to work for Bill Golden, art director at CBS, where I found I was just as incompetent as ever, except at a higher level.

Were you working as a designer? Yes, it was design work. After working at CBS, I like to think that I was a

Sketch for the comic strip shown on page 64. 1985. Pen and ink.

good designer. Everything I learned about type, I learned there. There were all these marvelous rules of typography that no one ever bothered to teach me and which proved valuable when I began to freelance.

This is obviously leading into your own debut as an illustrator. How did that happen? Well, as I said, I could not work and play well with others. I left CBS to take a job as an art director at an advertising agency, and I simply hated it. I hated the idea of a job. Who's to explain why some people love to get up at the same time every morning and others can't? I cannot stand routine. I am willing to accept working through the night or getting up at five o'clock and not having any weekends, or any financial security, for the marvelous privilege of being able to do things when I want to do them. I did not, at first, become an illustrator; what I became was a freelancer. I was perfectly happy to do freelance design as well as illustration, except that I lived on Eighty-seventh Street and there weren't any photostat houses in the neighborhood. And because it was too much trouble to go downtown to get photostats, I decided to become an illustrator instead of a designer. I'd say I got by for the first ten years of freelancing because I was able to copy anybody's style. I had no personal vision, but I had good hands.

Whose styles did you copy most? I copied Kurt Weihs, who was an art director at CBS and who drew with a kind of stitched pencil line, and I was still influenced by Milton's cross-hatched pictures. Because I was politically aware and wanted to do political commentary, I found that the decorative styles, which supported me as a freelance artist, were inappropriate.

What caused your political enlightenment? I grew up poor and realized that other people were rich. This made me sore as hell. Also, I went to school at the height of the McCarthy period, or at the beginning of the McCarthy period when the worst was yet to come. I saw the fear, especially among the designers and architects at Cooper. The artists were courageous only because they had nothing to lose. I am sure that if they were going to work for large corporations, they would have been every bit as frightened as the engineers and the architects. I think about half my political stuff is in some way or other a cry against authority.

In order to do political work, you had to change your approach. Decorative art techniques were not going to be convincing in a polemical situation. The two-dimensional illustrations that I did for a few years were impersonal. They revealed nothing about me. As soon as you do a pen-and-ink drawing, you reveal more of yourself.

Why is that? I think it's because it's much closer to signature. It can be analyzed. If you have a tight line, it's just possible that you're a deliberate or overly neat person. If you have a loose line, maybe you're spontaneous and a slob. As soon as you start illustrating ideas as opposed to being decorative, you reveal yourself. And clearly, to my way of thinking, it is a higher form of art. The purpose of art is to reveal the person who is doing it, whether it is music or writing or art. It was really very traumatic for me to go from the cold design illustration into something personal. And in point of fact, for the very first *Almanack*, I did all these flat, two-dimensional illustrations, but I could not do the last page, which had two small ads for the printer and typographer, because these small ads required a tiny line illustration. The illustration that was called for (and I'm not exaggerating this) was exactly ½ inch high by 1 inch wide. I couldn't do it because I hadn't done a line drawing in seven years. Finally, after I became physically sick because

Illustration from an essay in American Heritage *entitled "Lost Pleasures," showing the lost pleasure of smoking. Ink and watercolor on board. Art director: Murray Belsky.*

I couldn't do it, Seymour had to do it for me. I don't think too many people have had the trauma that I had in learning how to draw all over again in my mid-twenties.

But you found it once you started doing political work. If you look at my early political stuff, it was embarrassingly bad. For example, the first tiny bit of celebrity that I ever enjoyed was when I started doing "Sorel's Bestiary" for *Ramparts* magazine. I look at those drawings, and they're constipated, tortured, and the only good ones are the ones that look like David Levine's. The reason that they were well received is because any kind of political comment at that time was unusual. What was being applauded was not my drawing ability, but the fact that I attacked Cardinal Spellman.

Was it difficult to get political work accepted in those days? Well, it was difficult to survive just doing political work. But by the time I reached thirty, I had already developed bourgeois tastes. I had turned into an eager American consumer, I was unwilling to devote myself to any noble cause and suffer the financial consequences. So I kept doing commercial work and did political things in my spare time.

You did an awful lot of political stuff in your spare time. That was in the mid-sixties. By then, everybody was political. By 1966–67, everybody was playing the game of "more radical than thou." I mean, it wasn't simply good enough to be radical; you had to be super-radical. So that otherwise sensible and good people were repeating Mao's nonsense about morality starting at the barrel of a gun. Of course, by that time, I was in the thick of it. But in the beginning, when I first started doing political work, there were only a few outlets, like the *Realist,* that I contributed to. What I always tried to do was get my ideas across in such a way that it could reach a large number of people.

Is that why you chose caricature? I chose caricature because you *have* to be able to do it. I object when people refer to me as a caricaturist. I do caricature because I have to. To do just caricature would drive me out of my mind. I'm a caricaturist—also something of a phony: I live the life of an American conspicuous consumer and at the same time express my indignation at the moral rot that surrounds me.

That you were contributing to. Just so. The trick is not to show your hand when you express your point of view. You can't be heavy handed when you want to make a point. It's got to be funny even to those people who might not otherwise agree with you.

But you do *express your rage through cartoons.* Yeah, but I am putting it through a process, whereby it comes out not as rage but as witty comment. It is not unadulterated rage anymore. Unadulterated rage does not go well with four-color advertisements for Cadillac cars, which is the environment my cartoons are placed in. As a matter of fact, one time I was syndicated by King Features and had a thing called "Sorel's News Service." It was uneven, but occasionally amusing. It was syndicated to forty papers around the country, and based more or less on current news. The feature was limping along for about a year and a half until I did a cartoon that was heavy handed with absolutely no wit. It involved a picture of Richard Nixon juggling some skulls, which had to do with the Vietnam fatality figures for that week. And as a result of this thing, I got dropped from half of the forty papers.

Did the political cartooning affect your commercial work in any way? No. The only thing political cartooning did was to get me invited to a few more parties than I would otherwise have been invited to. It was all salutary.

Does your ideology come to play when you do commercial work? Are there things that you won't do? Unless one is born wealthy, one has to balance idealism with pragmatism. It's a balancing act that I'm pleased to say gets easier and easier. At this particular point in my life, I can't think of a single job I am doing that I hate. Even the commercial

jobs I take are fun—banal perhaps but not painful.

At what point in your life did you finally get your drawing down? I can almost pinpoint the time. It was when my wife, Nancy, wrote a book called *Word People.* It required about fifteen illustrations. The book was about people whose names became part of the language, like "Sandwich." Books are a marvelous chance for an artist to try out new stuff—it's like a murderer trying a new poison out on the dog. Every time I have done a book, it's always been with an eye to trying out something new. And in *Word People,* for the first time, I did drawings without any kind of tracing and slipsheeting.

What is slipsheeting? Slipsheeting is a form of tracing. It's when you slip a drawing under drawing paper so that you can see through it. Most tracing that illustrators do—pen-and-ink illustrators—is done by putting pencil lightly on a piece of paper and then inking it, which is what David Levine does, for example. For some reason or another, I have never been able to do that. Slipsheeting allows the illusion, at least, that one is drawing direct, although one isn't. But in these drawings for *Word People,* there was no tracing at all, and that was really the beginning of a style of personal drawing. It was as close to a signature as possible. Working direct is certainly the oldest way to work. That's what the cavemen did.

These pictures for Word People *were also caricatures.* Occasionally they were. The interesting thing was that I thought the style was utterly noncommercial, and that no one would ever ask me to do that kind of thing for ads because at the time those drawings were done, 1969, most illustration was very premeditated. The kind of sketchy line that I was doing in 1969 for the first time hadn't been done since John Groth in *Esquire* during the forties. It never occurred to me that there would be a revival of this kind of drawing line, but in fact there was. The funny thing about drawing direct is that it takes more time than tracing because you make more errors. I can run through a hundred-sheet pad without getting the right drawing.

What are you looking for when you're running through that pad? Gesture or expression? Mostly gesture. And hoping the composition works out right. To me, there's a kind of magic in working "direct," even if I have to go through a whole pad. When I do a commercial job, I don't feel like wrenching my guts trying to get it right with a direct drawing, so I do a tracing, because it goes faster and I want to get rid of it.

After all these many years, what did having the confidence of knowing how to draw do for you? You presume too much, sir! I have never had the confidence that I could draw, and at the age of fifty-five I still start every job with the gnawing feeling that it will turn out badly. There are occasional commercial jobs where I'm sufficiently unconcerned about whether they turn out well or not, so that I can work without any kind of pain. But as soon as a job is at all meaningful to me, I worry about it too much.

What happens with, for example, the political drawings? You come up with an idea, and then your job is to express that idea as best as possible. Doesn't having the drawing skill make it easier? I think we have to define our terms. To me, a person with drawing skill is a guy who can sit down to a piece of paper and draw upon his familiarity with the body and with gesture, and do whatever he wants to do. Such a person does not have to, as I do, go to his folder marked "Hands" when he needs to do a certain gesture.

You have quite an obsession with hands. Ever since I worked with CBS, when I drew hands like amoebas, and George Lois made some crack about them, I've always had an obsession with hands. But aside from that, I am seldom able to draw entirely from my imagination. I always need some kind of reference material as a starting point. This is my great lack as an illustrator. I think it stems from not having enough life drawing at a crucial time in my development.

You're talking about basic research matter. You need *research to do the kinds of things that you do.* For crying out loud, the greatest caricaturist of them all, Max Beerbohm, did most of his drawings after he met the people . . . and he did them from *memory!* I couldn't do a caricature of my wife without having a photograph in front of me. I don't know if that makes me inferior to Max, but I suspect it does.

What is it that causes you to go from one style to another and, in fact, invent a new style for yourself periodically, as you did recently with your pastels? The pastels came about because of my determination, when I started the "First Encounter" series for *Atlantic,* that I would never trace. I didn't care what technique I used, whether it was black ink, brown ink, light ink, pastel, crayon—whatever I did, it would be direct. And I started doing pastels because it would give me a chance to make mistakes, to correct mistakes without tracing. Pen and ink is a sudden death situation. You cannot erase it. And that is why my pen-and-ink drawings, when they are successful, have so much life and a lot of spontaneity. I was only successful in half of the pastels I did. Half of them turned out okay; the other half were as

overworked as if I had rendered them in pencil. So after doing about six of them with varying degrees of success, I went back to pen and ink. However, from doing the pastels I discovered that I could do realistic portraits. And I was pleasantly surprised that I could. That is the other thing that enrages me about school. Nobody taught technique! Nobody taught me pastels. It was as though they felt that if they were to teach you anything, they would be inhibiting your creative genius, when all I wanted was specific information.

The "First Encounter" series is just one of many essaylike things that you do. What prompts that? Is it a dissatisfaction with commercial jobs? Is it a difficulty to deal with politics at this time? If I just had commercial jobs, I'd be a basket case! All of the essays that I do stem from the fact that the advertising stuff is just *boring.*

And the advertising constitutes most of your commercial work. Well, to someone reading this, doing a magazine illustration will seem like commercial work. For me to do an essay that appears in the magazine is my fine art. I don't do any painting. When I do a pictorial essay, I am expressing myself completely, and it reflects my interests, and I generally work in a much freer style because it's my conception. I'm not illustrating somebody else's idea, so I can illustrate it exactly the way I feel it should be. The best work I've done has been to illustrate my own writing. The worst work I do is when I run across an editor or an art director who is scared and insecure. I think fear is contagious. When I come across an art director who is scared, I get scared. On the other hand, Walter Bernard is the most unflappable of art directors. He never seems worried about anything. It never occurs to him that I am capable of doing a bad job. So I only do good jobs for Walter.

You're doing more essays now than political work. Why is that? Because I don't like to repeat myself. In the sixties, I did cartoons protesting what the CIA did in Guatemala, and I suppose if I were doing political stuff now, I'd be protesting what the United States is doing in Nicaragua. The corruption is the same. The hypocrisy is the same. The paranoia is the same.

Did you always enjoy writing? That seems to be a major part of your work now. I always liked writing. Probably, had I been able to go to a good school, I might have become a writer rather than an illustrator. I always suspected I got caught up in the wrong art form.

Is that why you do comic strips? I started doing comic strips when I had a weekly gig at the *Village Voice.* When

Illustration from a series in The Atlantic *entitled "First Encounters," in which William Randolph Hearst meets Orson Welles; text by Nancy Caldwell Sorel, pictures by Edward Sorel. 1984. Pastel on paper. Art director: Judy Garlan.*

Clay Felker bought the *Voice,* he gave me space every week. Originally, I thought that this would be like "Sorel's News Service"; I would take some quote and make a funny picture about it. But this was not easy to do. There were weeks when nobody in public life said anything amusing. So the necessity of having to fill space every week caused me to do comic strips. The advantage of a comic strip over a late-breaking news item is that you can do it weeks in advance. So you can go away on vacation, and there are your comic strips waiting to run. I deliberately made them look as different from Feiffer—who was also appearing in the paper and had been there first—as I could. As far as the ideas went, I never saw much similarity between mine and Feiffer's. But strips are hard for me.

In what sense? It's almost impossible to do a comic strip direct, mostly because of the lettering. Maybe some day there will be a breakthrough, and somebody will be able to do a comic strip as spontaneously as a child would do it. But I am not free enough to do that. So comic strips have to be planned ahead. Therefore, it isn't as much fun for me as other kinds of work that don't require tracing.

Do you have a process? Aren't you really illustrating what you're writing? Well, of course, I do my illustrations first and write afterward.

So the writing is the illustration. Wait a minute. Is that a trick question?

MAURICE SENDAK

Maurice Sendak *(born on June 10, 1928, in Brooklyn, New York) defined the look of modern children's book illustration. His drawing styles are derived from illustration and comics of the past, but his stories are psychologically rooted in the present. Although his illustrations appear in many story and picture books by other authors, his most significant books are those he's penned himself;* Where the Wild Things Are *and* In the Night Kitchen *are two of his most popular. In 1982,* Maurice Sendak, *a biography and retrospective, was published. Recently, Sendak's love of music, especially of Mozart, has become a professional passion: he now designs operas. Indeed, his own* Where the Wild Things Are *has been scored, choreographed, and performed, with his own unique sets.*

There was no conscious decision to become an artist. The first awareness of artists was my brother always drawing pictures, writing stories, pasting and stapling; that seemed the most natural thing to do. I did it, without considering if I could do it. And it has continued ever since.

Did your brother continue? To the degree that he wrote at least a dozen books. I illustrated his first two.

Were there any other artists in your family? It's hard to say. My father ran away to this country in 1903, from a *shtetl* outside of Warsaw. So I don't know his family at all. He had a huge family, but they were all incinerated during the war. On my mother's side, I've heard stories about her father being an artist, but he died very young. And she so romanticized him that it's hard to know what's fact and what's fiction.

What were your earliest pictures like? Cartoons, mostly based on Disney movies. People with huge, round shoes. Of course, the most available influence was Mickey Mouse, *Snow White,* and all the biggies that came out just when I was of age to go to the movies. So what Michelangelo was to a Renaissance child, Walt Disney was to a Brooklyn Jewish child.

The comic strips as well? Comic strips and comic books, which we all read. Children's books were unavailable to a lower-class child in Brooklyn. My parents couldn't buy them. And library going didn't come until much later. I didn't read kiddie books, anyway, I only read older things. I wouldn't have been caught dead reading a book appropriate to my age, which I suspect is what children feel all the time. But comic books put you in connection with your peer group, because you read them and traded them out in the street. And a lot of my books—up to *In the Night Kitchen*—were

Cover illustration for Zlateh the Goat
and Other Stories *by Isaac Bashevis
Singer, published by Harper and
Row. 1966. Pen and ink. Editor:
Ursula Nordstrom.*

dramatically influenced by my early love of comic books, particularly panel movement. Animating the picture book has influenced me all my life.

When you were doing these drawings, was there any idea of turning it into a profession? I was fourteen or fifteen when I illustrated my first book. It was *Peter and the Wolf.* Like so many children, it was also the first piece of music I got to know well. My inclination toward classical music started very early, again, probably influenced by my brother. I did a book, which was a very bad Disney version of *Peter and the Wolf.* But it had pictures and text, and the word *copyright* on the front. So, I was wired to be an illustrator. The second book was the libretto for *Louise,* by Gustave Charpentier, the French opera.

Opera was an early influence, then? Very early. My first great experience was with Arturo Toscanini on the radio . . . Everything was radio. I didn't go to concert halls and to museums. Nobody would take me, so it was a logistical and financial problem that could not be overcome. Toscanini did Beethoven's *Fidelio* over a two-Sunday program. I'll never forget it. It was like St. Paul on the road to Damascus.

But back to books. I did my favorite story when I was about seventeen. It was "The Luck of Roaring Camp," by Bret Harte. Which is interesting, because it's a theme that has run through all my adult work. It is the story of an abandoned baby in a miner's camp and of what happens to the baby. There may have been more books, but those are the ones I remember. I have never let them be published. I have never let them be seen. So, you see, it was there all the time; there was no choice but to become an illustrator.

Why not music? I had no talent, but I wanted to play the piano. We moved every third year, because my mother had an aversion to fresh paint. (It's true.) And in those days, they painted your apartment, whether you liked it or not, every third year. We lived all over Brooklyn and I went to every school in the world, which made for a very dismal childhood. But that non sequitur had to do with the fact that one of these apartments we moved to had a piano that was too big to be taken out by the previous tenant. The terrible dilemma was, who was going to get lessons. And my brother got them, because he was the elder. I'll never forget that, because I wanted them so much. He never stayed with it; he became an accordion player, and then a writer and illustrator. So there was no musical gift, or if there was, it was never cultivated. But I whistle on pitch, and I can whistle the entire repertoire of Mozart's operas and symphonies. I'm very good with Beethoven. When I'm home listening to recordings and working, I become part of the orchestra.

Did you go to art school? Yes. To appease my father, basically. He was mortified that I was going to be a serious artist, because I would make no money. It also mortified him because of something I didn't think he could admit to; it embarrassed him. He would much rather have had a son who was a doctor or a lawyer or a professional, like the typical Jewish fantasies. Instead I went to the Art Students League for a very short time. At the same time, when I was about nineteen or twenty, I was working at F. A. O. Schwartz, the toy store, doing window display. I went there because my brother and I made toys together. He's a genius with mechanical apparatuses; I simply painted what he told me to paint. We wanted to sell the toys, so we brought them to Schwartz. They told us they were beautiful but impractical, and instead I got a job. I stayed for three years, as an assistant to the display manager.

Did you get anything from the Art Students League? Very little. The only teacher I ever had who was sympathetic to my peculiar nature and whom I could trust enough to learn from was John Groth. He had a course in illustration, which I took twice. He was the only generous teacher I ever had. The only one I could relax with and feel I could trust, and who was really like me. He gave us wonderful exercises. We had to carry a sketch pad wherever we went, on the subway trains and in the parks. I got in the habit of drawing all the time. Alas, I don't do it anymore. But for years I drew on subway trains—when it was safe to look at people on subways. The other thing was to look at the work and study the compositions of Goya and Daumier. Daumier was his favorite artist. But in order to make us look, he would whet our appetites by saying, "Go home. And this week I want you to do the rape scene from *A Streetcar Named Desire*. I want Stanley screwing Vivian Leigh in the style of Goya or Daumier." Well, we could hardly wait to get home. He knew about young people, and what our energies and our drives were, and would try to tie that into educating us, without any pedantry.

Did Groth encourage you to go into illustration? Oh, yes.

Was it editorial illustration at the time? Whatever I could do. I mean, his encouragement was, "Go out and work. Don't stay in school." That's just what I've always told the students I've had at Parsons or Yale, that if you're really talented and really excited, why are you in school? You should be out there working. You should do-do-do-do, not study-study-study-study. Because the doing is the studying. The experience is the learning. And John was for not wasting time. He thought it was a kind of masturbatory act, to just sit around studying and looking at work and thinking about what you do. And the fortunate thing was, that in the early fifties in New York, you could go out and get work.

Where did your first work come from? The first book I illustrated was back in high school, for my physics teacher. You can't really count it, but it was the first professional job. I was failing, as usual, in everything, especially in physics. He wrote a book which, I believe it's true to say, was the first book explaining the atomic bomb to a layman, called *Atomics for the Millions*. I also worked for All American Comics during the three years I was in high school, which undermined my grades, of course, but I did the backgrounds on "Mutt 'n' Jeff," "Tippy," and "Captain Stubbs." So all the worst habits of comic-strip drawing were in my work.

After I had worked at Schwartz for quite some time and littered their windows with my pictures . . . it was like putting your fishing pole outside on Fifty-ninth Street and Fifth Avenue, waiting to hook an editor . . . a very well-known children's book illustrator named Leonard Weissgart came by. He was doing a book he didn't want to do for the Jewish Seminary, called *Good Shabazz Everybody*. So

he got them to take me. My name is very small on the cover, and his name, as art consultant, is very big. I was happy to do it though. I had also been to publishing houses and been turned down, over and over again, because my pictures were considered old-fashioned.

You mean you were too nineteenth century? The prevailing look was sort of vaguely thirties. Simple, flat color. The prevailing attitude was generally that kids liked simple shapes, simple colors, pretty people. There was nothing disturbing. There wasn't a ripple. And my work was cross-hatching, because I was copying from Cruikshank and other English illustrators. So it was very out of fashion. I kept a little notepad of criticism of editors, saying, "No, no, you can't look like that; go look at what's contemporary . . . ." So it was rough, until 1951 or 1952, when I met Ursula Nordstrom at Harper's, who was a friend of the bookbuyer at F. A. O. Schwartz, Frances Christie (whom I owe everything to).

Before I tell you about Ursula, I must say Frances ran the best children's book department in America. That's where you found the out-of-print books, the European books, the American books. It was fantastic. I got away with murder in Frances's department, she let me be there, reading books, studying, looking, copying. Then she introduced me to Ursula, who was the editor at Harper, and that was the beginning. I did my first book, which was a collection of French fairy tales by Marcel Aimé called *A Wonderful Farm*. Again, the drawings are better than anything I previously did. But still, I had no training! I absorbed styles that were inappropriate. I think now they were inappropriate, but then I had no choice.

You were wedding Disney to Tenniel? I was trying to. Although, it's funny, my earliest portfolios had indications of more complicated work that look more like me now. But those were the things that were rejected by the early editors; cross-hatched, peculiar images, which later became what I was well known for.

Ursula Nordstrom had guts. Oh, yes, she had guts. Ursula's passion was for young people. If I can make a huge, generalized statement, and I shall, what's wrong with publishing today is that nobody has guts. I mean, they're all playing it safe, publishing safe, middle-aged people like me, who can sell books. The young people have a rough time coming in, because they can't guarantee sales. There's something wrong with the system when you can name only a few people. So you have to be very strong and gifted to break through that very commercial, immoral attitude. But Ursula was the opposite. I mean, a children's book department

Illustrations from Kenny's Window; *text and pictures by Maurice Sendak, published by Harper and Row. 1956. Ink and watercolor. Editor: Ursula Nordstrom.*

is something you made up, out of your head. So she made it up. Everybody was young. She went through the streets and swept them up like garbage. And we all worked; I had a job reading manuscripts.

The second book was *A Hole Is to Dig,* which put me on the map instantly. It was a *mad* success. That was by Ruth Krauss, who had written very inventive books, using children's language, children's gestalt, and children's attitudes toward life.

And this book was something that just fit perfectly into your style? Well, Ursula is an amazing person, and so is Ruth, for taking a kid off the street and giving him an important book. Because I know for a fact there were at least two very famous illustrators at the time who had been approached with it and thought it was too bizarre. So they came to me. And after seeing my sketchbooks with big-headed little Jewish kids and ill-drawn caricatures but full of animation and life, they said, "Why don't you do it?"

How did you approach that task? Every weekend I went to Rohatyn, Connecticut, where Ruth lived, and we worked together on the book. Her husband, by the way, was Crocket Johnson, the great man himself. So I had the best of two worlds. And Ruth was way ahead of women's lib. She wouldn't let me get away with any myths about what little boys did and what little girls did. We did six books together, and that was my education in bookmaking, book layout, and typography.

Were you surprised the book was a critical success? I was stunned. It was a tiny book with funny scratchy drawings and weird, crazy words. It's still in print. It was a bestseller for twenty years, and it is part of college curriculums. It's a very, very historically important book. And I was just lucky enough to be around to do it.

Once that critical acceptance was achieved, was it easier for you to get projects? Oh, sure. But my projects were mostly through Ursula. She spoon-fed me. I had no taste. There was no way I could have had taste. You're not born with taste. You accumulate it. You learn it. So she taught me. If I wanted to do this, she'd say, "No, you do that." And so my entire early backlist is superb, from the variety of things she made me do. Books that I thought were inappropriate for me she said were appropriate. Drawings for books that forced me to do homework on Dutch landscape and costume. So she taught me how to be an illustrator. I learned how to be a chameleon and change my style and change my look and change my emotional everything to suit the book I'm illustrating. That was a million-buck education.

Top: *Title-page illustration from* The Sign on Rosie's Door, *text and pictures by Maurice Sendak, published by Harper and Row. 1960. Pen and ink and watercolor. Editor: Ursula Nordstrom.* Bottom: *Illustration from* A Hole Is to Dig: A First Book of Definitions, *text by Ruth Krauss, pictures by Maurice Sendak, published by Harper and Row. 1952. Pen and ink and watercolor. Editor: Ursula Nordstrom.*

ROSIE'S DOOR

Story and pictures by MAURICE SENDAK

HARPER & ROW, PUBLISHERS   *New York, Evanston, and London*

Steps are to sit on

It's interesting, because in the fifties, when an illustrator picked a style, that was it virtually for life. That's what doomed a lot of the illustrators working then. And that was the one thing Ursula was absolutely not going to let happen to me. I was going to have catholic taste, and I was going to learn how to draw in a variety of styles. I think my books are identifiable, but they all look different because illustrators are secondary to the text. If you insist on being primary to the text, then you're a bad illustrator. Which is why I list Arthur Rackham as one of the worst illustrators that every lived—one of the best draftsmen—but he's one of the worst illustrators.

At that time, was the book the only form you wanted to deal with? No. Because it was very little money. The fees were small, the advances were small. I didn't get royalties in the early days. Life, happily, was cheap enough so that I could leave Brooklyn and live on my own in Manhattan. It was an enviable time, socially and historically, but there wasn't enough to really make out. Besides, one wanted to be commercial, to be in the magazines.

"Commercial" meaning advertising or editorial? Editorial and advertising, yes. The sad thing for me was that however gifted I was, I wasn't gifted in that direction. I required the density of a book. I'm a very slow and ponderous artist. It takes forever. The book was wonderfully my medium in that it allowed me to stew and steep, and each picture built and built and built, until at the end it all flowered into a kind of conglomeration that was suitable. Whereas a specific magazine picture had to be quick. I did drawings for *Esquire*, and they are terrible! My best friend in the mid-fifties and sixties was Tomi Ungerer. Tomi had the ability to round out, steep, and thicken in a book, and with the other to *blast off* in a given image. And I was jealous of that. But I was also aware of the uncanny quality of his talent. He could make an enormous success out of being a commercial, literature, and poster artist. I couldn't. I've learned, though, how to do my book jackets better.

Did you want to make statements, political, social, or otherwise? Not really. The most political statement I made was in my high school yearbook. I grew up during the war and lived off the business of dead Jews. So, Holocaust drawings and that kind of thing was an obsession with me. An obsession I rejected with violence as I grew older, because I felt like I couldn't get out of it. I couldn't be happy. I couldn't live in the world. But outside of that, politics was not my forte. Instinctively, I didn't want to do what didn't come naturally to me. I never have.

When did you start making decisions about your own

subject matter? I thought of writing from the beginning, but it was the wrong time. I had to keep illustrating, just to keep books going, to make some money.

Could you write? Yeah. I wrote for my own pleasure, but I had no confidence in what I was writing. Again, it was because of Ursula. The first book was *Kenny's Window,* which is still one of my favorite books. But it was done mostly with her propping me up and convincing me I could write. It was completely idiosyncratic writing and idiosyncratic subject matter. *Kenny's Window* was a story of a little boy who has contradictory attitudes toward life, and toward his toys and toward his parents. His parents never appear, and the whole thing is a series of dialogues. It's seven chapters; a series of seven fantasies acted out by himself or with toys, in which he is battling out forces within himself— it sounds grandiose, but I am not able to describe it better now. He has a dream at the beginning, and the book is an effort to fulfill it. The ending is an irresolution. He cannot fulfill his dream. Which is anti-American. Some of the reviews said, "What a terrifying book. We're led to believe he's going to get it, and then he doesn't get it." But it was mostly him acting out sometimes irrational rages toward his toy soldiers and then trying to compromise emotionally and get some understanding for those actions, because the assumption was there was no discussing this with your parents. He comes to a resignation, which is, "I've got to figure it out myself, and I guess I've gotta wait; and I guess I'm going to be alone."

Was this true for you? Yes. Except, in a sense, it was idealized in the book, because my rages and my quandaries were severe, and there literally was no one except my brother, and my older sister later, to work them out with. *Kenny* was a very forthright book. It's overwritten. It's not well illustrated. But it's still one of my favorite books, for its bravery. People liked it, but it never sold. It won critical praise, and it even won an illustrators' award, which it didn't deserve. I'm not being modest. I *wrote* better and stronger than I was able to illustrate.

Did Ursula encourage you to get in touch with yourself for new material? Oh, yes. The miracle was that she was encouraging me to write very uncommercial books. She wanted me to be me; to become the artist she smelled in me. She was Mama.

That kind of person is a rarity. She did that with everybody. We were known as the Ursula kids. None of us was jealous of the other. We all thought we had our distinct place in her heart, and that each of our gifts was different from the other. She was cultivating the best in us.

Illustrations from In the Night Kitchen, *text and pictures by Maurice Sendak, published by Harper and Row. 1970. Pen and ink and water-color. Editor: Ursula Nordstrom.*

The second book I wrote was *Very Far Away,* in 1958, which I am now considering reillustrating. I will not touch a word of that text, I love it so much. But the pictures are not good enough.

What is this book about? It's almost a rough study for *Outside Over There.* It's about a little boy who so bitterly resents his mother coming home with a new baby, that he leaves. He puts on a costume so he won't be recognized, and he goes very far away. He meets a horse, a sparrow, and a cat, and they go live somewhere else, where you don't have to put up with parents who come home with gratuitous unwanted children. And he finds, living with them, the vanity of these creatures. The stupidity and irrationality of all creatures is so wearying and tiring, that they have a terrible fight, and he goes home. And the going-home has to be rationalized, because basically he's going home because who else is going to feed him? He can't take care of himself. So it's, "Well, maybe I'll get used to the kid." But you don't know that he does.

Your books seem to subvert commonly believed myths. I sometimes think it's amazing I've had success, because they are so idiosyncratic and personal and run against the American grain that says if you persevere, you'll get what you want. What I'm saying is: you may persevere, but you may not and often probably won't get what you want, because, one, you don't deserve it, two, you're too young to have it, and, three, that's the way life is.

I think the American grain is actually a veneer, and underneath there's the hardwood that is difficult to penetrate. Yes, my books were vulgar, pushing and striving for inner things rather than for outer things.

I noticed that you have the Journal of the American Psychoanalytic Institute *in your home. Was psychoanalysis something that became an interest at the time of* Kenny? Those aren't my books. But yes, I was in psychoanalysis at a very early age. Maybe that, too, was fashionable in New York in the fifties. Maybe not. But I was in need of it. I was also entranced with the subject from a very early time. And *Kenny* is all about the *outrageous* rage that you inflict on inanimate objects, because you don't dare inflict them on your parents or your siblings. So *Kenny* is all about how to deal with rage. Even Martin, the hero of *Very Far Away,* is dealing with that issue.

The third book was *The Sign on Rosie's Door,* which is the most cheerful of my books, and I love it. It is also the first book where the pictures melded with the text. After that came *Where the Wild Things Are,* in 1962. *Wild Things* was an amalgamation of everything that had gone before.

Max was one burly little boy, a terrific, strenuous, volcanic embodiment of all the things that were unnerving Rosie, Martin, and Kenny. But the people who at that point said, "What a novel thing," "What a weird thing," "What a disgusting thing," "What a strange thing," hadn't read my earlier books.

Were the early books an attempt, consciously or subconsciously, to say to kids, "It's okay to have all these feelings"? No. To say it to myself. I wasn't interested in other kids. I was not a humanitarian or a social worker. Or even someone who understood children. I don't have children. So I cannot pretend that I set out to help other children. Primarily, my work was an act of exorcism, an act of finding solutions so that I could have peace of mind and be an artist and function in the world as a human being and a man. My mind doesn't stray beyond my own need to survive.

To share that need to survive is not so bad. Yes. If you can touch other people, as I apparently have, that's fine. I'm very proud of that. But those things are inadvertent.

Well, Where the Wild Things Are *was really an explosion.* Yeah, it was an explosion. But it was an explosion that only meant to me that I could render more concisely and precisely the theme that I had overwritten in the earlier books. I had also fallen in love with the picture book, because just previous to *Wild Things,* Ursula had given me my first picture books to illustrate—*The Moon Jumpers, The Giant's Story* by Beatrice Derenier, *Mr. Abbott and the Lovely Presents.* And the form entranced me.

What is the difference between a picture book and a storybook? They are many pictures with little words, but

Illustration from Where the Wild Things Are, *text and pictures by Maurice Sendak, published by Harper and Row. 1963. Pen and ink and watercolor. Editor: Ursula Nordstrom.*

combustible little words are really like time bombs. And the pictures are the explosion. What I could do with a picture book was to condense language into metaphor and symbol. The pictures are like the operatic stage, and the words are the orchestral accompaniment.

You couldn't, in fact, do without one or the other. So I abandoned the storybook completely. In *Where the Wild Things Are* I finally came to grips with what my theme was and found the form most suitable to me as a writer and an illustrator.

Where did it derive stylistically? From everything I had done previously. People think it looks different, but it doesn't! The drawing is better, but I was growing better. As I should have. God forbid I was going the other way. Curiously, by the time *Wild Things* came around, people thought I was out of the head of Zeus. I had been around for a decade, working very hard, having illustrated over two dozen books. It wasn't spontaneous combustion. And I was annoyed, frankly, that suddenly I was a star on the firmament, as though I hadn't been around all this time.

As the star, what was happening? I won the Caldecott Award and began to make money. But by then, I was sufficiently knowledgeable and savvy about life and people so that I was not impressed, nor have I ever been impressed, with being a star. Don't forget, I was thirty-three when that book came out.

So I proceeded on my way. I illustrated books for other publishing houses, which bothered Ursula a lot. But I had a very strong feeling that Harper books, at their very best, looked like Harper books, the way Viking books look like Viking books and Random House like Random House, etcetera. What I was afraid of was I'd start looking like a Harper illustrator; that all my books would have that cast. And my sense of self-preservation was strong. So I began illustrating other books. My ethical code was that I would only write books for Ursula, but I insisted on my freedom. My instinct was right. I learned to look different.

What was the next book that you wrote? After *Wild Things* was *Higgledy-Piggledy-Pop: Or, There Must Be More to Life.* I wrote it in 1956; it was published in 1967, the year of my coronary. I almost didn't get to see that book. But I'm very proud of it, because it's the only funny book I ever wrote. I'm not a funny writer. That's another weakness. I have a good sense of humor, but I'm serious when I work. And *Higgledy* is full of laughs. It's a sad book, though, being about death. I was then enamored of the English romantic woodcut artists; they were called "Artists of the Sixties," such as John Everett Millay and Arthur Hughes, and the Pre-Raphaelite brotherhood. Where *Wild Things* is big and noisy, *Higgledy* is all chamber music. I didn't write many books after that. In 1970, I did *In the Night Kitchen,* which again, is very different and offended people in a very different way.

Was In the Night Kitchen *influenced by Windsor McKay?* Absolutely. That's when I got into collecting Mickey Mouse nostalgia stuff and learning all about Windsor McKay. *In the Night Kitchen* is in homage to him. When I steal, I go all the way. But *Night Kitchen,* however much Windsor McKay it is, is mostly me. I just took from him what suited me, as I have taken from other people. That book occurred when my mother was dead, my father was dying, and I had a heart attack—rough years. And so, it was in homage to everything I loved: New York, immigrants, Jews, Laurel and Hardy, Mickey Mouse, King Kong, movies. I just jammed it into one cuckoo book. After *Night Kitchen,* I didn't write anything for almost ten years, because the very next book was *Outside Over There.*

And you worked on that for a very long time. I worked on that for five to seven years. I began it in 1972, and it was published in 1980.

What was so difficult about doing that book? It was the pursuit of the theme I had been tracking since *Kenny's Window,* but now I had it trapped in a corner. I was really like Sherlock Holmes, sniffing it out in myself. I'm not saying it was a religious experience, although in fact it was. And did it change my life? In fact, it did.

How? In terms of my attitude toward my work, and my attitude toward myself. The most significant thing that happened was, immediately after finishing that book, I did an opera.

You also said that it would be the last book you'd ever do. Yes, I said that. But I meant that in a metaphoric sense, in that it probably is unlikely I will do another picture book. I want to write books, but I don't know what kind. It was definitely the end of a certain kind of book that I would do. Maybe I will never write again. I haven't got a clue. But

Illustration from Outside Over There. *Story and pictures by Maurice Sendak, published by Harper and Row. 1980. Pencil and watercolor. Editor: Ursula Nordstrom.*

it freed me. I became another man. I became an opera designer. I began not only whistling, but attending rehearsals of, Mozart operas. Since 1980, when that book was published, I've had five years of not publishing, except books that were related to theatrical works, like *The Leopard* and *The Love of Three Oranges*. *Outside Over There* allowed me to be the person I wanted to be. And that, I assume, is what the work of art is supposed to do for the artist. I don't know what it does for the people who read books. But I can't worry about that.

It must have really scared you while you were doing it. Yeah. It gave me a mini–nervous breakdown. It was unquestionably the hardest book I ever worked on. It caused me the most pain. Psychically and physically the pictures drove me crazy, because they were so difficult and so slow that I had calluses all over my fingers. But the end result was that I knew it was my masterpiece. That's what I planned all along that it would be. Commercially it's been zappo, but that was never my concern. It's a disappointment, not because of the money, but because I think it should be read. By its noncommercialness, I know kids are not reading it. But that's secondary to what I set out to accomplish.

How did the opera work come about? I was working on *Outside Over There,* and Frank Corsaro, a great opera director—the greatest, I think, in America—called and said he admired my work. He's one of the few artists from another profession who crosses over. (Who else does that? God forbid we should ever meet, like in a Stendhalzian salon, and discuss things.) Well, here is Frank looking me up and telling me, "Hey, I'm crazy about your books. Have you ever thought about opera? Do you like opera? How about *Magic Flute?*" I was nearly having my second coronary on the phone while he was talking to me. I agreed to do the sets for *The Magic Flute,* and right in the middle of *Outside Over There,* everything turned Mozart. Mozart became the godhead.

Somebody said to me after looking at these drawings, "For some reason, this line feels like Mozart." Oh, that's the nicest thing anybody could say. If anybody could prove to me that Mozart was God, I would believe in God forever. But I do believe in Mozart as though he were God. If God is someone that's supposed to give you comfort, I think of him and I listen to him when I'm in trouble. When my dog died last summer, and I couldn't bear it, it was only *The Marriage of Figaro* that got me through the last two weeks of August. Because there is a truth, a revelation, spirituality, humor, and earthiness. What a break, to do *The Magic Flute.* And that began an opera career and a ballet career,

which hasn't ceased. Now, I'm just about to illustrate a Grimm's fairy tale. It will be literally my first proper illustrated book since *Outside Over There.* So it's going to be almost five and a half years since I've illustrated a book that way, and I'm looking forward to it.

How do you prepare for that book? You don't. There's no way you can prepare. The manuscript has just been recently discovered. So I'll be the first illustrator for this story, and it will be its first publication. It's a fabulous, fearfully sad little story. I know just what I'm going to do, emotionally. But technically, I haven't a clue. And what it looks like, I don't know. I never think about what it looks like. I just know that at the end of February I'm going to sit down on my backside, in front of my drawing table, and begin Grimm. And that's how I do it. Because I have total and complete faith in the fact that I've already done it, in my head. For however long, a year and a half now, I've been thinking about it. I was in England working, and I was in Los Angeles at the Huntington Library. Whenever I go and look at pictures, I'm looking at something. I say, "What am I looking for? Oh, I know. Cottages. Trees. German settings." I'm doing homework all the time. Even when I'm sleeping, I think I'm doing homework. So although I'm going to be scared and go through the same "I can't draw," "What does it look like?" "How do I compose it?"— the nightmare of beginning a book—the truer thing is that it has already been conceived and envisioned. The trick now is to calm down and schlepp those visions up.

ALAN E. COBER

Alan E. Cober (born on May 18, 1935, in New York City) was a pioneer of expressionist illustration. A stylistic marriage of Ben Shahn and Leonard Baskin marked his early work. His highly tuned linear skills are inspired by a childlike sensibility. He influenced many in the seventies, due in part to his teaching and in part to the national accessibility of his work. As a graphic journalist he initiated many stories, including "Willowbrook," a frighteningly objective account of life in a New York mental institution. This and other reports on prison life and the problems of the aged were collected into his book, The Forgotten Society. He is also a prolific children's book illustrator and continues to be a principal participant in "The Illustrators Workshop."

I was the class artist, like so many others. I was the best in my class, and that's where I got my pats on the back. I always enjoyed drawing and having attention paid to me.

Did you go to art school? I had always wanted to be an artist, but first I went to the University of Vermont to be a lawyer. I was so young that I thought if you went to college you studied college, if you wanted to study art you went to art school. I didn't know that art was taught in college. I did visit an art class with a friend and did a portrait drawing of the teacher, Francis Coburn. I asked him if I had enough talent to go to art school, and when he said yes, I left college.

But most important, college was rather difficult for me because I wasn't able to read. I had a learning disability and didn't know it then. Nobody had heard of learning disabilities in those days. I was dyslexic. I was certainly bright, but it's very difficult to be a lawyer, like my father, if you can't remember what you've read. So I decided to go to art·school. My mother was extremely supportive; my father was very upset.

Where did you go? First I went to the Phoenix School of Design in New York, and that was absolutely awful. An awful place, an awful school, and Mr. Phoenix was not a terrific person. So next I went to the School of Visual Arts, which is where I got a certificate in 1956. I'm certified, so now I can practice.

What convinced you to practice illustration and graphic art rather than painting? I was interested in the figure, and so it was suggested that I start my career in illustration; from there I could move into anything. I took the advice.

Were you influenced by other artists during your school

Postcards done on trips to Italy, Yugoslavia, Ireland, and Mexico, drawn from life. 1975–81. Watercolor and pen and ink.

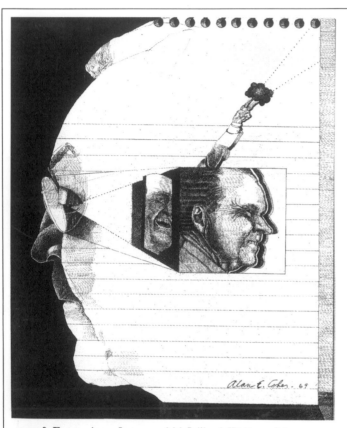

Alan E. Cober. 69

years? Ever since I was a kid I liked Wallace Morgan, an illustrator of the twenties and thirties. What fascinated me about his work was its spontaneity. I knew intuitively it was special, but what I admired most was the idea that he could sit in a speakeasy, for instance, and draw from life, making an entire journalistic image from what was before him. Well, that just knocked me out. The year he died, 1948, was when I discovered him. You know, it's funny how little things like that can drive you toward certain areas later in life. I was also fascinated by Thomas Hart Benton's illustrations for *The Oregon Trail,* as well as Dali's drawings for *Benvenuto Cellini.* And the most lasting memory, from when I was five years old, is Disney's *Fantasia.* It was a very important film. Moreover, every time I hear *The Rites of Spring,* I conjure up dinosaurs—what a lasting image!

Did Fantasia *spark you to think in pictures?* I think radio was the main thing. I'm sure the artists of my generation—particularly the illustrators—were all raised on the radio. "The Lone Ranger," "Jack Armstrong," "Superman," "Tom Mix," and "Terry and the Pirates." I didn't see them in the comics, I saw them in my own mind's eye, and I always

had images in my head about what was happening on the radio. It was an active medium, not a passive one like TV. What I heard in my ear was translated into big pictures in my mind. So I guess I was always illustrating.

When you were in art school, how were you drawing? Were you following your own methodology, or were you copying the conventions of realists such as Norman Rockwell? One thing is constant from the beginning—I still don't fit things on a page. They always get cropped somehow. But I had no method, because I was just a student. I always loved caricatures and I've been a big fan of caricaturists—William Auerbach Levy and Eugene Berman. But, as for my own style, I just drew. In fact, I mostly did men's fashions.

Was that because there was money in that area? Well, it was a commercial vehicle. But I always liked clothes, and so fashion illustration fit my predilections. While I was still in school I went to see Eric Simonson, a big agent at the time. He visited the school to see the annual show and asked the teacher to send me to him with all my things—no promises. He liked the work, told me that I had a future, but said I should simply draw *more.* So I bought reams of typewriter paper and a clipboard, and I drew, literally, two thousand drawings that summer. I think that exercise made me a better artist. I never lost the habit.

In what manner were you drawing at that time? I was using a crow quill pen. I think it was the manner that I draw in today. I was attempting to be more realistic, but that was impossible. I will say, though, when I drew then and when I draw now, I really think I'm rendering photographically. I'm not aware when I go off and make one eye higher and another lower; I don't know when one ear is too far out and the other isn't. I simply don't see that until after the picture is done. I just draw, and I'm smart enough to let what happens happen.

That's interesting, because you wouldn't be able to do what you do as well as you do it, without having a vocabulary of realism or representationalism. I would never have been called a realist. I never could really draw photographically. I can draw well, and that's intuitive and automatic. I see well. I just happen to see differently. It's always been that way.

In art school, were there other influences that seemed to affect you directly? Albert Werner was my instructor then, and he's still a close friend of mine. I can still show him my work, because I know that he comes to it without prejudice. I mean, he will tell me what's good, what's bad, and why. It's like a golfer going to a pro's pro. Werner is my pro. He was a great influence, inasmuch as he said,

Series of illustrations for book reviews in America Illustrated. *Page 84, illustration for* Making of the President 1968; *page 85, illustrations for (top)* Hemingway: A Biography *and (bottom)* Fire on the Moon. *1969. Pen and ink on D'Arches paper. Art director: David Moore.*

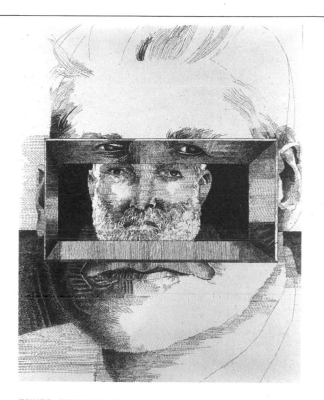

"You draw, you draw, and then you draw some more."

Your work exhibits two characteristics, the journalistic approach of the Ash Can School and the emotional qualities of the expressionists. Would you agree? I always related to the Ash Can School because they were journalists, but I consider myself an expressionist, although a bit late. It's interesting to note that the Ash Can artists were also illustrators, and only later were they accepted as painters.

When you came out of school and were working in your particular style, how did you see your work in relation to other illustration being done? I drew a certain skewed way, but in my mind it was representational drawing. I didn't know I wasn't the same as Coby Whitmore or Norman Rockwell. I mean, these were artists I respected and liked. To me, I was the same. When my success came, I didn't know that I was a young Turk. I just thought it was my turn, that it was normal for careers to move in this way.

You mean you didn't know that you were bumping against existing styles and trends? Well, today I do. Today I see that I was helping to create a new field, but then I thought I was in the same field as everybody else. I couldn't see why I shouldn't work for *Redbook* and *Ladies' Home Journal.* In fact, in one year I did five illustrations for each. I just thought that was the way it happened, that it was my turn to get work. I had no idea I was "hot."

When did success happen? It came through *Redbook* and *Sports Illustrated* around 1963. Until then I was working for very small magazines—*Antique Airplanes, Caper,* and *Escapade.*

Do you remember how you were approached in terms of what was required? Did Redbook *and* Sports Illustrated *let you have a modicum of freedom?* Dick Gangel gave me my first job for *Sports Illustrated.* It was called "Deep Sea Fishing in Malindy." Unfortunately, they were not about to send me to Africa. But you know what I did? I hired a model—an agency sent me an African woman to draw from—and I did seventeen finished drawings. Later, when I'd get a job like that, I'd probably do much fewer. But I wanted to do a great job. I was insecure, and it paid off. I did fifty jobs for Gangel in twenty years. My first assignment from life was for Bill Cadge of *Redbook,* about a famous locomotive. He sent me to Philadelphia to the Franklin Institute to spend the day with it. I walked around, looking at it for an hour, and then did the drawing on the spot. I finished when I got home that night, but the result was very spontaneous. That felt absolutely right.

At what point did you feel the need to do journalistic picture essays? I always thought of myself as a journalist.

Self-portrait with medical figure, from giant sketchbook. 1974. Sepia and black ink.

Two Italian sketchbooks. 1980. Sepia ink and watercolor.

I always tried to work from life, and whenever I did a job, I always worked from a live model. That's the way I did it because I could explore my subject better, look around it, see how things hooked together—I couldn't do that with a photo, so I didn't.

So research is integral to your methodology? I always did homework. Whether it was to go to a museum or a library or anyplace else to find information to accompany my figures. Moreover, I had roots in that approach. When I was a kid I would accompany my father to court, and he would get me permission to draw the trials. I was, therefore, very impressed by the court artists for *Life.* That's what I wanted to do.

When did you begin to cover stories in the field? One of the first jobs I did as a "professional" was a series of drawings of jazz musicians for *Metronome Yearbook.* My first major journalistic assignment, though, was in 1971 for *Newsweek;* I did prison drawings for a piece entitled "Justice on Trial." These led to the fifty Willowbrook drawings that I did for the Op-Ed page of the *New York Times* and then to my essay on the aged. All these became my book, *The Forgotten Society.*

What did you do as preparation for this experience? My preparatory work was that I was raised in it. When they said at *Newsweek,* "You're going to the Tombs" [a jail in New York City], I had already been there when I was eight; I'd been in the courts my whole life. We'd go with my father on Sundays—to his office in El Barrio or to the courthouse or the Tombs to see a client, then to the museum or movies. So, what background did I need? They didn't know it, but I was the perfect guy for that job.

Why did you add written commentaries to your drawings? That relates to *Sacco and Vanzetti,* a very important series of paintings by Ben Shahn, commissioned for *Harper's* magazine. I always look at his paintings and think of how my own work relates to his. I often talk about my process as looking for the Holy Grail. Actually, I'm looking for my own

Sacco-Vanzetti. To me, that's high journalism. James T. Soby, Shahn's biographer, said, "Sacco and Vanzetti could not have existed without Shahn." And that's true for many of us. I understood Shahn's need for further explanation as a model for my own commentaries.

So when you did the prison series, you were drenched in personal history—you were searching for your Sacco and Vanzetti. What other background did you bring to that assignment? I was searching for Sacco-Vanzetti but probably didn't know it. Things happen as they happen. I just start on a drawing; I have no predetermined idea of the space or what I'm focusing on. I simply dip the pen into ink, then see, and then draw. I never quite know what I am going to end up with. I design intuitively; I draw intuitively. If I talk through the whole process then it is really intuitive because I've divorced my right side from my left side.

Do you start from the center of the page? Do you have a point of demarcation where you always begin on a sheet of paper? I'm trying to think about how I started a drawing the other day. I make my space . . . start with a logical focus. (You're making me think about it, so I'm trying to get some sort of reasoning.) I draw one part at a time and don't see another part until I get there. If I'm drawing the left eye, I don't see the right eye or nose. It's like shooting a roll of film in my head.

Do you use a camera in your work? I bought a camera a few years ago and took it on one assignment. I wanted to experiment with it but ended up feeling guilty that I was photographing and not drawing. I shot a lot of film on this particular assignment and did many drawings (although not as many as I would have liked) and brought them back to the art director. He said, "You know, it's absolutely amazing to me that these people really exist and that you actually design the photograph the same way you draw."

How did that comment make you feel about using the camera? I found that I really didn't need it. I decided that if I were to use it, I would simply take pictures for themselves,

not as background for my work. My reasoning is, why waste valuable drawing time by shooting photos?

How do you reconcile personal biases while covering a story? An artist cannot avoid making commentary. I believe I work without biases. Let's talk about the Willowbrook drawings, for example. To the viewer, they may seem slanted to a particular point of view, but they're not. Maybe the choice of what I draw is where the so-called bias is.

In America we are conditioned by the media to think that objectivity, as seen on the evening news, is the ultimate test. When I look at a Willowbrook drawing, I see a lot of feelings conveyed—by accepted standards, that's subjectivity. I felt a great deal when I was there. Although I'm trying to overcome it, it's hard not to hear the sounds and smell the smells. Ultimately, though, I am simply drawing a portrait of a person, as if I were drawing you. I like to think that I come to each drawing as if I had come from Mars, and that I'm seeing an individual for the first time. So this guy from Willowbrook could be the first human being I've ever seen, and all human beings look like that. So he's atrophied. So he has club feet. I'm trying to look at him objectively. What happens, though, is when things like these are printed, someone edits, someone picks two drawings out of many. Someone else's prejudices or biases are coming into play, not mine.

How would you define the act of illustrating? I think a lot of us tend to get into bad habits. Not so much the shortcuts, but we start to repeat ourselves by creating a predictable vocabulary. I know that I start to fall back on mine at times. I fight it, but I know I can do perfunctory procedures. That's what I call illustrating—that reliance on the old reliables, the lack of expression, or just a rehearsed attitude. The risk taking is called drawing, whether it is for an illustration assignment or not.

Are you content with the limitations of the print medium? I'm not, although I love the printed page. I think every illustrator will give you that answer. But I am less and less content. When I show in galleries I'm not sure it means anything to me outside of ego satisfaction. It does give me a different forum, and it is seen by a limited amount of people. It makes me bona fide in terms of being an artist and says I can go beyond magazines. But magazines reach the largest number of people. However, I always want to expand on a number of things begun as illustrations. Ultimately, I want a larger forum.

What is your typical daily schedule? First, I swim in the morning. Then I go into the studio around 9:30 and begin to do assignments. I thrive on projects, particularly projects

Drawings done at Cape Canaveral during the launch of the third space shuttle. 1982. Top: watercolor; bottom: pen and ink. Originally commissioned by NASA; art director: Robert Schulman. Published in Technology Illustrated; *art director: Bruce Sanders.*

Illustrations for the Limited Editions Club edition of Franz Kafka's The Trial. *1975. Colored ink and watercolor on D'Arches paper.*

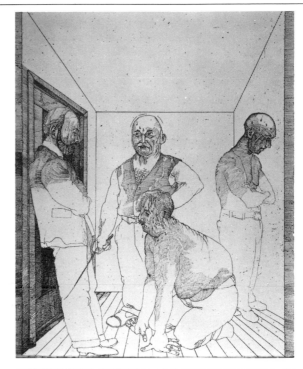

for myself. Lately I've been doing portraits of swimmers. I also have press credentials to cover an important trial, which I will do once or twice a week, the way I used to cover the circus. I don't think anybody realizes that I practice what I preach. I go everywhere with a sketchbook and do a *body of work;* my sketches may be notes or ends in themselves. Whenever I go on a trip I fill many books. I love the idea of documenting where I've been and what I've seen. I learn from these, too. When I was in Yellowstone National Park, I drew the landscape. My pictures began to get very abstract, and all of a sudden I started to have a firsthand understanding of Georgia O'Keeffe's work. I saw how the landscape dictates what you do. It's not that each drawing is good, but they are real documentations. In a sense, these pictures are the most important things I do.

Do you know how many jobs you've done in your professional life? Yes—1,493 since 1963 when I started keeping a book and numbering my assignments. And for each job, on the average, there are two to four drawings. For some I might do twelve, for others twenty. That's 6,000 to 7,000 drawings I've done just for jobs, and then 10 million drawings for myself, and 14 million drawings in sketchbooks.

What are the differences between your journalistic work, your more commercial illustrations, and your children's books? In theory I want to do everything as well as I can. I've gotten old enough now to know which things are important, however, and where I must place my effort. That's what it comes down to. I love children's books. Unfortunately, they don't pay well, so when I do them it's because I really want to do them. And yet, when I take one on, I find it's a *job* because there is never enough time to do it right. Remember, most people who make a living doing magazine work cannot make a living doing children's books. Every book I've done, especially my very best, gets remaindered. Worse, reviewers don't respond. Once in the *Times* someone reviewed a book like this: "... by Myshka Milles, with sufficiently weird drawings by Alan Cober." He thought that that was a sufficiently high compliment.

Are you also saying that magazine work is no longer satisfying? Once it was great to be in the *New York Times Book Review,* among others. It's still nice to be there if I could do something that meant something. I'm not interested in busting my hump to do a spot; I'm interested in a vehicle for doing good work. It means if I can work somewhere for a couple of hundred bucks, and do what I *love,* that's one thing. But to do work overnight so that a jury will look and say thumbs-down or thumbs-up, I don't need that. Thank God, I'm beyond that.

JAMES McMULLAN

James McMullan (born on July 15, 1934, in Tsingtao, China) is an unswerving realist and rationalist. Though his iconoclastic adherence to watercolor, once deemed retrograde, if not uncommercial, by painters and illustrators, may have seemed irrational, McMullan's belief in his art form is in keeping with his personality. Consequently, his illustration has a rare credibility. Moreover, his belief in fine draftsmanship has made him a significant educator in a field where style ofttimes takes precedence over form. McMullan's book, Revealing Illustrations, *a highly personal, yet precisely detailed, exploration into the art of making communicative pictures, is a progressive milestone in the literature of illustration.*

When I was a kid, I really looked forward to getting the *Saturday Evening Post* because the pictures in it were so rich. I felt a special interest in Norman Rockwell because it seemed to me that Rockwell was given the opportunity of creating a world of his own. Although this world was based on observing reality, his illustrations were really a fantasy of what he thought the world should be like. And rather than responding to texts, he made it come true, based on his own ideas and his own cast of characters. At least half of those covers during World War II probably originated as suggestions from editors—for example, to think of something that represents Thanksgiving—but nevertheless he was able to express the themes in his own inimitable way. Even as a kid, I thought of those covers as his *invention,* and that is probably the beginning of my conviction that illustration had an integrity as a unique art form.

Because of Rockwell, then, you felt the possibility of creative freedom in illustration. I was definitely *affected* by Rockwell's pictures and the idea that he opened up to me that illustration could be strongly emotional and pyschologically affecting. This was true even though I wanted to affect people very differently with my own prejudices.

Tell me something about your childhood. Weren't you raised in Canada and then lived in China with your family? I was born in China. Because of the war, I did a lot of traveling in my early years. My mother, my sister, and I left on the second-to-last repatriation ship from Shanghai. We lived with my grandparents in British Columbia, and I went to a boarding school in Vancouver. During the war, we took passage on a boat to India, where I went to another boarding school. Before I was graduated from high school, I had gone to twelve different schools.

Were you drawing or painting at this time? Yes. My

Illustration from the New York magazine article "Tribal Rites of the New Saturday Night." 1976. Watercolor. Art director: Milton Glaser.

mother didn't save my drawings from those years, so I can only dimly remember what I was doing. But I was a rather timid and nervous child, as I think anyone would have been in my situation, being sent to different schools all the time, in different countries, and being separated from my parents for long spaces of time. So art was a way of coping with this nervousness. It was something that I did reasonably well, and it was simply a way of feeling that I could do *something*. Children my age were learning completely different subjects in each of the schools that I went to, so except for art I always felt like an idiot.

It was your native language, in a sense. I was always talking in the wrong accent, so I suppose art was coin of the realm wherever I went.

What were some of your other artistic influences? I was influenced by much of the Chinese painting that was around me. I grew up appreciating gestural art and was fascinated by the idea of the brush stroke suggesting muscularity. When I went to art school, I was introduced to the work of Ben Shahn and Max Beckmann. You can hardly see it in my illustration now, but I learned and borrowed a lot from Beckmann.

What art school did you go to? I first came to this country when I was seventeen, having just been graduated from high school in Canada. I was lucky to have slipped into the United States before I turned eighteen, because being born in China, I came under the China-born quota, which would have prohibited me from entering. Fortunately, at that age I was allowed in under my mother's Canadian quota. So, I went to a small art school in Seattle, Washington, called the Cornish School of Allied Arts. When I was eighteen, I enlisted for the draft, so that I could try to control the timing of military service a little bit. I was inducted into the Army just after my nineteenth birthday and stayed in for two years, stationed at Fort Bragg, North Carolina. Just before I was to be discharged, I went to Yale for an interview with Josef Albers. I decided afterward that Yale took an approach to studying art that was too intellectual for me. So I took the initial exam at Cooper Union and found out they didn't have life drawing, which dissuaded me from taking the second part of the exam.

By that time, did you know that you wanted to be an illustrator? Judging from what you said about Cooper not having life drawing, you must have known that you wanted to do a certain kind of art. My whole reason for being an artist was that I liked to draw. Furthermore, I had a very clear sense that you had to know how to draw to be an illustrator, so it didn't make sense for me to go to an art

school where drawing skills wouldn't be honed, or where I wouldn't be able to draw from the model. I've changed my mind about a lot of things, but never about that.

Where, then, did you end up going? I finally enrolled in Pratt Institute, but I didn't have a very good time there. I was not a valued student, because it was the era of abstract expressionism, and all the teachers saw me as kind of a reactionary. But Pratt's virtue was that it provided a background in the arts, which I'm very thankful for. Also, Richard Lindner was teaching there then, and he opened my mind to various possibilities.

What were some of those possibilities? I was exposed to the ideas of modernism; I learned that realism is a platform from which a great many exciting ideas spring. And that the levels of expressiveness in art can accelerate and become much greater than what usually appears in illustration. Specifically, with regard to the fashionable illustration at that time, such as the Jon Whitcomb and Coby Whitmore school, which was technically quite superb but in terms of its psychology and content was saccharine. Many of us were affected by German expressionism. It was a figurative art that dealt with the underbelly of life, which as a young, somewhat neurotic twenty-three year old, I was also very concerned with.

It was a hard time to be beginning, though. Many of the people I went to school with never survived professionally. They started out as illustrators, got socked with the possibilities of *art,* and ended up in a limbo where they could neither paint nor illustrate. It was difficult then because the parallelism that you have now didn't exist. Now it doesn't take more than a hop, skip, or jump to go from an illustrative vocabulary to the imagery in galleries.

Actually, German expressionism wasn't accepted by the art world at that time, so you and your classmates were out of synch. You're right. The critic Clement Greenberg, who held philosophical sway, had decreed that subject matter was *verboten.* So without swimming against the tide, you could not have painting with a figurative base. Now that the whole era is being talked about again, you see that de Kooning, for instance, was never as nonobjective as Greenberg claimed.

Were there illustrators who broke down boundaries and helped you to develop? Ben Shahn was probably the most useful artist for me in providing a pathway. He was doing all of the things that Rockwell did for me as a kid, but he was doing it on a much higher level. Also, Milton Glaser, my senior by a few years, had a one-man show at the Pratt illustration department that was very impressive. What Milton

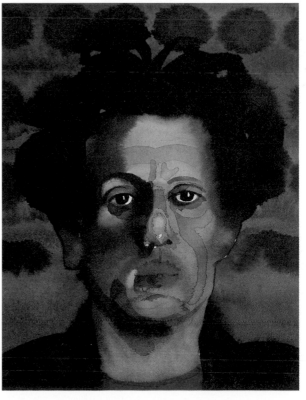

dramatized for me was the link that could exist between design and illustration. Bob Weaver was someone else who affected my ideas about illustration in those years. His art seemed like a wonderful amalgam—the emotional bite of the German expressionists, the energy of the abstract expressionists, and the clarity of Ben Shahn all rolled into one.

You've pointed to Shahn's painting, Sacco and Vanzetti, *as an important discovery. How do you feel about the fact that the image was taken from a photograph?* It clarified something for me. I had always been fascinated with photographs. I think that my point of view is basically voyeuristic, and that's the way I perceive photography.

By voyeuristic, do you mean guarded or removed? Well, it's drawing from an angle or a protected position, which allows you to encounter things without confronting them. My pictures suggested that the artist is not part of the scene. For me, it comes out of an indelible childhood feeling that I was never part of the game, I was the watcher. Photography is a kind of snatched record of something, which holds all kinds of hidden meanings. Photography was always a way of allowing me to go through the embarrassment of being there. It was a big step for me when, years later, I started taking my own photographs, because it signaled a change in my life. I had become somewhat more outgoing. I got married. I had become much more connected to the world. And also, I think, I wanted to take much more control of my picture making. Finding other people's photographs was stimulating and a little like discovering buried treasure, but now I wanted to take my own and be more confrontational.

What medium were you working on in your early postschool years? I derived methods from expressionism and, I suppose to some degree, abstract expressionism. I once saw a reproduction of a Van Gogh in which his underdrawing started to show through. God, that was so wonderful! I was tremendously interested in that idea of layers, transparencies, and revealments. But I was doing it with rather murky kinds of media. I was working with a lot of diluted inks, using Japanese bamboo pens, different steel pens, and anything else that produced scratchy textures. I combined this ink layer with caseins and tempera. So I ended up with a dense, dark palette for a while. I look back at some of those pictures and still rather like them.

That's the approach I was using for my first commercial work. A little later on in the same period I began to paint over photographs with the same combinations of inks and temperas. I was interested in the contrast between the realism of the photograph and the textural, more stylized

Illustration for the Inside Sports *article "The Ten Best Tennis Games of All Time." 1982. Watercolor. Art director: Gail Segestrom.*

quality of the hand-drawn things. The impetus was always the idea of having images partially concealed and partially revealed.

When I started to use watercolors, I quickly found that they didn't stand a lot of monkeying with. You couldn't combine them with inks. But what they could do very naturally was evoke the sense of layers that I had struggled so hard to get with my combination of inks and opaque media. So fairly quickly—in the space of a few months—I switched to painting only with watercolor. When I did, it seemed as though I had come home, to the watercolors I had known on the walls of our house in China and in the English storybooks I had read as a child. So you might ask, "What took me so long?" Well, I think part of the answer is that watercolor was very much against the spirit of the times. In the late fifties and sixties, watercolor was regarded as an insipid, antiexpressionist medium: *it didn't have bite.*

Curiously, a lot of the German expressionists worked in watercolor. Yes, they did. But I didn't know that then. And actually, except for Nolde and some Kandinsky paintings, I'm not enamored of expressionist watercolors. To me, many of the expressionists struggled against the medium and overused black to establish their forms. My timing was also bad, because soon after I started using watercolors, we entered the psychedelic era, and watercolors weren't fluorescent enough. Everybody was in love with saturated colors, and there I was, at Push Pin Studios, the hotbed of drama and color saturation, laying down subtle washes of Rose Dore watercolor.

But Milton Glaser and Seymour Chwast saw something in your approach to take you on at Push Pin. Maybe they saw something that I wasn't entirely tuned in on myself—

Top: *Album cover for Columbia Records'* Poco: The Songs of Paul Cotton. *1979. Watercolor. Art director: Paula Scher.* Bottom: *Sketch for* Graphis *cover, unpublished. 1981. Watercolor.*

that despite all my interest in drawing and a kind of psychological narrative, I was also very much a designer in my work.

There are things that happen in one's life that are very important but whose actual influence is hard to define. Push Pin was like that for me. I spent a great deal of my time there resisting the influence of their success and fighting for my artistic identity but, nevertheless, I think my whole sense of how you are an illustrator in the world was lifted by the time I spent with Milton and Seymour. Certainly I became more conscious of how I designed a picture and how I made myself clear in a picture as a result of my association with them. Not that it has ever been my way to work with the kind of directness and economy that is natural for both Milton and Seymour. I found out during those years that I had to reach the clarity in my own work through many steps and stages.

So your process involves a lot of preparatory work? It's preparatory, but it's more evolutionary. Each step takes me further into my understanding of what the picture is going to be, but it never quite decides what the picture is going to be. So you might say that the finish is just one more evolutionary step.

You could go further with a finish, then? Yes. Because it was (and is) usual for me to do sometimes as many as ten versions of a painting. I realized then that part of it is insecurity, but part of it is an understanding of my own aesthetic. Internally, there is something that I am trying to reach in a picture that isn't just an illustrative effect. It depends on a fortuitous mixture of gesture (particularly the way a figure moves), light, and color. Although this may add up to a variation of the same psychological or formal qualities that you have seen in other work of mine, in all my good pictures I'm doing something that in one way or another I've never done before. I am very affected by the subject matter. Each subject affects me very, very differently.

Are there subjects or themes that you regularly turn to? I don't think of them as subjects in the sense of trees or interiors, but as a recurring aura that seems to envelop many different kinds of subjects. So on the one hand I am very affected by subject matter and my pictures tend to be different, in a way, because of subject matter, but on the other hand many of my illustrations seem to be connected by what you might call a pervasive psychology. Generally, in terms of subject, I would say that I am interested in people and their body language.

How often do illustration assignments give you the opportunity to expand your aesthetic boundaries? That's a difficult

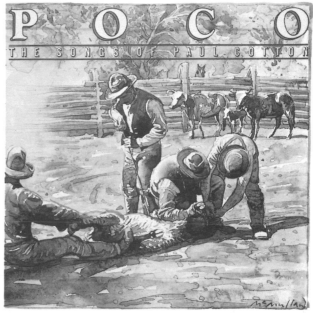

Finished poster for the Hampton Classic. 1981. Watercolor. Art director: Tony Hitchcock.

inspired Saturday Night Fever—*representative of this new kind of illustration?* The disco pictures do not represent some kind of pinnacle in terms of picture making for me, but they do represent a high-water mark in that my view of the world and its character is probably more revealed in those pictures than in any others I've done.

Those pictures were, in a way, like Shahn's Sacco and Vanzetti. *They crystalized a phenomenon into iconographic images.* Well, there were some criticisms at the time saying that they didn't do what you've described, that the real scene was very different from what I painted—and there's probably some truth to that. What I was painting was the scene as experienced by *me.* Even though I took photographs and I was, in a sense, faithful to the photographs, I think what came through very strongly was a lot of feelings in response to that scene. I felt isolated. I felt out of touch. I didn't feel comfortable for a variety of reasons. That I was really a voyeur came across very strongly. I couldn't cross over and say something to these people that would give me an insider's view. The pictures were, in fact, very much an outsider's view.

I felt you captured a certain truth, though, if only a truth about yourself. Of course, I was picking up their isolation too. Because a lot of these people were faking it. What I saw was how lonely, how isolated, how dismal, in a way, the whole scene was. To whatever degree they are powerful pictures, that's what made them so. Now, in terms of what I said before, that they represent a certain distinctive quality about my vision; for once, I wasn't hyping the information, nor was I glamorizing or romanticizing it. I wasn't manipulating at all, I was just allowing my feelings about what I saw to be as clear as possible. And in that sense, they were not illustrations as we know them, because there was not that sense of controlling the information, of turning it toward one view or another. They were the most left-alone pictures, in a philosophical sense, that I have ever done. And I think it's that other, more manipulative quality about illustration that, as I grow older, becomes more and more difficult for me to deal with. There is always some kind of hyping going on. If you're not having to hype it for *Mother Jones,* by saying that the world is worse than it is, you're having to hype it for *Reader's Digest,* saying it's a lot better than it is. I try as much as I can to use my authentic feelings. And they can be very good feelings—I'm not saying that my feelings are always down. They are what they are! I try to keep in touch with them as much as I can so that my pictures will have a spirit that gives them a credibility, and that is the most important aspect of illustrating.

question in light of today's illustration market. Illustration has changed in that artists are being more *art directed.* Also, there are political magazines with particular points of view, which I find very hard to work for. Because with them, I'm being asked to speak with a kind of vociferousness that I don't actually feel. I'm not interested in political subjects. My ideal material is still literary, and fiction is my favorite form. I'm interested in psychologically based stories, and magazines either are not doing that kind of fiction or, if they are, the art directors tend more than ever to impose their ideas—there simply isn't as much opportunity to do interpretive work for magazines anymore. The other thing is that I've changed, and what I want from my work is subtler and perhaps quieter than it used to be. Much of the illustration work I see seems stridently and falsely emotional, or perhaps I am more aware than I used to be of the melodrama that is always lurking as a possibility in illustration. If I were given an income right now, I don't think I'd stop illustrating, but I might illustrate stories of my own choosing, or put books together, or do something where I could illustrate texts of some substance.

But isn't that type of illustration akin to the art that is hanging in galleries now; the so-called illustration on canvas that stands alone without regard for a text. No. I think I've always been interested in the connection of words to pictures.

What is the process of connecting with words? What kind of magic occurs? Are the disco illustrations—the ones that

Left: *Poster for* Let's Find Out, *a magazine directed at kindergarten-age children. 1983. Watercolor. Art director: Carol Carson.* Right: *Poster for the play* Comedians. *1976. Watercolor. Alexander Cohen Productions.*

PAUL DAVIS

Paul Davis (born on February 10, 1938, in Centrahoma, Oklahoma) joined Push Pin Studios when he was twenty-two years old as a second-string designer and illustrator; soon his own vision emerged. An interest in regional American and primitive painting was wed to an appreciation of surrealism, resulting in a unique style of narrative and symbolic painting. His pictures became lasting icons in an art form known for its disposable imagery. In recent years Davis has revived the long-weakened art of the poster through his emblematic New York Public Theater bills. His most recent book is Faces, a collection of personality portraits. Today he experiments with illustration and design in a manner that reveals continual growth and courage.

I decided to come to New York from Tulsa, Oklahoma, when I was fifteen and arrived when I was seventeen. Coming to New York and becoming an illustrator were one and the same.

How did you get interested in illustration? There was never a time when I wasn't. It was one of many interests, but it was the one that I followed.

When I was fifteen, I worked for Dave Santini, a Tulsa illustrator. Dave would have been good anywhere, but in Tulsa, you didn't have very many choices, so he did everything. One doesn't have many choices anywhere, in my opinion.

There's the illusion of choice. Well, it's rare to be exclusively an editorial illustrator or an advertising illustrator. Everyone has to do as much as they can, as far as I can tell. I don't know artists who limit themselves to one or the other.

Yet some would never be accepted in the advertising community. Advertising has more restrictions than editorial. No, editorial people are just as cautious as advertising people, only in a different way. And artists will take as many chances in advertising as in editorial. Advertising people have no lower limit on bad taste nor an upper limit on good taste. That's not a factor when you really get down to it. Editorial artists are in fact creating a context in which advertising looks good. It's a different job, but it's still a way of helping advertising.

You seem to have a good, if not ideal, situation in terms of the collaborative process. Yet I think with a lot of advertising that rapport between art director and illustrator doesn't exist. Well, generally, the problem is that illustrators are not called in at the beginning; they're called in at the very end to pretty the things up. It's a bad attitude and a bad work

Cover for Monocle *magazine special issue on the C.I.A. 1963. Tempera on wood. Art director: Philip Gips.*

habit. The Public Theater posters are advertising, but from the very beginning the art director took me along to meetings with Joe Papp. If I had been called in at the last minute just to make a layout look nice, it would have been done with much less interest or sense of challenge.

How long have you been doing posters? My memory goes back to the Ché Guevara subway poster for Evergreen Review, *done in the sixties.* I did a couple of posters in the sixties. Then no one asked me to do a poster again for five years.

You were one of the Push Pin crew. How did that come about? I went to work there just out of school. They hired me to be an assistant but immediately gave me interesting things to do—little illustration and type jobs. When I had been there for about two months, they said that they were going to make me a full-fledged designer and illustrator. It was like going from sweeper to member of the board at twenty-two years old.

Is that where you learned about typography? No. I had studied typography in school, and I had worked in studios from the time I was fifteen, off and on. But that's where I refined my knowledge. I knew how to do it, but I didn't have very much taste as far as type went.

As a matter of fact, I don't think I had *real* taste when I went to Push Pin. I learned about taste from Milton and Seymour. In some ways, though, it was a kind of narrowing. There was a Push Pin way to do things that I learned first, and then I gradually learned to move outside. Also, I always knew that I wanted to have my own kind of look.

How did the Paul Davis look come about? I have had many influences. But allow me to back up a little bit and say that I painted a lot in high school. Then I got into art school, and I drew, painted, worked, studied, and finally, at the end of three years, threw everything away and began to draw like a ten-year-old kid—which was sort of infuenced both by Leonard Baskin and Robert Andrew Parker, if you can imagine a cross between them. I did watercolor cartoons. Although I didn't know Tomi Ungerer's work then, when I saw it years later, I felt certain connections. I did that for about a year, and then I got the job at Push Pin Studios on the basis of this work. But at Push Pin, they couldn't really sell those things.

So you were forced to move in a different direction? I found that what I was doing was limiting. I thought I had found a voice, but it was very limited in terms of what I could express. So then I began thinking about how to express a broader range. I began looking at folk art and things akin to that. I saw some primitive German targets and began making targets of my own. I found some breadboards for

Illustrations for the Push Pin Graphic
featuring the artist's targets. 1962.
Oil on wood.

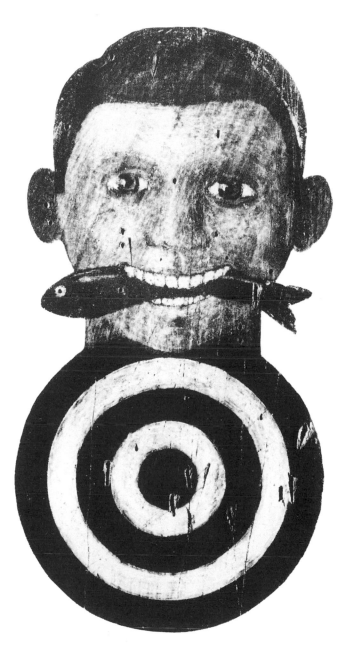

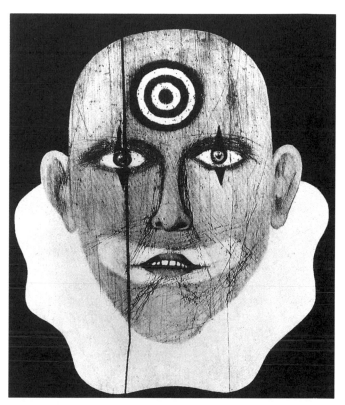

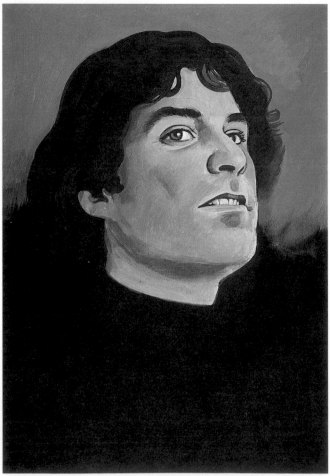

sale, which were cheaper than canvas. I made them into targets, threw darts at them, and painted on that surface.

I remember some of those. There was one black-and-white painting of a top-hatted gentleman, done for Monocle *magazine's election issue.* Yes. Then I started doing wooden signs as a motif. Gradually, I began to take a slightly different attitude, which was that the plainer and more simply painted, the better. I did a few illustrations for *Show* magazine in the manner of American Colonial paintings. I was trying to distill their essence and not make them eccentrically styled or distorted. When I was painting one of them, Milton Glaser said, "That looks like a Magritte." Well, I didn't really know much about Magritte then, but I quickly got very interested in that surrealistic approach as a way to convey ideas.

It would take a while to sort out all the details, all the threads, but at that time, when I was twenty-three or twenty-four, everything was influencing me. It was funny, I would do something, someone would react to it, then I would react to that reaction. All my assumptions were altered as I went along. I remember one of my first things that could be called "magic realism" was a bestiary Irwin Glusker, Ed Sorel, and I did, which we were trying to sell to *Horizon* magazine. I had done some cross-hatched cartoon characters, and Glusker said, "Why don't you do this in that magic realism style, like the targets?" I started to say, "But that wasn't magic realism," because it wasn't; it was very, very primitive. I thought, "Well, maybe I *can* do magic realism." Then, I started painting with the idea of trying to make them more magical. I listened to all suggestions, and usually one thing would lead to another.

I think of the primitive approach as a rural art, and here you came from the West into the most urban surrounding, painting in that fashion. Well, "primitive" is not the right word, because my approach was deliberate. I knew how to paint. It derived from a Western art background, which included Alexander Hogue and Charles Banks Wilson, who in the thirties painted tightly rendered Dust Bowl paintings. I knew a lot about that, and the people who liked that work were my teachers. I was also aware of Thomas Hart Benton, whose work is very stylized; in fact, there is an Americanness about all of this stuff. Anyway, this is the kind of thing that would be held up to us in high school. Benton, John Steuart Curry, Edward Hopper never were thought to be primitives. But there's something straightforward about their work that's very much in the tradition of primitivism.

What was the next step in the evolution? The bestiary opened up some doors. Also being at Push Pin, there were trends that we either created or were on the crest of—the Americana phenomenon, for instance. Woodtype and paintings on wood. I loved wooden signs, and I always loved combining type and pictures. I did various sign paintings for *McCall's* and *Redbook*.

Were there any art directors or editors who encouraged you? Well, at that time I began doing work for Henry Wolf, at *Show*. He was a terrific art director, who would not really criticize things until after they were printed. Also at the same time I began working for Robert Benton at *Esquire*. His was a hands-on approach; Benton would ask for specific changes, which I don't remember Henry ever doing. Henry would say, "If it doesn't work, try something else." But Benton would be very specific and say, "This whole area needs to be more blue."

Talking about art directors, I was looking at magazines the other day, wondering what happened to the glorious ones. I worked for Otto Storch at *McCall's*, Bill Cadge at *Redbook*, Art Paul at *Playboy*, Benton at *Esquire*, Wolf at *Show* and later *Harper's Bazaar*, and Ken Deardoff at *Evergreen Review*. There was a really high level throughout. They were all very different to work with, but they were all great.

Do you think that the profession was more respected then? I'm sure of it. I think that magazines were really on their last legs then, although we didn't know it at the time. The postage situation was partly responsible, but also there was a big change in attitude about what a magazine should be. At first, when they started folding, I thought, this might be better; there are going to be more specialty magazines. But I cannot think of a single art director today who has the kind of arena that any of those art directors did. Not one. After that period was over, there was *New York* magazine, with some interesting possibilities, but right now it just seems to me to be a bygone era.

The collaborative spirit was very infectious in those days. Yes, it was. I guess that was until 1973. When it began to change, it changed in such an imperceptible way that I don't think anyone really noticed it at first.

Until it happened. Until it was over! It's like when a certain model car begins to disappear from the streets. At first, they're everywhere; then there are not so many, but they are all rundown and junky, and all of a sudden only three or four of them are left, and you think, "Oh, my God, what a wonderful thing that was!"

Going back to the Evergreen *cover of Ché Guevara, I don't know how you perceived it, but when that came out, it was iconographic in the way a Rockwell painting of a soldier*

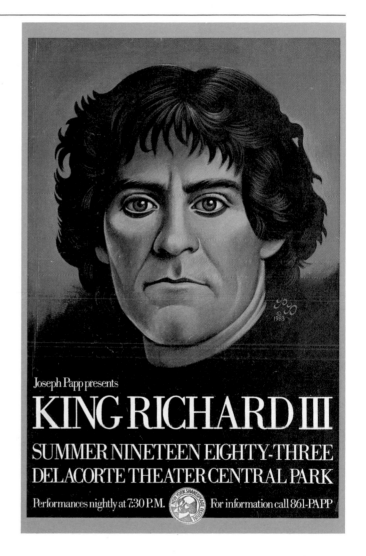

Joseph Papp presents
KING RICHARD III
SUMMER NINETEEN EIGHTY-THREE
DELACORTE THEATER CENTRAL PARK
Performances nightly at 7:30 P.M.   For information call 861-PAPP

Poster for the Mobil Showcase Network's television production of King Lear. 1984. Acrylic on board. Art director: Paul Davis.

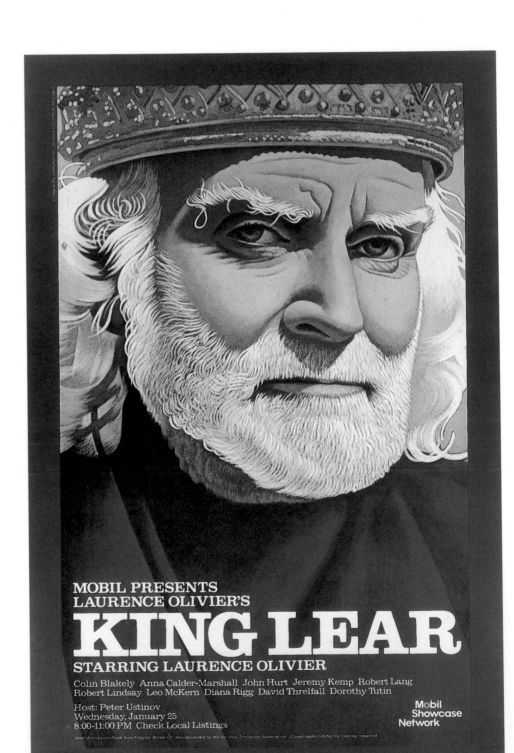

Bus-shelter poster announcing the
Mobil Showcase Network's "Sherlock
Holmes" series on public television.
1985. Acrylic on board. Art director:
Paul Davis.

coming home from the war was. *For better or worse, my
generation was hooked on characters like Ché Guevara as
symbols. Was that your intent?* Well, "iconographic" is interesting. Icons are another potent influence on my work.
By the time I did the cover, I was very interested in Italian
art and religious iconography. I painted Guevara as if he
were a sort of saintlike figure. Yes, I was trying to make
an icon; I was trying to make the image of a martyr. I
didn't understand the politics very well at the time, except
that I remember when that cover and then the poster
appeared, *Evergreen's* offices got firebombed. Later, when
it was reproduced in *American Artist,* a bunch of people
canceled their subscriptions. I wasn't aware of the potency
of the symbol when I did it. And that was from a photograph
to boot.

How do you ordinarily work? From photographs, mostly.
I prefer to take my own, but I often can't in situations like
that.

Do you work with a sketchbook at all? I've begun to do
that more frequently. When I draw in a sketchbook, I draw
ideas. I don't really draw much from life, although I'd like
to try a little bit more of that.

Can you define what you mean by ideas? I sketch out
composition or color ideas. They are really practical more
than aesthetic problems. Certain ideas recur over and over
and over again until I get a chance to use them. I'll figure
out a way to use type, a way to do a title that doesn't
work for the first ten things I try it on but finally does. It
seems the way I work is to have many solutions that I
continually call upon. A solution is held in limbo until there's
a moment when I can use it in the right way.

*Can you describe a piece whose time hadn't come for a
few years?* Well, there's the Sherlock Holmes poster. I had
been working with ideas about using type (in a way new
for me) where it is sized arbitrarily and laid out with color
bands. I've been looking at constructivist work, so I am
very interested in that approach. In the past, direct application
hadn't worked out, but with Holmes, I thought it might
work and it did.

*Your Shakespeare Festival posters are the closest thing
to a contemporary poster revival that I have seen. So much
poster design today is based on tiny, ephemeral elements, a
style that is called "modern." Did your poster approach derive
from the Golden Age of posters, the single, stark, beautiful
image with an integrated title?* I really think that my posters
evolved out of my book covers. But yes, I've always admired
those dramatic posters, though I appreciate Russian and
French posters of every kind. When you look at thousands

Poster for the television drama "First Lady: Celebrating the Eleanor Roosevelt Centennial," presented by Theatreworks/USA. 1984. Colored pencil on board. Art director: Paul Davis.

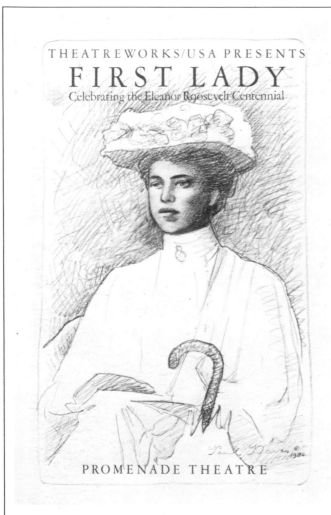

and thousands of posters, the ones that stand out are always those singular ones. If you're going to be influenced, be influenced by the very best. And if you're going to steal, steal from the best. I don't think there's anyone better than Toulouse-Lautrec when it comes to posters. There's a complexity to his that's layered over simplicity—I wish I could do that. My posters on the other hand have been getting more and more complicated.

I thought what you said in your book about your poster for Streamers *was interesting. It succeeded in its purpose, though the composition is very complex and very unusual; it made me want to know about the meaning of the play's title and more about the character. I think a poster should sell but should also provoke, and that one certainly did.* Yes. I was pleased.

Did you demand typographic control? No. I didn't demand anything. The first poster I did was *Hamlet,* and Reinhold Schwenk, the art director at Case and McGrath, and I worked out all the type together. We took the painting to a silk-screen shop and had the type silk-screened right onto it. We wanted them to make a sort of mistake. We wanted it to be blotchy so that it wouldn't look perfect. Even so, the result was not blotchy enough to suit us.

That was one of the happier collaborations I've ever had. But the Shakespeare Festival left that agency years ago. Now I do all the festival's design myself.

What is the major difference between your theatrical posters and other theatrical posters? I think that many designers don't take the time and trouble to find out what the play is about. I like to go to rehearsals or readings, talk to the directors, talk to Joe Papp. It occurred to me the other day that I was doing this revolutionary thing by actually reading the scripts.

That's where your comment about Lautrec makes sense, because he was at the Moulin Rouge. He also did everything on the spot. I wish I could do that. There is something special that happens when you draw on location.

Are posters now the main body of your output? I do many projects for the theater, but I am also doing murals, book design and illustration, packaging, and I'm looking for new areas all the time.

Do you get typecast? I try to avoid it, but it is inevitable. You do something for a little while, and then you are considered a specialist. As far as theater advertising goes, I do think the ads for the New York Shakespeare Festival productions look better than most. One of the reasons is that Joe Papp and I both agree that an ad should be specific to the production and focused in its message.

You obviously feel a part of the Shakespeare Festival family. Much of my best work comes from long-term relationships.

Do any of your images derive from other than visual sources? I think a lot of them do: literary, religious, philosophical. But I can't quite tell you exactly how.

I didn't see much television until I was in my twenties. Now I watch it all the time. But I always looked at comics, and I was fascinated by them. When you're about six or eight years old living in Oklahoma and reading comics like "Bringing Up Father" and "Katzenjammer Kids," they seem bizarre; they don't look like anything you ever see in real life. I used to study the curls in people's hair, instead of what the comic was supposed to be saying. They were so surreal, and somehow I learned from them.

ROBERT GROSSMAN

Robert Grossman (born on May 18, 1935, in New York City) learned to use the airbrush from working in his father's sign shop, and he soon applied it to the drawing of caricature and cartoon. Not since Ottis Shepard airbrushed the Doublemint Twins was the tool used with such flair. Grossman's balloonlike creations were soon copied, but the mordant wit was not duplicated. Also an accomplished pen-and-ink artist, Grossman continued to draw black-and-white comic strips, such as "Zoo Nooz," an anthropomorphic political commentary. He also pioneered a form of animated sculpture, which has been used for television commercials and for a short feature starring former president Jimmy Carter as a peanut singing "Georgia on My Mind."

My father, Joe Grossman, was a commercial artist who had a small design studio as part of a silk-screen printing business he operated. When I was a little kid, three, four, or five years old, Dad would do drawings for me of cars and planes and tanks—this was during World War II—before he went off to work in the morning. I have a vivid memory of a blue airplane model he made for me during that time that he attached to the handlebars of my tricycle so that I could imagine I was flying. Drawing and painting came easily to me and my parents encouraged it, sending me to Saturday morning art classes at the Museum of Modern Art. In high school and college I became interested in doing artwork for publication—in the school papers, the yearbooks, and so forth, which led directly to the work I am doing today.

Working as a cartoonist? Sure, if you count my attempts at humor as occasionally successful—"illustrator" in that most of my pictures are done to augment some text or other. I prefer "artist" because it's the most vague and, somehow, the friendliest. Have you ever noticed how practically everyone knows someone who is some kind of artist? Tell someone you're an illustrator, and the first thing they are likely to ask is whether you also do paintings "for yourself" in your spare time—these, presumably would be the true "art" as opposed to the terrible hack work one does to avoid starvation. Like most people I believe in giving all I've got to whatever work I'm doing. I don't feel I have to apologize because my art appears in a magazine instead of on a gallery wall.

Well, even so, I can't help asking—are there other Grossmans we don't see in print? Maybe one or two.

I sense you're still not completely comfortable defining yourself and your work. What keeps you going? I find the

Illustration for an article in Time entitled "Reagan: The Ship of State." 1980. Watercolor and airbrush on illustration board. Art director: Rudy Hoglund.

Sketches for an illustration on the decline of American industrial power. 1982. Pencil.

process of drawing endlessly magical. The idea that there are an infinite number of little worlds waiting to be created on a piece of paper excites me as much today as when I was a child.

How did the silk-screen business figure into it? When I was old enough, Dad had me run errands for his business around New York. I soon saw that there was a network of people and professions occupying a sort of visual arts spectrum—publishers, printers, photographers, a million different artists and designers—and that their efforts, taken together, determined how we saw our world—the "look" of a particular place and time. It was exciting to feel you were a part of this process. It made it easy to feel a kinship with artists of other times and places, as well. I find it amazing that while we have no idea what language people in the south of France were speaking twenty thousand years ago, their approach to drawing animals was much as it is today.

Complete with airbrushing? Well, you know, some people who have studied the matter think that there are areas in those old cave paintings where pigment *was* in fact blown onto the damp walls in order to achieve a soft shading.

The three-dimensional look. That's important—the eye welcomes reminders that it isn't just staring at a two-dimensional surface.

While we're talking about the remote past, tell me about your college experience. I majored in art at Yale. At that time—I was there from 1957 to 1961—the influence of Josef Albers's teaching was very strong, and great emphasis was put on how one area of color related to another within a painting—almost to the exclusion of every other consideration. You remember Albers's paintings—three or four squares of solid color nested one inside the other. I think I am as far from being a "color field" painter as anyone could be, and yet I know I acquired a taste for a certain kind of precision from those Albers courses. At the same time the campus humor magazine, the *Yale Record,* provided a ready outlet for silly drawings. In junior year we did a parody of *Time* magazine with a Boris Artzybasheff takeoff on the cover by yours truly; in senior year we published a *New Yorker* parody, the *Yew Norker,* of which I was the editor. The *Yew Norker* led to an introduction to Jim Geraghty, the *New Yorker*'s then art director, who, after I had graduated, gave me a job helping to sift through the magazine's unsolicited cartoon submissions. It seemed like the ideal opportunity to actually become a *New Yorker* cartoonist, but I just couldn't get the knack of it. I managed to see a total of two of my cartoons published in two years; I wrote a few jokes that other artists drew and finally decided to call it

Finished illustration for the Forbes *article "America's Shrinking Industrial Base." 1982. Watercolor and airbrush on illustration board. Art director: Everett Halvorsen.*

Illustration for an article in Rolling Stone *on the effects of marijuana. 1974. Watercolor and airbrush. Art director: Mike Salisbury.*

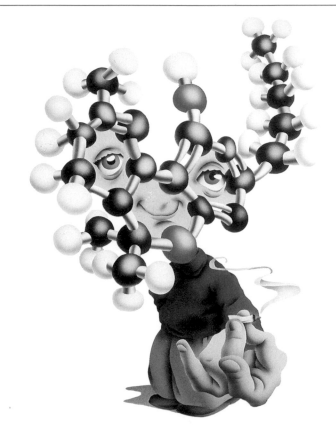

quits. *The New Yorker* is still my favorite magazine.

These were line drawings you were doing at the time? Strictly pen and ink. This was also the period when I started doing comic strips—"Captain Melanin," a black superhero, and "Roger Ruthless of the CIA" appeared in *Monocle* magazine—this would have been about 1963.

When did you get started with the airbrush? That was later on. I was impressed by the way David Levine and the Push Pin artists were using line to develop a bulgy three-dimensional feeling in their work. I found an old airbrush in my dad's shop and discovered a jiffy method to outbulge them all. For a while I diligently pursued outline-less-ness as the secret to a real stereoscopic three-dimensional look. I felt my line work belonged to a different world that had nothing to do with the airbrush and went its separate way. Lately I find a strong outline reasserting itself in all my pictures.

The airbrush look has certainly taken hold in the world at large. I am thinking especially of all those TV station breaks with the giant metallic numerals rotating through space. Yes, the airbrush has turned out to be everybody's friend—computers are learning to do it beautifully too.

So now it's time for you to go back to your line work. It sounds like you are still wavering between precisionist Albers-type art on the one hand and Yale Record *cartoons on the other.* My God! Can it be? No, I'm taking a stand right now! Make sure that tape-machine is running. I hereby declare that the outlines of a picture are more important than any surface treatment or color. A friend of mine who worked in the space program was visiting from California. After watching me work for a while he tells me, "All you are doing is edges and fields." It seems that every dot in a picture that is sent from a satellite in space belongs either to the edge of an object or to a field—a surface or empty space between edges. Those are the only two kinds of things that can exist inside any picture, according to my friend anyway, and of the two, it is the *edges* that are by far the most important. They contain most of the information. Ergo, go for the outlines!

Isn't this just an elaborate description of what happens when a picture comes into focus? I suppose it is. But the fact that the eye wants a focused picture shows it is looking for *meaning* first of all. Even so, the determination of what "looks good" might have more to do with color and surface qualities. It does seem as if photography, the movies, and television are creating a worldwide consensus of what is pretty as far as color, lighting, and composition.

That sounds like a new version of "social realism." Only if you leave the question of the *content* of pictures entirely aside, which of course cannot be done. An East-West agreement of what "in focus" means could probably be reached tomorrow—agreements on what is "fair" or "funny" will take longer.

Caricature plays a big part in your work. How did that come about? I think I've been attracted since I was a kid to forms that deliberately distorted everyday reality. I loved the magic of *Alice in Wonderland,* the time travel of the *Connecticut Yankee,* the alien worlds of *Gulliver's Travels. Mad* magazine obviously also left a deep impression. I think much of the appeal of the cartoon world lies in our desire to bring complex matters down to manageable size. It is possible to imagine the mind as a kind of combination toyshop–puppet-stage–model-railway layout in which we test out alternative courses of action as we confront real-life problems. In that mental world the rules of space, time, and causality can be suspended or violated at will. Cartoon art may simply be a true depiction of this interior visualization system of the mind.

Illustration for a Forbes *article on population indexing. 1982. Watercolor and airbrush on illustration board. Art director: Everett Halvorsen.*

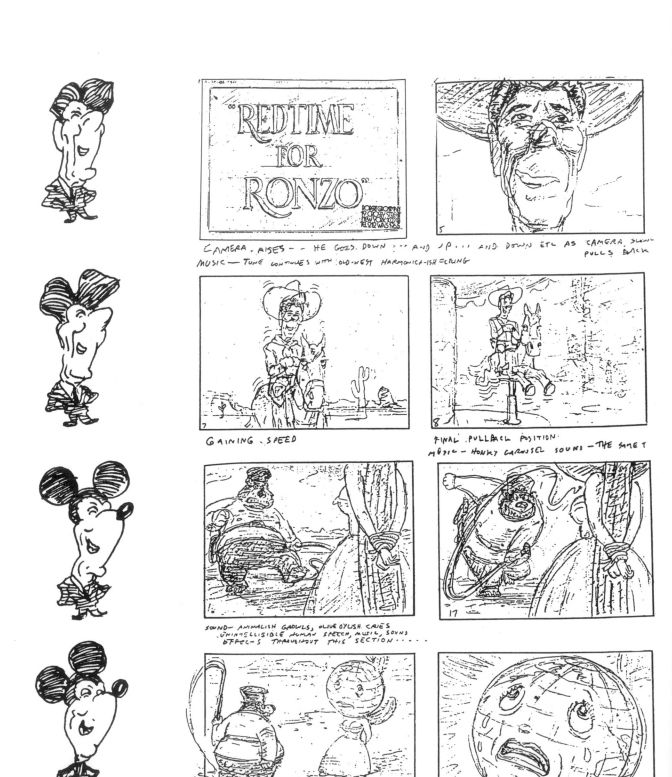

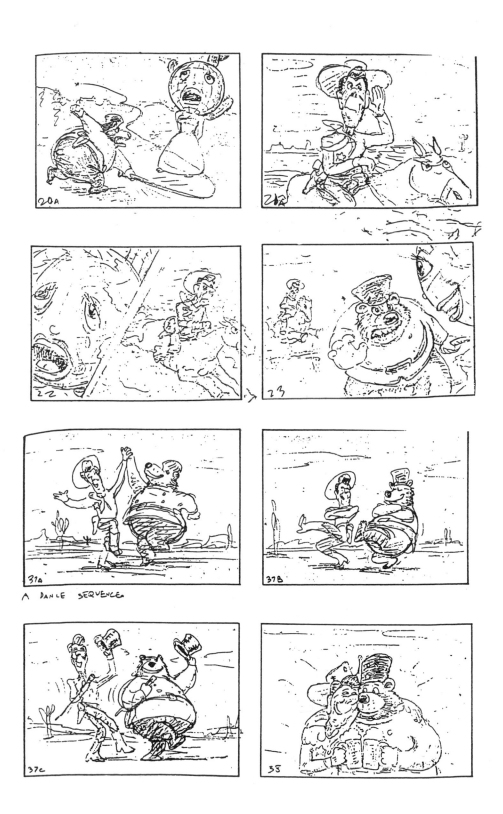

A DANCE SEQUENCE

Still from the set of an animated commercial for Carrier air conditioners. 1982. Mixed media. Agency: G.G.K., New York.

Cartoons are snapshots of our mental playschools? I'm not sure I buy it. Well you can't deny that cartoons are occasionally said to be "true." And yet they are all obviously "false" from the photorealistic point of view. I'm suggesting that the distortions that may make a caricature "truer than life" may actually conform to the curvature of our internal "thought-space."

My thought-space is starting to ache. How's about an example? Take this magazine cover. The editors of *Forbes* were attempting to visualize—of all things—"America's Shrinking Industrial Base." We came up with this concept of Edison and Ford and the industrial giants of the past gazing down from Valhalla at a tiny dwindling factory building. A bit of heavy-duty visualization, I think you'll agree.

Well, at least we're getting down to cases, but frankly, I can't get too excited about caricatures of dead inventors. Tell me about your politics—you put the likes of Nixon and LBJ up to ridicule. To a dedicated caricaturist, leaders only exist to be ridiculed. You start by doing your teacher when you are a kid and eventually graduate to the presidents.

I remember your Nixon as Pinocchio—what is this thing you cartoonists have with noses? I was surprised to read the other day that Freud as a young man subscribed to a weird theory that the nose was the most important organ of the body. He would refer patients to his friend Dr. Fleiss, who would then wreck their perfectly good noses as treatment for depressions and various physical symptoms. Later on Freud abondoned this idea in favor of the psychoanalytic theory we have all come to know and love today. Wouldn't it be funny now if it turns out he was right in the first place? Cartoonists could then be seen as the heroic vanguard keeping faith with the "nose theory" down through all the years when people foolishly thought it was dreams and the unconscious mind that mattered.

Is that what you're striving to deliver—the graphic punch-in-the-nose? I am aware that in the struggle to get people's attention a certain degree of "cartoon-i-ness" is a recurring strategy. People seem mysteriously drawn to it. The huge marketing successes of Garfield, Snoopy, the Smurfs, and all—I've read that there is now an industry devoted entirely to developing and licensing these kinds of characters—proves my point. These businessmen are turning imagination directly into cash—it's more amazing than Michael Jackson. I believe there really is a Michael Jackson, but Smurfs?

You sound jealous. How's business? I feel so fortunate to have been able to raise a family by doing the work I love best, I could never complain.

Surely you are aware that in the art gallery world in

SoHo artists are getting many times more than the best advertising clients pay in your market. You're talking about much bigger paintings than I ever do.

How big are your paintings these days? What kind of materials do you use? Do you have any technical tips to pass along? For the past five years or so I've been doing all my work on pieces of very smooth, flexible Bristol board about 15 by 20 inches in size. An art director told me this was the largest size copy permitted in a certain type of laser scanning machine that makes good color separations. I work out my drawing with a number two pencil, then preserve the lines I like in watercolor applied with a fine sable brush, and erase the rest. I make friskets from glassine paper with spray adhesive on the back and develop my picture

with gouache and watercolor applied with the airbrush and more sable brushes. I always feel I have a roster of tools and materials I can depend on, but I also enjoy the way it evolves and changes over time.

I notice clay work seems to be taking up more of your attention. How did that come about? I wanted a way to bring the voluptuous tactile quality I was getting with the airbrush to animated films. Stop-motion photography of three-dimensional models was the perfect solution. It gives a magical other-worldly look I never tire of.

But it sounds so difficult to do. I've heard you've built whole series of models like three-dimensional cels for a single effect. That's one of the techniques we've used—it's called animation by "replacement." When the panting dog begins

to melt in the air-conditioning commercial, you are actually seeing a series of more than twenty dogs that were painstakingly sculpted by my brother David and placed before the camera one at a time. We use a bunch of other techniques, but that really was a killer.

I get it—Dave does all the dirty work. He does a lot. I do some and we hire a crew of highly skilled obsessive people to do the rest. There *is* a lot of grueling toil, but we've found the results worth the effort and expect to be doing a lot more filmwork in the future.

A final question—what do you think is the best-known work that you're done? That's easy—the picture of the airplane tied in a knot for the movie *Airplane!*

Did you *do that?* Who else?

BARBARA NESSIM

Barbara Nessim (born on March 30, 1939, in New York City) found it difficult to be a female illustrator with a distinct, if not hard-edged, vision. Even during the mid-sixties, women were primarily accepted as children's or fashion illustrators, and not much else. Nessim was incapable of doing cute or beautiful renderings of women. Hers was a sometimes grotesque imagery born of complex personal emotions. With the premier of Ms. magazine in the late sixties, her work finally found an outlet and an appreciative audience. Today she continues to employ many different expressive media, including computer graphics.

I always knew that I wanted to be an artist, because I wanted to be just like my mother. She was an incredibly talented clothing designer.

When did you begin to formulate your art? I had formal training in the seventh grade and went to an art class for gifted students each morning, an hour before school began. In the ninth grade, I broke my leg while ice skating in Central Park. Because I had a cast to my hip, I couldn't go to school. I had some instruction that included three hours of regular education and three hours of art a week. That was fantastic! I hadn't learned as much going to school from nine to three every day. I learned how to learn. During that time, I had a teacher, June Howard Mahl, who taught me the basics of art, like working with black and white and gray. We did things that might be taught in the first year of college, and I was only in the ninth grade. I learned stippling, drawing from what was in your pocketbook, and how to break down shapes and forms. That's what really got me focused. And that's all I really needed, for somebody to show me what it was that I was supposed to be learning and doing. She suggested that I go to the High School of Industrial Arts (now called Art and Design), which I did.

What kinds of courses were taught there? We had four courses of art and four courses of academics—it was a perfect blend. We had lunchtime dancing, where I began to blossom socially. It was a small, very integrated school, two hundred in the graduating class; one-third Hispanic, one-third black, one-third white. That was the fifties—I was graduated in 1956. Those were the rock-and-roll years. I was right there, because all the black kids would bring in the latest records. And the Latin contingent would have all the Mambo records.

After high school, you went to Pratt Institute. Were you interested in going into illustration then? I had no idea about illustration. All I was interested in was going to art school. At Pratt in my second year, I had the option of going into

Illustration for an article in Domus Moda *on the fashion scene entitled "Fragments from New York Fashion." Published in 1981; original drawing taken from sketchbook, 1979. Gouache on D'Arches paper. Art director: Franco Raggi.*

industrial design, advertising design, or illustration/painting. I liked industrial design, but I couldn't quite figure out exactly how I would fit into it. Advertising I had had in high school, so I understood how to do color separations and had learned a little bit about type. I figured, "I know about advertising," but I didn't know anything about painting. That's what I took. That's where Fritz Eichenberg, Jacob Landau, and Richard Lindner were my teachers.

You say illustration and painting were combined. Did you lean toward one or the other? No. For me it was all mixed together. When I got out of school in 1960, the Society of Illustrators had just started having shows, so there was little or no history on which to model myself. Also, I had no idea how to get illustration jobs. I barely knew what an art director was then. I knew that one could get a nine-to-five job in advertising design and photography, but that wasn't possible in illustration.

Were you aware at that time of any illustrators? Bob Weaver and Bob Gill were influential teachers. I could relate to Gill. He was animated, and he did interesting work. Bob Weaver—I didn't understand him at all. Then when I got out of school, I started doing etchings, and it was Weaver who told me to enter my prints into the Society of Illustators' Show, which I did.

Had you been published at that point? Just barely. I got a job the first day I went out—for a *Playboy*-type magazine.

Your etchings seem quite unusual for that period in illustration, yet they are contemporary-looking now. Their beauty, for me, is the unfinished quality, the looseness and the energy. I'm surprised that the society accepted you. I was, too! And the fact that they gave me an award on top of it was just incredible to me. Anyway, that's when I got friendly with Bob Weaver. It was only then that I started learning from him—on a one-to-one basis. He would go through my sketchbooks with me, asked me questions about them. He really made me understand what I was doing.

What was it that you were doing? I was tracking my thoughts. I was doing my work as a subconscious effort,

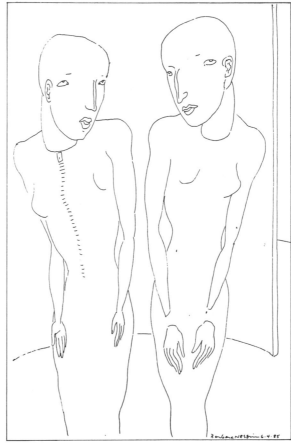

and it was coming out as a conscious thing. There were certain things in my books that were very narrative, were explaining my life to me. Certain feelings that I had about looking at the world through a man's eyes, or how women and men related to each other. Those were concerns of mine at the time, and we used to talk about them. He made me feel comfortable with who I was.

Was the linear work that you were doing then similar to the etchings? Yes. I started doing linear drawings with applied local color. I did those etchings at Pratt Graphic Center, where I won a scholarship for the summer right after I was graduated. Michel Ponce de Leon was the teacher at the time, and he would criticize my method, saying, "I'm sorry. What you're doing is not allowed. It's not considered a print or a series, because you're not taking a plate and doing the same thing all the time." I said that I felt they were a new form, which I named *monotype etchings.* I used oil paint on paper, which was also not acceptable. After I completed all my work, he congratulated me and said he

was going to rethink what I was doing. Obviously, I felt good. I always liked inventing or discovering things. The etchings still look good.

You weren't playing by the rules, either. I rarely played by the rules.

Since what was in your portfolio wasn't conforming to the requisites of commercial art, how did you get accepted in the profession? I mostly did work for *Playboy*-type magazines. I couldn't make a living from my illustration. I worked three days a week as a textile designer, doing plaids, stripes, and colorings. The art directors said they loved my work but never used it. Henry Wolf used me sporadically in *Show* magazine in the early sixties. He was very supportive.

The girlie magazines offered freedom? Absolutely. And I did a lot of interesting etchings for them.

Did you have any philosophical problem about working for girlie magazines? I didn't like it, but if that was the only place I was going to get work, so be it. It was better than getting married. I tried everything else: for advertising

125

Top: *Sketch for cover of generic disco album for Columbia Records; unpublished. 1978. Pen and ink and watercolor on D'Arches paper. Art director: Paula Scher.* Bottom: *Drawing from sketchbook. 1983. Pen and ink.*

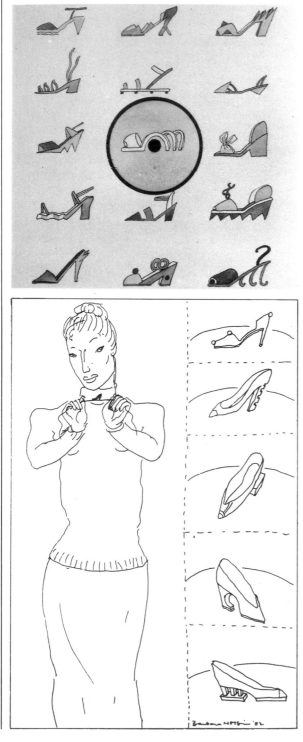

agencies, I was too weird; for regular magazines, I was too strange. But, you know, I never realized that at the time I was one of the few *female* illustrators around. Only looking back did I realize there were so few female illustrators. So when I would walk into an office, I was a novelty, rather than somebody to be taken seriously. I had several art directors in the early stages ask me why I wanted to do this. Why didn't I consider getting married? What kind of life was this for a nice girl? I always responded politely and nicely—I guess I had to be acceptable in a lot of other ways in order to succeed at this maverick life-style.

Were there any female models at this time? Others who were working in the arts? There was Lee Bontecue, who I didn't know but whose work I thought was very beautiful. There was Marisol, whose work I respected, too. I later found out that she was wealthy. People who didn't have to earn a living and were in the arts—even if I liked their work—were not role models. A person who had to earn a living—I had to earn my own living—and still could do their work, that was a role model. And I didn't know one woman who was freelancing at the time.

Were you always working in many different media? When I first got out of school in 1960, I did illustrations, many etchings, and worked in my sketchbooks, and I didn't do any large paintings. But people kept telling me that I was a fine artist and not an illustrator. And I kept arguing because I felt that fine arts was surviving and suffering, and illustration was making a living. Finally, after three years of everybody telling me I was a fine artist and not an illustrator, I decided to go to the Art Students League. I went every night for six months, and I thought even every single night wasn't enough time to really do meaningful paintings. So I got myself a studio and painted furiously.

By that time, what themes were you working on? Pretty much the same kinds of themes I'm working on now. Female imagery and women relating to the world.

So you were adding painting to your oeuvre, and you were making prints and drawing. At what point did things start improving in the illustration world? Eight years after graduation. Actually, I thought to myself many times, "Maybe I'm in the wrong business." Because by then I was twenty-eight, and I still couldn't make a living. I was getting awards right and left. (That's one of the reasons I stopped entering shows, because I realized that awards didn't mean two cents.) I thought I must have been doing something wrong since I tried to bend myself as much as I could to make my work more acceptable.

Was it that art directors didn't feel comfortable with your

Illustration, The Bronx Martini, *for the Hotel Barmen's Association of Japan calendar. 1980. Watercolor with pen and ink on D'Arches paper. Art director: Shinichiro Tora.*

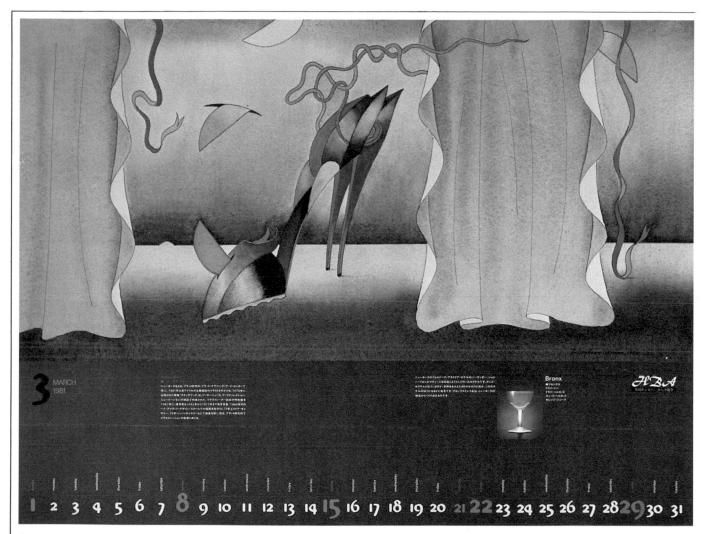

imagery? That was one reason. Another was that I didn't know how to make women really attractive in a conventional way. It was difficult for me to portray *pretty.*

Why was that? It didn't come out! I'm not the kind of illustrator that uses a luciograph and copies a photograph—I rarely work from photographs. I work basically from my head. And whatever comes out, comes out. That's what my work is all about!

You were also an interpreter. I never get the sense that you are forcing a symbol or forcing an idea. It's very natural imagery, and I could see that being a handicap in the illustration world. If you look at what illustration was then, you can see very well why my work wasn't being accepted so readily. My work was very painterly and didn't seem narrative in

the usual way. Even though I thought of my work as narrative, it's only in a very subconscious way. It's not narrative as in "now I'm going to tell you a story," but it twists and turns and bends.

So what made it click? I think that there were other illustrators who were influenced by my work, and they in turn made my work more acceptable to other art directors by example.

What do you mean by that? They made me see *how* my work could be more acceptable for publication use. At the same time I became good friends with an art director, who was also an artist, Uli Boege. He taught me how to use the work I did for myself as reference; to use my personal symbols and translate them into a picture that

127

would represent the story. He would show me an illustration that was derivative of mine and explain why art directors and editors could relate to it.

What were some of the things said that allowed you to gear yourself up commercially? It was just *working* with me, basically. He would give me jobs, go over every aspect in detail. He would go through all my personal work, pull out some paintings that he felt applied, and we would use them for inspiration. Often he made me do a job over, sometimes four or five times. Then he would choose perhaps one of the earlier pieces that I did, saying, "This one has just a little something the others don't have." The whole process was very enlightening *and* so frustrating that sometimes I felt like bopping him over the head. But it helped me enormously.

Were you developing a process? One thing about my work then and now is that I don't have preconceived reasons for doing things. So that's probably why it took me so long to understand what others were doing. When I saw how somebody else could interpret my work and make it commercial, then I could see clearly. I too could make my work more acceptable by making a conscious effort to change, whereas before I would just do everything intuitively.

Can you give me an example of one of those conscious changes? Was it changing a face? Repositioning people? Or dealing with a story on a more literal level? I think I just better understood how to make the work relate to the job.

And how did that happen? By controlling and changing the symbols, making what was once cryptic more understandable to the reader—while still trying to maintain the spirit of the work. Being more conscious about how I was drawing the figure. Sometimes I was more successful at this than other times.

Did you consider that a compromise, or did you feel comfortable with it? I wanted to pay my rent!

But in terms of the artwork? You know, it's difficult to say whether I considered it a compromise or not. I was very glad when I could make my work relate to a story— I was thrilled, in fact. Because I somehow felt I could now do work that was acceptable to people who had been telling me for years and years, "I love your work but I can't use it." That offered a little bit of freedom. It turned out that even though I thought my work was slanted more commercially, clients still had a hard time with it. But little by little I made more money. I can't say that I ever made a great deal of money.

I remember that at a certain point in the mid-sixties, your work was all over, meaning it was more accepted, at least in editorial markets such as New York, Audience, *etcetera. Was that, in fact, a time when you were becoming more accepted and sought after?* In 1968 *Print* magazine did a cover story on my work. That was the *first* time any kind of public notice was taken. I didn't start working frequently for *New York* magazine until the early seventies, because the editor did not understand my work at that time. Milton Glaser's positive influence encouraged my eventual publishing.

When you think of an illustrator as a hired hand, you do not conform. You are coming to it not with hands but with heart. But in those days you seemed to be emerging as an artist. I was! For me every year got better. Furthermore, more women started becoming art directors, and that made a big difference.

You're right. There weren't many women before 1970. Bea Fietler, Ruth Ansel, and, of course, Cipe Pineles were among the few editorial art directors. Ruth, Bea, and I all started at the same time. They were assistants to Marvin Israel at *Harper's Bazaar* around 1962. So when women started becoming art directors, it changed for me. Women like my work, much more than men. I'm not saying that no man likes my work, but nine times out of ten a heartfelt compliment will come from a woman.

Were there any other significant changes in the business that accelerated your success? Well, *Ms.* magazine came out in 1972. The whole women's movement started flowering, and that's part of what my work was about.

What kind of assignments were you getting at that time? What were your favorites? I liked everything I got.

Everything opened up a different door for you? Always, when somebody gives me a job, I think about it. I won't accept a job that I don't think I can handle. Sometimes I'm called by someone who might know my name, but doesn't really know my work. Usually the jobs that people call *me* for are really interesting. Illustration for me has always been a way to force myself to think conceptually about the work I do. It's another way of contemplating and seeing. I'm now very specific when I do an illustration. I try to address all the issues at the same time.

You're always working. You have hundreds of sketchbooks. You work in numerous media. And you have themes that you consistently deal with. How do you do an illustration? I go right to my sketchbooks, and *that* is my illustration.

What motivated you to work in sketchbooks? I just like to draw. I like to know what I'm thinking about, and so I keep a visual diary. A lot of ideas come out there that ordinarily would not. I don't *think* about anything when I do my sketchbooks, I just do them.

Top: *Illustration for article about cosmetics in* Mademoiselle *entitled "Colors Coming Up." 1982. Collage and gouache on Canson paper. Art directors: Paul Greif and Marilu Lopez.* Bottom: *Cover for the Dutch translation of* Outrageous Acts and Everyday Revelations *by Gloria Steinem, published by BV Uitgeverij De Kern. 1984. Pastel on Canson paper. Art director: Jan Van Willegen.*

In the sketchbooks, are you transcribing ideas or working out stylistic problems? I do everything. It's my place to jump around. I like the fact that it's a book, and I never tear anything out of it. It's like life, you might be sorry you said or did something, but you did it, and nothing will change that.

Do you use other kinds of resource material? Yes. But not in the usual way. I surround myself with beautiful objects, and when something appeals to me in a book or magazine, I'll leave it open or hang it up. These references aren't specific to a job, but a way of life, a way of looking.

It seems to me that illustration and your more personal art are almost one. Am I right? No, I have two different lives. The work that I do for myself is different from the work that I do for illustration. The illustration is inspired by the work I do for myself. That's the way they intermingle, but I consider them worlds apart.

How do you proceed with an illustration? Do you do sketches? I like doing sketches. I didn't like them early on. For some reason, I thought sketches were demeaning. If somebody wanted to see sketches, that meant they didn't trust me, and if they didn't trust me, forget it, Charlie. And now, I wouldn't even consider doing an illustration without a sketch; I mean, a detailed sketch. And I *want* the art director to look at it. I want *everyone* to put their eyes on it. I make Xeroxes of it, and we make notes—everybody has the same Xerox—because I've had enough misunderstandings. You asked me how I start, what my process is. The art director calls me and tells me the subject. I either read the story or talk about it. Sometimes it's carte blanche, like for the *Time* cover. They said, "Do something about the women's movement. It could be editorial, it could be political, it could be years ago, it could be now, it could be the future. Anything you want." They wrote the cover line, "Climb to Equality," based on my illustration. Other times I get an article where the illustration has to be very specific.

Does the sketch process slow you down? Does it unfreshen the work? No. I'm very comfortable with my work. I rarely transfer it. Each drawing is something new. If I do sketches or not, there's no difference. The sketch becomes a reference for the finish.

Another thing that interests me about you is how organized and business oriented you are. Have you always been? No. I realized many years ago that I needed a "wife." I didn't understand how everybody got things done, got jobs delivered, entered illustrators' shows. I was not in a lot of the early shows because I didn't have the time. It was hard

enough just to pick up the job, do the job, deliver the job, do my own paintings, and do the laundry. When I finally realized that most of the male illustrators I knew had wives who did it all for them, it finally made sense. So I got an assistant to help me.

Did it make doing art more pleasurable or easier? Both. It also freed me to do other things. This is going to sound really strange. But I've learned a little bit about public relations. It might take me a little long to catch on, but once I catch on, I've got it. I was never as organized as I am now, but I am basically the one that keeps it organized. The only thing that my assistants do is take things to the photographers for illustrators' shows, wrap my paintings if necessary, do errands, and Xerox things. But I write the letters and everything else.

How did you get into computer art? Well, I'm always interested in doing different things. In 1980 Peter Spackman, who was then the head of the Council of the Arts at MIT, called me up and said, "Barbara, I think it would be great to have an artist come up here and do some work on the computer." It sounded great to me! So we corresponded, and I got information about computers. I talked to many programmers. I was told to get *Byte* magazine and some other computerese magazines and read the ads. And that's what I did. I got it that way. I never went up to MIT, because I had just gotten married, and there were lots of other things to do. It wasn't until a year and a half later that I thought I could spend the time. But by that time, Spackman was planning to leave. Then computers started getting popular, and it was difficult to get funding for me to work at MIT. Meanwhile, I had developed a good background in it, even though I had not been on one. So I decided to find a computer here and was invited to use one at Time-Life. It was really difficult, because everything was so secretive.

Was anybody doing imagery on computers at that point? Well, they were doing some commercial work then, working on developing a videotex information service. I would go over there at night and wasn't permitted to talk about what they were doing.

What prompted your imagery? Did you work off of the limitations of the computer? Did you decide that you were just going to do what you were going to do? I did both. This computer only had a limited amount of resolution, colors, forms, and patterns. The fewer things I had to work with, the more fun. Not that I'm saying that I don't like lots of resolution, that would be fine, too. But that's not what I was given, and I tend to like economy. As far as the imagery

was concerned, the resolution was so low that it was difficult to do detailed drawings. It had a rough feel, like a woodcut.

You didn't feel that the computer was taking anything away from your drawing ability? Not at all. I don't think I've ever used an art form where I felt that anything was taken away from me. I don't care what you give me. I'll do something with a stick and whipped cream.

How far are you taking the computer art? I'm going to get my own Macintosh. I already have plans for it, and I want to market the drawings, which will be hand-colored xerography on a very good paper.

These are not intended as illustrations? I never think about illustration. This is totally mine. Then, if an illustration or a job comes along where I think that the process would fit, I may use it.

Your devotion to the computer has not supplanted your devotion to other art forms? No! I still like doing it all. It's just an added attraction. It's a tool and a medium all in one, which is historic. It responds to you. You can make a "family tree" off of your original work. I coined that phrase because I can't think of anything more appropriate—you're branching off the original and, after many stages, you still have that original image intact. No other medium or tool has enabled artists to achieve this.

You've been teaching for a long time. What is it you teach? The basics of illustration, how to get a concept. I also teach a little bit about business. I try to demystify this hocus-pocus. I don't glamorize the field, because I don't think it's glamorous. In fact, if I had it to do over again, I doubt very much whether I would do illustration.

Even knowing that the route you took led you to this point. I would still have gotten to this point. I would have made my money another way.

So it comes down to dollars and cents. Absolutely. When I started illustrating, the available money was more than it is today. I don't see how illustrators make a living at all. It's one of the only professions in the art field that hasn't kept up with the cost of living. I would never want to be an illustrator today.

And in terms of creativity, would you say the same thing? No, I think it's more creative now. I love the new illustration. I would fit right into it if I were twenty. Illustration today is strongly influenced by the Chicago-based "Hairy Who" from the early sixties, Jim Nutt, Gladys Nilsson, etcetera. It's narrative and fun. But it's hard to make a living. And in a way, books like *American Illustration* promote the myth that maybe you *could* make a living. It's like running after a carrot.

Unpublished computer image entitled
African Queen *(Computer Image*
#117). 1982. Computer graphics,
adapted from painting in a 1979
sketchbook.

MARSHALL ARISMAN

Marshall Arisman (born on October 14, 1938, in Jamestown, New York) achieved critical notice in 1972 with the publication of Frozen Images, *his book of black-and-white graphic commentaries on violence. A regular contributor to the* New York Times Op-Ed *page, he further earned a reputation for dealing with hard-edged and controversial subject matter, which he continues to practice through strikingly expressionistic paintings. Since 1963 he has co-chaired the media arts department of the School of Visual Arts and now directs its unique master's program, "The Illustrator as Visual Journalist."*

I started out as a graphic designer. Having graduated from Pratt in graphics, I got a job at General Motors, where I helped design the Delco logo. I stayed there three months and realized I didn't like working with groups of people. I also realized that I wanted to do more drawing on my own.

Had you been drawing much before that? Not much. I started taking drawing classes at night at Wayne State after work. I got so involved in drawing that I didn't want to go to GM.

What kind of drawing were you doing? Figure drawing. It didn't relate to anything I do now, and I wasn't sure how to make a living from it.

So when did illustration become an option? When I came out of the army, all I had was a graphic design portfolio, but freelancing as an illustrator didn't look all that impossible. My first drawing portfolio was influenced by André François— it was a typical kind of humorous European poster style.

Was this something that you picked up while you were in Europe in the army? Yes, it fit my limitations. I *couldn't* draw, but I *could* do humorous posters.

What do you mean, you couldn't draw? I could *style* things, but I couldn't really draw. I had a primitive style, which I suppose was the charm of my first portfolio. I got work, but after a year or two I realized I had reached a dead end. I had a formula and a style, but it was at the sacrifice of any real drawing. I wasn't becoming wealthy, so I decided maybe it was time to back up and take the step I skipped: learning to draw.

Did you take drawing courses? Basically I taught myself. That's when my work began to change. I went back to black-and-white sources—Goya, Velazquez, El Greco. I spent a year doing a series of black-and-white paintings while studying the masters. At the end of the year, my former illustration agent, who had opened up a little gallery, gave me a show.

Illustration for a cover story in the Boston Globe Magazine *about mental patients. 1983. Oil on paper. Art director: Ronn Campisi.*

Top: *Sample portfolio piece. 1964.
Gouache on board.* Bottom: *Sculpture
entitled* Man I, *shown at the Allan
Stone Gallery, New York. 1968. Aluminum window screen on Masonite.*

What kind of drawings were they? The review in the *New York Times* said, "A curious combination of Goya and Beardsley." Looking back at that work, I was doing illustration. The drawings had ideas; they were a combination of mass and line. I had a little trick of mixing turpentine with India ink, so there were little bubbles here and there.

Were they conceptual drawings? Very much so. The content had become less cute. For example, I showed women with men around their necks in place of fur collars; women with horse heads instead of hairdos.

Where did that imagery come from? Heinrich Kley was an influence at that time. I would look at his drawings and steal.

After the show closed, the gallery owner started talking about the next year's show, and I realized I was in the middle of a change again. I wanted to do sculptural forms and to paint, which I hadn't been able to do before. Curiously, I began getting illustration work as a result of the show.

Editorial work? I had been trying to get into *Playboy* for two years. I sent slides, but nothing happened. Then I sent them an announcement for the show. Obviously, they didn't make the connection between what I had sent before and the show, because I got a phone call in which they not only gave me an assignment but apologized for it. They said, "Well, we know you're a fine artist and don't like to do commercial work, but we're *Playboy* and we have this black-and-white drawing we would like you to do." So that was my first taste of the contradiction. Looking back, it did make total sense; my work was more like illustration than anything else.

Define, then, what you mean by "illustration" with relation to those drawings. They were socially oriented. They were highly figurative. They told stories, had a narrative line of some kind. They weren't just drawing for drawing or form for form.

Was this a period of other realizations? Yes . . . my father had a stroke, and it was the first time I sensed my own death. And it was terrifying. I began to work these sensations into my art. This is hard to explain, but I was attempting to show in sculptural form a transparent skin as an outer layer and internal organs as an inner layer. I spent three years developing these curious, large figures that represented mortality. I would paint them white, then ink the top surface like a woodcut. The outer skin was made out of window screen, which one could actually see through. Between the grid of the screen and the groove of the under layer, you got moiré patterns. From twenty feet they look like huge charcoal drawings of bronze figures.

134

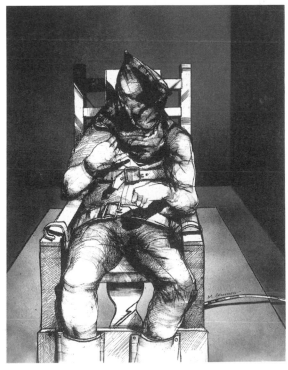

This form was a major influence on the way I drew after that. I can go back to all of my black-and-white drawings and see the origins of these forms.

At some point, you began to do more conventional drawings for illustration purposes. Yes. The problem with those large pieces was that I couldn't get any detail in them simply because of the building process. So I went back to drawing again and started working on a series conceptually based on handguns. From the four or five drawings I originally planned, it grew to ten, then twenty, finally seventy-five, and I had spent something like a year and a half doing work that became a series about violence.

What inspired you to pick handguns as a subject? I was raised in upstate New York, and as a kid, guns were very much a part of life. Almost everybody I knew, including my brother, carried a gun. Also at that time, there was a proliferation of photographic violence in mass-market publications. When I did these drawings, Vietnam was going strong, the Watts riots were occurring, there was a never-ending stream of violent images in magazines. On one page, you'd get an ad; on the next page you'd get a horrific photograph. I was beginning to feel numb, and in an effort to raise my own consciousness—to feel again—I put this series together about violence, trying to make it relate to the *idea* of the photograph. I even cropped the drawings like photographs. It was the first time I put tone into my drawing as an attempt to make them feel more photographic.

I started spraying backgrounds with gray spray paint. I also learned about light and dark. I remember reading that Goya attributed a great deal of his knowledge of light to tapestry designs. For me, it was the first time I really understood how to look at and get information from a photograph.

What did you do with all these images? I decided, since I had seventy-five of them, that I had a *book*. I walked around New York and saw many publishers. Everyone said: "This isn't enough; you need a text for a book. You need a famous writer to write an introduction." So I sat down and thought, in the best of all worlds, who would I like to write something about my work? I dismissed all the art critics. However, I was reading Kurt Vonnegut at the time. I got his address and sent him photographs of the drawings. He called me one night and asked if he could lend me money or send me some booze. I explained to him that he was certainly more famous than me and publishers might be interested in publishing the book if someone famous wrote the introduction. He said the book obviously didn't need any words, but he would write an introduction.

Were the publishers at all in tune with your subject matter? No. On the way to interviews, I would buy a copy of *Time.* Invariably, the editor would look at my seventy-five drawings and say to me, "My God, these are much too violent. Why would you spend your time drawing subject matter like this?" And I would open *Time* and point to a photograph and say, "This *really* represents violence, my drawings are just commentaries." The editors would look at the drawings and then look at me like I was crazy. I would try to point out that this was a reflection of what was happening in the real world. The irony is, I think I did just what I was objecting to: I put too many images of violence together, which ultimately made people numb.

How, then, did you get the work published? The School of Visual Arts started a press and wanted to do a series of picture books. So I finally got it printed. It was one of the most important things I think I've ever done. It became my portfolio and became the basis for the illustration work I got.

Is that when you began to work for the Times *Op-Ed page?* The work on the Op-Ed page was directly linked to what I did in the book, and there was certainly enough violence in the world to keep me relatively busy.

Once the book was published, did you find violence was your forté? People were calling me for it. I was not getting general phone calls saying, "We want you to illustrate this or that." I was getting specific requests, such as, "There's a riot in Uganda, they're executing people, we would like you to do a drawing."

Do you think that the needs for illustration in general at that point were changing and more receptive to your unconventional subject matter? I don't know if illustration was changing. There was certainly a phenomenon taking place on the Op-Ed page. The page was quite exciting. There was a unique group of artists doing black-and-white work. The images were dissimilar, but there was some sort of connection to content. It didn't last that long, though. Like most things that get that much exposure, it became a little school, was copied, and is now the conventional black-and-white drawing that people think of as editorial illustration.

So I started painting at that time but was determined not to mix my painting with my illustration. I continued to work in black-and-white for illustration and was painting for myself. The inevitable, however, occurred. Someone at *Playboy* had seen one of my paintings and called me to do a series on the Gary Gilmore execution, for an excerpt of Norman Mailer's book *The Executioner's Song*. I was painting very strange heads at the time—large faces with metal forms in them—not narrative in the usual sense of illustration. I felt they were emotional but didn't express anything specific. The source for much of it was a medical book on the Civil War, full of lithographs of miniballs stuck into bone marrow. I'm fascinated by the contradiction of metal in something organic, such as bone.

Your paintings are so personal. How could you apply them to illustration? I had made a vow that I would not do a painting for commercial work. So *Playboy* said, "If you are willing to paint a portrait of Gilmore for the first installment and paint a kind of breakdown of that portrait in the second installment, we will reproduce one of your head paintings in the third installment." It perversely interested me because I hadn't shown these head paintings to anybody, and I thought it would be a good way to have people react to them.

So you did the assignment to get exposure for your personal work? Yes. I sent the three paintings to them, and they called me and said, "We love the portraits," but they didn't say anything about the head. Finally, they admitted that it didn't work. And it didn't, really. It was just an excuse for me to print a painting. So I only did Gilmore, which proved more successful. After the *Playboy* series, I suddenly got calls for color. I guess it was the right time. The black-and-white market was drying up on me, and I was also getting tired of doing it.

Was it becoming too routine? Too symbolic. One of the problems with doing drawings dealing with national or international issues is that you have to simplify enormous ideas without personalizing them; so you have to find symbols for them. If you do enough, you repeat yourself.

Did you feel that your earlier illustration was more per- *sonal?* Yeah. There was a time when the articles I was assigned to illustrate suggested something much more personal.

Therefore, the article became a vehicle for you to express yourself? Absolutely. Moreover, people began to ask me if they could reproduce some of the drawings that already existed as illustrations for certain articles. So many of my personal statements were being published, in fact, it started looking like I was doing a great deal of illustration. The truth is I have never done a great deal. I don't have an agent, and I don't take out a portfolio to look for work. Every three weeks or so, I get a phone call for an illustration job. I like the immediacy of illustration. It has a beginning, a middle, and an end. It takes me out of the head I'm in when I paint.

What kind of illustration are you being asked to do now? I have been categorized as someone who deals with violence. I've made no attempt to stop that. In fact, it serves me in a curious way. I've always felt that art has a variety of functions, and you have to choose what function you want it to serve. There's art as amusement, art as concept, art as theory, art as propaganda. I've always been interested in art that expressed emotion, whether it's an illustration

job or a painting. So when someone calls me and says, "We want you to deal with violent subject matter," they are on some level asking me for an emotional statement.

But you don't think of yourself as a "generic" violence illustrator? No. But a typical phone call starts with, "Marsh, you're going to love this one."

You sick bastard, you. Right. Sixteen people got shot in the middle of so-and-so. I'm aware of that. As I said, I've made no attempt to change it. I'm really not interested in taking the emotion out of my painting.

The problem I have with most illustrators is that they don't think of themselves as artists; they think of themselves as illustrators, which is very different. If you think of yourself as a service, then ultimately you are producing style and not content. I see illustration simply as another outlet for the work I do. I think the publishing industry is using me, and I am using the publishing industry. It seems a fair exchange most of the time.

Do you ever take on jobs where you cannot exercise control? Sometimes I make mistakes with jobs and get in over my head. I have to be a little careful about context. For example, someone asked me if I would do a Budweiser ad for *Rolling Stone*. I was asked if I could take one of my large heads and substitute beer cans for the metal forms.

Sounds like co-option time. Exactly. So I'm a little careful about how far I go. I'm willing to admit that I'm a whore, but I do have some guidelines. More importantly, I began to recognize my levels of tolerance for pain. Certain kinds of illustration work were so painful for me to do, it simply wasn't worth the money.

You appear to know what you want and where you want to go with your art. I also understand my process better. I haven't done anything "right" in this field. I don't do sketches for illustration. The reason for that is the way I paint. I like to use my hands, and I prefer not to know exactly what's happening; in essence, I'm sketching with the paint. So to do a sketch in pencil or in charcoal and then paint it means I have to try to make the paint do what the charcoal will do, and that usually doesn't work. When I work with somebody for the first time, I give them a finish on their sketch deadline, with the understanding that if it doesn't work, they don't have to pay me. I know the Graphic Artists Guild would kill me for this, but I am willing to take that risk. The truth is that 99 percent of the time, it has worked.

Do you generally have to explain the work? To some degree. I will obviously call the art director and tell him or her what I'm doing. If he or she gets real uptight, I'll take the painting in wet to show. It's not an arrogant position, it's just a *process.* Most art directors are not idiots. If you don't burn them by turning in something that's unusable on the last possible day, they're open.

Illustration and painting are one with you; that's not the usual way in the art world. Painting is another dilemma. I realized a long time ago that painting was very necessary because it makes me feel better—that it is a real function for me. Whether my paintings are good or bad, or whether my illustration is better than my painting or vice versa, I don't know.

Are your paintings influenced by Francis Bacon? I've spent most of my life in the illustration and painting world being compared to Francis Bacon. He was certainly a major influence. In the late sixties, at a time when pop art was dominant in New York, I saw my first Bacon exhibition at the Guggenheim. It proved to me that emotional painting was possible. I found that at the end of the ramp at the Guggenheim, I was stunned by the emotional impact of what I'd seen. So there's no question that Bacon is an influence.

I've always believed that you don't teach anybody anything through art; what you do is remind people of their own knowledge. And it's knowledge that is not totally conscious. The pictures that hang in my brain and not on the wall are the ones that have reminded me of my own knowledge. I think Bacon reminded me of some curious knowledge.

When people say you have borrowed or stolen from Bacon, are they referring to content or style? I suppose a little of both. I feel that a lot of people don't see much in terms of subtleties, that people tend to categorize most things. What happens is, people see the work and there is an emotional association that I suppose is negative. I mean, there's something unpleasant happening. That is obvious in a Bacon painting; whether you see the subject matter or not, you can feel it. Even upside down, there is some sense that unpleasantness is happening. I think that as I continue to paint, the obvious influence of Bacon gets less and less. My hope, obviously, is that I will eventually absorb it. My optimism in art is believing that there is real influence. The fun for me and the meaningful part of showing work is finding people who actually do connect to it.

You don't take your portfolio around to sell your illustrations, but you do some unconventional things to get your paintings noticed. Didn't you once publish a calendar of paintings? A friend of mine, an illustrator, suggested that I do something perverse like print a calendar using my paintings and send it to galleries. All of my fine arts friends

Illustrations for Fitcher's Bird, *the unexpurgated story of Bluebeard, published by Creative Education. 1983. Oil on paper. Art directors: Etienne Delessert and Rita Marshall.*

went crazy. They said, "That's an illustrator's idea. Galleries will hate you for it." But I was getting nowhere anyway, so I sent out five hundred calendars. This was before the neo-expressionist movement achieved notoriety. I got a letter saying, "It's hard enough for me to get up in the morning and come into my gallery without having to face this kind of thing." I had people saying that if I were the last painter on earth, they were not going to show my work. Out of the five hundred, I got one response that was positive, a call from the Sinden Gallery. The director called and said, "I'd like to see you this afternoon." I ran over to the gallery before he came, and it looked okay. Then he came over here and bought four paintings. He put them up and couldn't sell them but gave me a show anyway.

You've given up your gallery and are now working on The Last Tribe, *a series of narrative paintings that seem to be a synthesis of your illustration and painting. They are very ambitious. Do you see this as a culmination of a heartfelt theme?* I see it as a personal relationship. If I had to pick one book that has been more important to me than any other, I would probably pick *The Ghost and the Machine* by Arthur Koestler, which is primarily about the primitive instinct and the capacity for violence that we have. Koestler said, "The loudest sound in history is the sound of the war drum."

It's that primitive instinct I have been trying to get to in all my paintings. I'm very aware that I am painting the same painting; all my pictures are from the same emotional base. I know I've done a good picture when the picture comes to me through my stomach. Many times I have painted fakes of my own paintings. The surface quality is there, but there's no real hit. So *The Last Tribe* is somehow a culmination of things I've tried over the years. Visually, I wanted to reach that primitive level of the brain and relate it to a traditional form of painting.

Primitive art is my favorite, probably because it was never meant to be art. It was meant to be an expression of feeling. So tribal objects are very important to me. Someone needed to create them, and they have the power to match the intent.

Doesn't the paint actually slow you down and make the work somewhat contrived? No. For the last year, I felt very much like George Catlin, the artist who painted Indians; I get up every day and paint another member of the tribe. I think Howard Pyle, the father of American illustration, said that the real issue in illustration is the ability to project yourself into your picture. The issue is, if you can't live within your pictures, you'll continually paint style and surface.

So I actually feel like I'm one of the tribe members.

I don't know where all this goes. I see myself in some curious way conducting an as yet unresolved experiment: is it possible to be an artist and use illustration as one of your outlets and galleries and calendars as others? Or, are there very real lines that exist, making it necessary to choose?

By example you are changing the current limits of illustration. In what direction do you see the form going? I think the initial change is to move off the single page. Some things cannot be done in one image. Most of the time, for one illustration, I'm being asked to read twenty pages and come up with one image. If somebody gave me a manuscript and said, "You've got four pages to explore this manuscript," you immediately get into different problems. The page-to-page, the narrative form, the time sequence, and the space sequence can be explored. It immediately takes you out of that awful interpretation of Magritte—the symbolic symbolism, convoluted concepts.

How do you go about working on an illustration? I do a lot of research. I try, in essence, to put myself in the situation of not trying to illustrate. For a drawing on the execution of the Reverend Jim Jones, I actually went out and bought the shirt, a cheap polyester red shirt, and I painted the picture while wearing it. They are games for me, but they are process games. In illustration I can't start at one point and then totally change it in the middle, the way I can in painting. Meaning that simply, if I start out to paint a dog in an illustration, it can't turn out to be a pig—in a painting, it can. Many times my final paintings are totally different from my interest in the beginning. The illustration pretty much ends up where I started.

This sounds negative, but the truth is, I don't think I've ever learned anything from an illustration experience. I have learned informational things. But what I haven't been able to do in illustration is fail. And consequently, I tend to take fewer chances. But that's okay; it seems legitimate. It's not too much to ask, to come in with a dog instead of a pig. But I'm quite regular in terms of work habits. I have an obsessive personality, so the minute my wife goes away, I fall back to my old pattern. I am up all night long. I am painting till five in the morning. I can't get up till one in the afternoon. I start painting at two o'clock. Luckily, marriage has kept me on some kind of a schedule, so I can have some kind of an outside life. Before I got married, I had no outside life. I hated everything. I think what happens is, the idea of failing gets so terrifying that the only thing you can do to protect yourself is work yourself to death.

Paintings from The Last Tribe, *a series of narrative paintings (also a proposed book). 1984–85. Oil on paper.*

BRAD HOLLAND

Brad Holland (born on October 16, 1943, in Fremont, Ohio) began his career as an illustrator in such odd environs as a Chicago tatoo parlor and the Kansas City headquarters of Hallmark Cards. He arrived in New York in 1968 and was immediately given an assignment by Herb Lubalin for Avant-Garde. *With success within his grasp, he periodically left the overground for the underground, always with the intention of expanding his boundaries. Not content to be tied to one governing style or point of view, his graphic incarnations have been numerous; but with each change of line or of conceit, he has caused a rippling effect throughout the illustration field. Holland has influenced many artists and art directors. His belief in the power of illustration as a vehicle for personal expression has contributed to its now diverse applications.*

It's hard to say how I started in this business. It seems like I just barged in, and nobody ever chased me off, so I stuck around. You know, there're always more artists than there's room for. You never see articles in the *New York Times* about how the Russians or the Japanese are getting ahead of us in art. So you just have to wedge yourself in where you can. When I set out, hardly anybody made it in this racket before the age of forty. It was like the Masonic Order or the Brotherhood of Raccoons. You worked your way up by degrees to the higher orders, had a comfy middle age, and ended up painting portraits somewhere. So it was hard for somebody as young as I was to break in. I got so used to being called "The Kid" in those days that I still answer to the name.

When you started drawing, did you have any knowledge of illustration? No. I'm not sure I do even now. See, where I grew up everything was pop culture. Howard Pyle, Michelangelo, the Katzenjammer Kids—it was all art to me. But I didn't know how a person earned a living doing that stuff. I knew most of those guys had been dead for years. But Walt Disney had these programs on TV, showing how they made their movies and that seemed a little more accessible. So in the seventh grade I started getting work ready to send to Disney. I knew I'd have to do something to earn a living in a few years, and I knew I didn't want to go to college.

What was so terrible about college? Well, I'd learned to read before I went to kindergarten, and I went to kindergarten when I was four. So things moved a little slow. I remember in kindergarten we had to stand up and recite this silly poem about a duck. It was easy to memorize. It was so dumb you couldn't forget it if you wanted to. I still can't.

White Man's Magic, *illustration for article in* Science 85 *entitled "The Politics of Mistrust." 1985. Acrylic on Masonite. Art director: Wayne Fitzpatrick.*

Left: *Unpublished illustration entitled*
Short Orders. *1961. Ink on paper.*
Right: *"I Came Back to Jesus" cover*
for The East Village Other. *1971.*
Acrylic on board.

"Little Ducky Duddle went wading in a puddle." When my turn came I wouldn't recite it, though, because I thought the name was stupid even for a duck. I didn't want to say it. They kept making me get up in front of the class until I started to cry. I told them I just couldn't learn it. I hoped they'd think I was stupid and leave me alone. A bunch of kids started to laugh, somebody called me a dummy, but I just stood there crying. I never did recite that poem. They sent me home with a note saying something like, "Bradford seems unable to learn." Meanwhile at home I was chugging through Oscar Wilde's *Happy Prince*.

Was that what most of your school life was like? Yeah. It was an all-American education. In high school we had a science teacher who used to ask if Mickey Mouse was a real mouse.

Were you drawing all along? I started submitting cartoons to magazines when I was twelve or thirteen. Then I sent my portfolio off to Disney when I was fifteen. I figured if I got a job there, they'd let me quit school. So I did a lot of stuff. I had storyboards for *The Song of Hiawatha*, Pecos Bill, Paul Bunyan. I did some dirty stories, too, but I didn't plan on sending those to Disney. I had drawings showing camera angles, backgrounds, animated flip books, character model sketches. I even had songs that I had written. I wasn't messing around.

Did you intuitively know how and what to do? No, not the technical things. I found that stuff in a book in the library. I just checked it out for four years and returned it when I was graduated. Also I found an old WPA pamphlet about cartooning that said Disney ran a school for animators. This, of course, was true back in the Depression, which was how old the book was. In the fifties, they were firing people, although I couldn't have known that. I hoped that Walt Disney would come down like the duck in "You Bet Your Life" and hand me a ticket to Burbank. I figured once I got to the studio I'd learn the rest and, you know, maybe meet Annette. In fact, I figured with all my talents I'd be able to help Walt run things. I thought their movies were too cute, that they should be more satirical.

Did your parents encourage you? Yeah. My mother encouraged me daily. Sometimes she'd encourage me several hours a day. Then she'd warn me that my father would encourage me when he got home. She claimed that when I wasn't getting into trouble, I was drawing, which was nearly as bad. She was concerned that I was going to be a dreamer or a deadbeat, which I probably would have been if I had stayed in town. She'd say, "Bradford, it's fine to have a hobby, but you've got to learn to live in the world." In retrospect, I think it's helpful to have people discourage you early. If an artist can be headed off at the pass, he will be, sooner or later. Only the strong survive. Anyway, by the time I was fifteen, I had about a thousand drawings piled up in the closet or out in the barn. I mean, this wasn't your average teenage hobby, like collecting Elvis records.

How did you submit these to Disney? Like junk mail. I didn't really know how else to do it. I didn't know what a

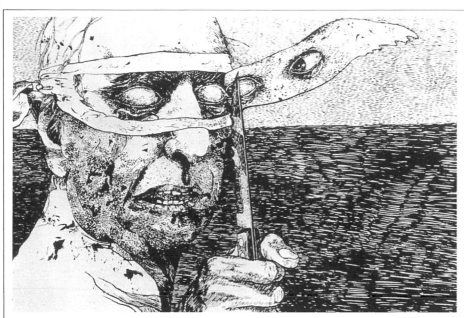

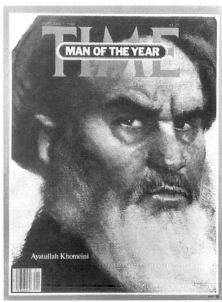

portfolio was. We didn't even have a bookstore in town, let alone an art store. But we did have a stationery store where I got typing paper and Ebony pencils. When I wanted to paint, I'd go to the five-and-ten and buy a mess of model airplane kits and throw all the parts away to get those little jars of airplane dope, and those cheap camel hair brushes. Then I'd get some shirt cardboard and do these awful, shiny paintings. For charcoal drawings I used briquettes, you know, saturated with fire starter. God! Have you ever tried to do a drawing with a charcoal briquette on shirt cardboard? Anyway, when I was fifteen, I got several hundred drawings together and put them in a cardboard box. I typed up a letter on a neighbor's typewriter, saying I was twenty-one, and sent it all off to Walt Disney Productions, Burbank, California. Then I waited for about a year. There wasn't even a note from Walt saying, "Thanks for the box."

Too bad you didn't know about registered mail. Well, about a year later, I got a note from the local post office saying there was a box for me from Burbank. By this time I was so sure they'd rejected me that I wouldn't even go down and pick the thing up. I didn't even want to see it. Because in the whole time I had thought about being an artist, I never allowed myself to think what I would do if I got rejected. But I didn't want the post office to throw the stuff out, so I finally went down to get it. Well, the box was in pretty bad shape. It looked like it had been around the world a couple of times and been thrown down a flight of stairs. When I opened it, I found the drawings

all folded over and wrinkled. Some had big thumbprints on them. I was wondering, "Are those Walt's thumbprints?" And at the bottom of all this was a little two-color rejection slip on heavy stock, with a picture of Mickey Mouse saying something like, "Mickey doesn't want you." So who wants to work for a mouse anyway, right?

Were you reading a lot when you were young? Well, I always read, except what I was supposed to. But I didn't illustrate what I read. I just played with it. Like, I'd take *Don Quixote*, which I've still never read, and make up a story based on the images. I did Pecos Bill the same way. The stories were just a point of departure.

Were your concerns aesthetic or conceptual? Were you illustrating an idea or making a drawing? I was essentially thinking in pictures, I guess. At the time I was just feeling things out. I wasn't illustrating anything. If I wanted to tell a story as such, I'd write. I'm a good writer and I always wrote a lot—stories, skits. I had a little acting group and an Indian dancing group. We toured, had our own trailer, lights, sound system. We performed in three or four different states, at camps and county fairs. When I wanted to write, I simply wrote. But I always felt I could get multiple feelings, even contradictory feelings, into pictures without having to name them the way you would in prose.

Did you understand things best through pictures? I don't know, but I liked the immediacy of pictures. I'm kind of like my dad. Dad's a carpenter; well, a lone-wolf builder, really. He can build a house without blueprints. He says he can just see it finished in his head. And he gets awfully impatient whenever he's got to explain anything to somebody else. So that's probably where I get it. Although I'm not like him in one respect. No matter how I imagine a picture when I start working, I just let the thing make itself up. I never even know what colors I'm going to use.

When did you decide to look for real illustration work? When I got out of high school, I hung around for the summer, helping Dad build a house. In the fall I went to Chicago and took my drawings around, in a fashion about as inept as I sent them to Disney. By this time I was doing some very strange drawings. They were all very crude, like drawings done with a sharpened stick dipped in ink.

What were you aiming for? I meant to be satirical. But they were darker, less cartoonlike by then. My big influence then was a *Mad* magazine artist named George Woodbridge.

I never knew anybody else who modeled his style after Woodbridge. I liked the way he drew teeth. He drew these guys with about a thousand teeth. When they smiled they looked like they had corncobs sideways in their mouths. Very intriguing. But as I said, my drawings were a little too dark to be really satirical, and there wasn't much of a market for satire in the first place. In Chicago, as I came to absorb the notion that I might be a failure for life, I began to identify with all the losers and drifters and drunks I used to find on Madison Street. I lived in a flophouse there for a while. Back home in Ohio, I'd been drawn to the migrant workers. I'd do sketches of them sometimes as they'd come rolling into town on the backs of trucks to pick tomatoes or sugar beets or something, or I'd see them living in shanties on the edge of the fields, or hanging out downtown at the Spanish Inn. I'd just do scribbles of them then. It was more a way of imagining I was them than a conscious attempt to make art. But in Chicago, as I found myself sinking lower on the totem pole myself, the drawing of the derelicts took on the intensity of self-portraits. And since I was never able to peddle anything I didn't believe in, that was the kind of stuff I took around.

Why did you go to Chicago? Because it was close. From Ohio, New York seemed about as far away as Paris. Chicago was just a bus ride. You got on the Greyhound, rode all night, and got off in the Loop. My grandmother gave me a breaded-veal sandwich to take. I remember standing in her yard, by the clothesline, getting ready to leave. My dad's pal Arkie came over to say goodbye, and I heard him ask my mother with a big grin, "Did you warn him about the boys?" And my mother said, "Oh Harold, I don't even want to think about that." And my grandmother said, "Now,

Bradford, when you get to Chicago, you're going to see these storefronts with women sitting in front of beaded curtains. Now you daresn't go in them places. Because there are A-rabs behind them curtains, and they'll take all your money." Anyway, with that advice, I started up and down Michigan Avenue. Didn't find many A-rabs, though.

What did you do in order to find work? I'd walk into buildings and look at the directories to see if there was anything that said "studio." If there was, I'd go up and apply for a job. Well, my drawings looked very homemade, especially for the commercial art business in those days, when everybody wanted to be Bernie Fuchs or Bob Peak. I got everything from blank stares to teen counseling. One art director flipped through my stuff and offered to introduce me to the Savior. He said he was afraid a psychiatrist wouldn't do me much good.

Didn't you finally get a job in a tattoo parlor? Yeah, I just walked in to keep warm one day and walked out with a job. I was never really keen on tattoos for myself, although I thought they improved some people. Especially the kind that hung around tattoo parlors. Wasn't much of a job, I was just there a little while. After that, I got a freelance job at a studio. It was a crowded little cubbyhole with three, sometimes four, of us crammed in. Whenever one of us got up to leave, the others had to get up to let him out.

Was that John Dioszegi's studio? Yeah. John's a great guy. Very gentle, very generous. One day, when I was still seventeen, he told me, with great respect, that people like me only came along once in a lifetime. Well, I'd heard that kind of stuff before, but not usually as a compliment.

Did you learn a lot from him? When I met him he was thirty-four, twice my age. As a man he taught me a great deal. As for drawing—well, I was pretty accomplished. Even in those days I often did the pencil sketches for his jobs. It was my rendering and my ideas that seemed to horrify everybody.

Did you leave because you wanted to learn more? Well, I had to make a living. The second year, we weren't making much money, so I worked for IOUs. I had a job at a supermarket, to survive, loading stock at night and on the weekend, and working at the studio during the day.

Did you stay in Chicago after you left the studio? Oh, I got around. I was headed for New York, but I ended up in Kansas City.

And then you went to work for Hallmark, right? I met somebody who said Hallmark had offered him a job for $425 a month. Said they were starting a department to do book illustrations and were looking for pen-and-ink artists. Of

course, I wanted to go to New York, but I needed some money to start up. I was always hearing stories from guys in Chicago who had just returned from New York with these tales of horror, you know, like Kurtz being brought out of the jungle. New Yorkers were vicious. They'd beat you, rob you, steal your ideas, steal your style, and send you back home with tin cans tied to your tail. Anyway, I went to see Hallmark about a job. Figured I'd work there a couple of months, earn a few hundred dollars, unless, of course, they paid in IOUs.

How did Hallmark respond to your work? Cautiously. They could see I had talent, but the fact that I was applying for a job in wheat jeans made them cautious. They knew I wasn't going to stay long, so they took me on the condition that I start producing immediately. And they only offered me $300 a month. I said I had heard they paid $425, but it seemed that was only for college graduates. They paid even more for a master's degree. I was only nineteen, but I knew I was better than the guys with degrees, so I said, "Nuts to this," and hitchhiked back to Ohio, where I tried to get a job in a washing-machine factory. Stood in line with about a thousand guys at the Whirlpool plant one day. But I took one look at those blanks on the application forms where you have to list your experience, and I saw that my goose was cooked. You know, the words *tattoo parlor* always look impressive on a job application form. For my last salary I had to list my IOUs. With the kind of employment record I had, even the local seatcover factory turned me down. So at last I called Hallmark, said I'd take the $300, and became a one-man department there, illustrating books.

Did working in Kansas City improve your self-confidence? Oh, I didn't lack self-confidence. If anything I was self-confident to the point of arrogance. At least that was a common rap against me in those days. See, people in fine art kept telling me I was a commercial artist, and people in commercial art kept telling me I was a fine artist. So I knew I was doing something right, but I wasn't sure what. And I certainly didn't expect anybody else to understand it, so I didn't try to explain anything. If people couldn't figure out what I was up to, it didn't bother me. I figured time was on my side. So, no, self-confidence wasn't my problem. It was money. I was flat broke and each day seemed like one more checkmark on an endless calendar.

Were you unhappy there? Well, I learned things I hadn't counted on. For example, the way people use a power structure to define themselves. It was a great lesson. See, one of the ways the company tried to discipline me was to make me a supervisor and give me some of the company

misfits to boss around. But it was a miscalculation from the beginning. I was late for the little ceremony where they promoted me, the way I was late every other day. Then when they called me in to tell me that I was now "management" and had to wear a necktie, I insisted they had to pay overtime to my people when they worked late. It was a good education. Anyway, after I had saved a few dollars, I headed for New York.

Wasn't Herb Lubalin the first person you saw when you came to New York? Yeah. That was back when he hired artists to do whole issues of *Fact* magazine for five dollars an issue or something like that. So when I got off the train, I went to Lubalin's studio and dropped my stuff off. I returned a couple of hours later and he offered me a page in the first issue of *Avant-Garde.* He asked where my studio was, and I said, "I've got a locker at Grand Central Station."

Did you know what you were doing? Sure. I got a room in the old Taft Hotel. It was about the size of a filing cabinet. I went to the five-and-ten in Times Square and bought some art supplies, a spiral notebook, some Scotch tape, one of those little plastic sharpeners, and a number-two pencil. I drew on the floor that night and took a sketch in the next day. It was several sheets of spiral notebook paper taped together. Lubalin laughed and shook his head. That night I got more art supplies and did a finished drawing.

Was your work akin to what you were doing for Hallmark? In terms of style, yeah. The Hallmark stuff never did look

like anything else there. I was definitely not attached to the mother ship. They were doing cards with bunnies and skunks and so on. I remember one that had three beavers on a raft. Stuff like that. Since I wasn't doing beavers, the organization never did find a way of dealing with me. I got a lot of vague complaints. Things like, "You know, your people aren't very friendly. Can't you make them nicer?" They complained that a whale and even some of my trees weren't "friendly." Still, since I was actually illustrating stories, I did some decent things there. But when I got to New York I decided to go for broke. I swore I would only do my own ideas, my own way, and I wouldn't make changes for anybody. I figured with that kind of attitude, I'd either starve or go straight to the top.

But you must have also realized that with an attitude like that you'd meet resistance. Well, what that period in Kansas City really did for me was to give me a year out of the mainstream of art. I began to think of my work in terms that had no relation to any of the clichés of contemporary art. I said to a friend one day, while we were walking around, that I had identified three kinds of artists: fine artists, commercial artists, and real artists. And real artists were the ones who didn't worry about which of the other two kinds they were. See, the work I was doing then didn't look like what galleries in New York were showing, and I reckoned that if I came here and took my stuff around they'd say, "Hey, this isn't pop art," and I'd get the bum's rush. So I began to think of magazines as an alternative. I figured I didn't necessarily have to illustrate anything to get work published. I thought I could just get art directors to give me a page or two in their magazines to do whatever I wanted. I was just a trifle self-confident.

What I remember of your early work is that it was all black-and-white. For any reason? Originally I decided to do a really bold black-and-white style because it would reproduce without halftones. But when I got to town I realized that editors had no interest whatsoever in running art by itself. So I decided I'd have to trick them and pawn off what I wanted to do as illustration. And I figured that since they tended to treat black-and-white art as secondary work, they'd give me less flak over it. I wasn't quite right. I got all kinds of flak, but it wasn't really surprising, given my methods. The first step was to explain why I would have to do my own ideas. Then there was the manuscript to weasel around. I always read it, of course, but I treated it as just a frame of reference, as if the writer and I were simply doing separate assignments on the same subject. Then, I'd internalize the whole deal and just draw whatever

God's Business, *the finished illustration for a cover of the* New York Times Magazine *entitled "America's Activist Bishops." 1984. Acrylic on rag board. Art director: Ken Kendrick.*

came, without trying to rationalize it. And I did pretty well with some of the early jobs, especially some of the stuff at *Playboy* where Art Paul let me run loose.

But not every art director was Art Paul. No, and worse than that, I couldn't always pull off what I was trying to. I got a job from *Redbook* early on that really showed me the limits of my approach. It was some dumb story about a girl who didn't have a dress to wear to the prom, and I never did find a way around that manuscript. What I finally did for it was a hodgepodge of intentions that added up to nothing. I even liked it at the time. But when I saw it published, I just cried, "What have I done?"

And yet that one got into the Society of Illustrators' Annual. You were, in fact, becoming successful, but didn't you retrench after that? Well, in a way. I began to get tired of having to finesse my way through every job. A lot of editors were accusing me of not having mastered the art of reading. One told me my work was perfectly meaningless. I said that didn't bother me and couldn't see why it should bother him. So yeah, I dropped back. I was looking for a hidden door through that commercial stone wall. I decided to look for some people in the business who hadn't figured out what they were doing yet, since I figured there would be a better chance of influencing them.

You began working for underground papers. I was the only artist I knew who started with *Playboy* and *Redbook* and worked his way up to *Screw, Rat,* and the *New York Ace.* But those crazy papers were great for what I wanted to do. They were all so new that their editorial policies were nearly indistinguishable from anarchy. You could do a drawing and paste it up and see it printed a few hours later. Of course you couldn't make much money, but I had low overhead. The best part was that we had fun. There was nobody there stroking his chin and scratching his head trying to decide if all the readers would get it. See, I knew if I kept going around to *Redbook* and *McCall's,* I'd be as successful as I could stand to be. But I was learning new things in New York, and I didn't know if I could stumble around for ways to express those things when people wanted illustrations about prom dresses. Of course, I was never your typical underground cartoonist, either.

I do remember getting angry with you—the way people got angry when Dylan changed from acoustic to electric—when you started doing that R. Crumb–like cartoon exaggeration. Well, actually, the exaggeration owed more to David Levine or Gerald Scarfe. And the style I began using was more influenced by a cartoonist who called himself Yossarian and some Puerto Rican friends of mine, guys I met when they were robbing my apartment. We got to be quite good friends, and I think some of their attitudes rubbed off on me. But I did take what Crumb was doing as a challenge. He was taking pop values as an end in themselves and putting a spin on them, whereas I was trying to trash them outright. And I realized that his approach was cozier and probably carried a greater charge. I was always more the outsider during that period, like Huck Finn on a raft, neither in society nor outside it, with a cold eye fixed on everything.

What particularly were you trying to learn during that period? I never knew for sure. But I always knew when I had found it. I suppose discipline, for one thing, which in art means craft. Beyond that, I was just trying to learn how to describe the life I was leading on the Lower East Side. I was fusing really crude cartoons with Japanese woodcuts. As usual, I picked up anything, anywhere, and threw it together by instinct. Sometimes by mistake. When I was a kid I learned from *Mad* magazine, Gustave Doré, Popeye, N. C. Wyeth. When I got to Chicago I discovered Ben Shahn, Leonard Baskin, Hokusai, Cuevas, Diego Rivera.

149

And when you moved to the Lower East Side . . . I embraced disorder and ugliness. I made one false start after another. Lost the battles, convinced I'd win the war.

Your models were not unusual, but what you did with your knowledge seemed to buck the accepted role of the illustrator. In commercial art—well, even in fine art, since one's no less commercial than the other—you're supposed to find a style, get on a roll, and then run it into as much money as you can. But I was just trying to lead an interesting life and to spin off some work, so my style kept changing. When I was still living in Kansas City my style was baroque. Like life in Kansas City.

I remember it being the ultimate in chiaroscuro. There was no tone at all, but it gave the impression that there was. Yeah. But when I moved to Eleventh Street that all changed. Somebody who knew me in those days said I reminded him of all three of the brothers Karamazov, struggling for possession of the same soul. He said that like Dmitri, I was a creature of my senses. Like Ivan, I was harsh and intellectual. And like Alyosha, I seemed determined to throw away everything that came easily or was dear to me. Since I could draw well, I chose to draw crudely. Since success came easily, I treated it casually. I suppose he was right, but I knew I wanted to learn to live without the crutch of my strengths, to learn to live off guard, out of my born element, to live by my wits. I wanted to ignore everything that most people think they have to have. You know, there's a sense in our culture that you can never drop back and punt. That you can never fall lower than whatever rung of the social ladder you happen to be on. And in a sense, I knew that an artist who's unwilling to lose is a loser by definition. So the move to East Eleventh Street affected me, mostly because I became close to all the people I had previously identified with from the outside. I wasn't going down to look at animals in the zoo. I wasn't drawing migrant workers on the back of trucks, then going home to the subdivision. I wasn't slumming. That consciously ugly style of mine came from embracing life down there.

You tried to do light, humorous work, but it never seemed to jell. Well, congeal might be a better word. My intent wasn't really to be light and humorous; humor and tragedy are just the front and back ends of the horse. I was simply trying to feel my way through what turned out to be the grotesque. Maybe I was overreacting to my experience, but then maybe you have to be a kid from the Midwest just arrived in New York to actually notice what is grotesque. What I was doing then, in the late sixties, would look quite up to date in an East Village gallery now. Except that now

the grotesque is rather a cliché of fashion. With me it was steps in the dark. I was completely caught up in the life I was living. I didn't get up in the morning and wonder what I was going to draw that day, or what my next career move would be. I'd get up, check the mailbox for dispossess notices, and look to see if there had been any break-ins. Then I'd go out on the street to see whose car had been burned the night before and make the rounds to see if any of my friends had to be bailed out of jail. Life was a free-for-all. I loved that time.

At what point did things change? When I fell in love. I mean, really in love. I met a beautiful woman, I wanted to be alone with her all the time, and my place had become virtually a clubhouse. So I moved to a little brownstone in the Village, where my whole life took on a different color. Of course, a lot of my pals found their way over anyway. One was a guy who called himself Babi Jeri. He was editing a comics magazine called *Yo-Yo*, and he got me to write a story for it. It was a long rambling thing, told in flashes with drawings that had very little storytelling paraphernalia, very little text. We worked on the magazine off and on for a year, then threw it together in a weekend.

Stylistically, there was something fresher about that work than most of what I see today. And probably better drawings and ideas than I've seen of late. It was the root of your Op-Ed approach, I believe. Right now there's an awful tendency to parody what went on in the Op-Ed page in the seventies, worse than ever before, to the point where I believe the symbolic drawing is better off being buried for a few years. Yeah. It's become pretty limp. To me, my drawings weren't symbols at all, they were images. Symbols by themselves carry no weight. But images come from the subconscious, like music you hear from another room. Maybe you hear it without noticing. Later you catch yourself humming it. That's what art is.

Was it difficult to persuade others to let you make use of personal imagery? It was really just an ordinary war of nerves. But yeah, when the time comes to write my autobiography, I'm going to call it *He Takes a Licking and Keeps on Ticking.*

But you have succeeded, ironically so, in creating an approach that has spawned imitators. Somebody asked me years ago how I made it up the ladder of success so quickly. I told him I never found the ladder. I just stumbled up the stairs in the dark, and when the lights came on, there I was. He seemed disappointed. I think he was wanting something surefire.

Would you say that the drawings for the Op-Ed page of

Illustration entitled Equatorial Zone, *for a special issue of* Mother Jones *on Ronald Reagan. 1984. Acrylic on Masonite. Art director: Louise Kollenbaum.*

the New York Times *really established your reputation?* Well, the stuff for *Playboy* paved the way. But since it was erotic, it did have a rather limited audience. So, yeah, the stuff for the *Times* was the big breakthrough, although it was probably the least likely place for me to break through. When J. C. Suarès called me to show my work there, I thought he was kidding. The page was just starting, and I figured the *Times* would never use the kind of things I was doing in the underground press. But Suarès persisted and finally got me up to see Harrison Salisbury. Harrison was different from most of the editors I had dealt with before. He went through the drawings with real interest and picked out several to use for articles. I had done a drawing of a junkie, so they got a junkie to write an article about himself to go with it. The first time in my whole career that an editor had actually understood the work exactly the way I intended it! Harrison seemed to understand instinctively that magazines don't have to use art just as illustration. The time he was editor there was a great period.

Did that work for the Times *grow out of your concerns about the Vietnam War, the Nixon presidency? Is that too simple an explanation?* For me it's too simple. I wasn't one of those people who loved to draw Nixon. And I wasn't really doing drawings about war or poverty or drugs either. Those things are too abstract to get a handle on. What I did was personal. For example, the drawing of the junkie was just a guy I knew on Eleventh Street. He overdosed after getting out of jail on Riker's Island.

But many of your drawings were applied to outside issues and given additional meanings. Did that bother you? No. I've always been a practical fellow where tactics are concerned. For me, the drawings were really attempts to be specific without being literal. But to get them published I was willing to apply them to whatever was handy, the way congressmen piggyback bills to one another. You know, illustrators are always supposed to "solve the client's problem," as the cliché goes. But I figure if I solve my own problems, they can be made to apply somehow. So I never thought of myself as a political artist.

As you said, we all categorize too much in this country. But categories aside, your drawings became a new form of political art. Yeah. Then a new form of careerism. The *Times* started all these supplements and just adopted the so-called Op-Ed style for everything. After a few years, the place began to look like Santa's workshop. There was one new art director who always had about a half-dozen artists sitting on cabinets and window ledges or hunkering

down in the corners making changes on drawings while he ran the stuff back and forth into an editor's office for approval. It was amazing. Then he began handing out copies of my drawings to these artists. For pointers, he said. Finally he began to hold these guys over my head, telling me how happy they were to make changes and how they never argued with him. Well, I could see the handwriting on the wall. The day Nixon resigned, I was trying to come up with something that would sum up Watergate without being a cliché, and I remembered an idea I first had when Nixon was elected. So I did it and took it in. It was a drawing of Nixon as a bunch of Easter Island statues staring out to sea. Well, when I showed it to the guy, he laughed out loud. But he said, "How do I explain this to my editors?" I said, "Don't try. If you don't let them think about it, they'll get it. The minute you start monkeying with explanations, you're sunk. They'll start intellectualizing about it, and the whole thing will come unraveled." Well, I left there with moderately high hopes, but in my heart I knew it was an illusion. I could see over by the windowsill that he had several elves on duty. The next day, when the paper came

151

Sketch and finished illustration for The Inspector, *for a* Science 85 *article on nuclear regulatory agencies. 1985. Art director: Wayne Fitzpatrick.*

out, they had replaced my drawing with a rendering of an eagle with a big tear in its eye. Of course, everybody thought it was quite lyrical, but that's the kind of dull platitude I had gone into the underground press to avoid doing in the first place. So I just gradually quit doing work for that outfit, except for the few people there who had some integrity. The guy kept calling me from time to time to tell me he had found "the new Brad Holland," and I'd just say, "good luck."

You were doing work elsewhere at the time. Otherwise things were going well. T. Y. Crowell had just published a book of my drawings; magazines were calling. But at that point I broke up with a woman I was living with, and between that and everything else, I just got a little down in the dumps for a while. I decided to take a trip to California for a few weeks. I went out there fantasizing that I was going to change my name and start writing for a living. In an odd way, I rather fancied the idea of starting over.

But obviously you didn't. No. I got an offer from a publisher in Zurich to go there and do some lithographs. I took a sketchbook with me and did some landscape drawings for the first time since I was a kid. I came back with dozens of ideas for paintings.

Was that the point at which painting became the important medium for you? No. I'd always painted, but the volume of work I was doing in ink kind of pushed it aside. I had done several paintings of women I was seeing. Then there was one painting that was a watershed of sorts for me. It was of a man with cat's eyes. Now, a sense of dignity requires that I point out this was years ago, before cats had become a national resource. What made it really different, though, was that it looked like it had been painted with pea soup on canvas. I did it for no reason and hung it on the wall for a couple of years. Then one day Suarès called and said he was doing a cat book. I sent it to him, although I figured he'd say it was unfinished.

I don't understand what you mean by "unfinished." Well, a lot of people who saw my paintings in the seventies said that they didn't look finished. You remember, back then everything had to be rendered to a fare-thee-well, with local colors and hard edges. Then there was the whole army of Paul Davis imitators. So the cat picture was really different. Just two yellow eyes staring out of a sea of mud.

Did you follow that up with more paintings? Did you recognize that at the time as something new? Oh, I probably thought it was unfinished. But curiously, a lot of people saw it. Then *Playboy* asked me to do some more paintings like it, and within a year the calls began coming in.

Was the Ayatollah cover for Time *another benchmark?* Professionally, sure. Of course, given the situation with the hostages in Iran, I knew the cover would be a sensation, so I wanted it to be strong. I did it originally as a waist-length portrait, but at the last minute I cropped it and asked them to run just part of the face. It was great having something so notorious for a week or so, and besides, how often do you get a chance to do a guy in a turban? But the real breakthroughs for me were several years before when I did a whole bunch of small paintings just to amuse myself. It isn't that I just got better all of a sudden and did the Ayatollah. The time just seemed to have come for what I was already doing.

Are you doing anything that you consciously see as a movement away from your present work? Well, see, all my life I've been everybody and nobody. And my experience has been one of the Everybody in me trying to educate the Nobody. So I learn essentially by instinct or maybe blind luck.

Do you seek out artistic models? Not intentionally, no. I'm kind of like one of those birds that makes his nest out of grass and tinsel. I just rummage through life and take whatever interests me. Since I'm interested in most anything, it isn't difficult to find material.

Are there artists you feel influenced by right now? Most of my favorite artists are dead. There are several advantages to that; the main one is that you don't run into them at parties. The problem with most contemporary artists is that they've all gone to college and learned that to be taken seriously you have to cause a revolution in art history. But ask yourself, how many revolutions can you have in art history every year? So most of them just end up acting like Stanley Kowalski with a paintbrush. I tend to identify more with artists like Mark Twain or Duke Ellington. I remember reading when I first came to town that Duke Ellington was still playing morning shows at the Apollo. I'm sure he wasn't crazy about it, but maybe that's the price you have to pay for being an artist in our time. I think if you're secure enough you can push out the commercial limits, the way these guys did.

Do you feel you do that now? Well, some days are better than others, but yeah, I've felt it for years. That kind of confidence is where all the false starts were leading. The last couple of years have been like batting practice. I've just been trying to hit balls to all fields. I never think about style. It just comes. Somebody calls me to do a job and I just take it. I know something will materialize when I start. I've been trying all kinds of stuff.

GUY BILLOUT

Guy Billout (born on July 7, 1941, in Decize, France) came to the United States in 1969, at which time New York *·magazine reprinted his entire portfolio. He developed an exquisitely meticulous linear and color style—a marriage of Japanese woodblocks and the cartoon strip "Tin Tin"—underscored by mordant (usually deadpan) wit. His first book,* Bus 24, *marked both a stylistic and content departure for illustrated books. He continues to create highly sophisticated picture books for children and adults.*

I've been in New York for sixteen years. Before that, in France, I was an advertising designer.

For whom did you work in Paris? I was lucky to start with some of the best teams in big advertising agencies, where I discovered Swiss design. But I always had the fantasy that I would become a poster artist; at that time, the real master in that field was Savignac. My other influences were André François and Ronald Searle.

What was your drawing like then? I was doing typography mostly. I did comp and layout sketches that didn't require any style. And I hired illustrators, never imagining that I could do illustrations. After five years, though, I realized I was going nowhere.

Some people go into advertising and stay there; what was it that caused your restlessness? I knew I was not good at it. I could have survived, but actually it was right after the 1968 student demonstrations in Paris. There was a lot of social and political tumult at that time. Talk about restlessness, there was plenty of it in France.

Did you take part in any political activities? One couldn't avoid it. I was captivated by the mood. So I would go to meetings and would follow demonstrations—everything seemed possible. I handed in my resignation later that year and then I came to New York. (But I am not sure that there was any correlation between these two events.)

Had you been to the U.S. before? I had come two years previously, trying to find a job as a designer. Once I made the decision to return, a friend of mine suggested that I be an illustrator. He gave me the idea for a unique autobiographical portfolio, because he thought Americans would love the illustrated story of a Frenchman's dream about coming to New York. So that's what I did: fourteen sequential drawings about my life. The pictures came out of me without too much suffering. As though they'd been waiting a long time. Since it was a portfolio, I wanted to show all sorts of styles and techniques.

What kinds of techniques were you using? Mostly what

Top: *Detail from the artist's first portfolio, entitled* J'arrive a New York, *published in* New York. *1969. Magic marker, watercolor, and ink. Art director: Milton Glaser.* Bottom: *Sketch for the announcement of an illustration show at the Schiller-Wapner Gallery in New York featuring the artist's work. 1984. Pen and ink.*

I used as a layout man: the magic marker. I also used colored pencil, gouache, and even a little bit of oil paint. As I wanted so badly to be versatile, I was surprised to discover a very consistent style.

Were you aware of Push Pin Studios? Yes, indeed. The idea of meeting Milton Glaser was really my dream. At that time, I had a friend who was going to Glaser's night classes. She insisted that I come and bring my drawings. I was paralyzed with timidity and was glad not to be able to speak English. Well, Milton Glaser invited me to visit him at *New York,* which I did. There he announced to me that he was buying the portfolio of drawings for publication. It took me half an hour to realize what was happening.

Well, that's an incredible way to start, to have your "portfolio" published in its entirety. When did you begin getting jobs? Bob Ciano, who was then at *Redbook,* gave me my first job. I started to realize that I was influenced by Jean-Michel Folon in terms of sense of space, the isolation of the character, and also in the use of watercolor.

And conceptually? Were you using his Everyman character? The small character was the most obvious temptation, and it comes back again and again. But I have never been aware of copying him. It was more like absorbing a mood.

You came to the U.S. as a designer and became an illustrator. You planned to return to France after a year but that was sixteen years ago. Were there other surprises? The most important happened with Harlan Quist. He gave me an extraordinary opportunity: "Do a book, your own story, your own theme." I felt no fear or apprehension, very much like with the first portfolio.

This was *Bus 24,* a story without words. The idea came from a picture I noticed in an old German book of tales for children called *Slovenly Peter* by Heinrich Hoffman. In one of these tales, a mother pleaded with her son not to suck his thumb because a man with big scissors would chop it off. Suddenly bursting into the picture is that frightening apparition of a tall, skinny man with huge scissors.

It is that dramatic effect that inspired the ominous fantasies of the boy waiting for a bus in my book.

Did that harken back to your childhood, being born in German-occupied France? I have no memories of the war, but my mother did remember and probably communicated her anxiety. What I remember are scary children's books full of witches and snakepits, dragons and children. Hungry ogres. I loved them!

So Bus 24 *was your homage to fear and anxiety.* It was only later, after people had seen the book and reacted to it, that I realized that I had made a book about these kinds

Drawings from Bus 24, *the artist's first children's book, published by Harlin Quist Books. 1972. Dyes and inks.*

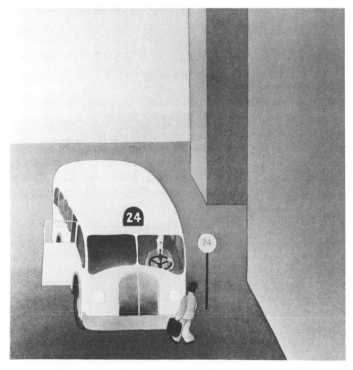

of emotions. It wasn't a conscious decision.

After Bus 24 *came out, why didn't you do another book right away that exercised that kind of freedom?* I did some sketches for another wordless story, but I was not sure I wanted to work for Quist again. However, I need a deadline to work, and I didn't look for another publisher to give me one.

About five years later, I was in the country going through the agony of a break-up. In order not to spend time alone and brooding, I took my pad and began to draw from life, something I was always afraid to do. Aside from the therapeutic effect of the process, I was amazed by the result. It did not look like my illustrations. There was no humor, and above all, I started to enjoy the freedom. While there are given colors in a landscape, I didn't have to adhere to them; I could use a red where there was a brown; I could make blue what was in reality gray. I felt something incredible about taking such simple liberties—surprised that nobody could say, "You can't do that."

Going back a moment, do you consciously try to make illustration funny, or is humor second nature to you? I don't have to force the issue, it is a normal inclination. The process of finding ideas still surprises me, though. Somehow I know how to create the right conditions for me, but I don't feel that I control much.

What are the right conditions? I read a story and then start to draw; if that doesn't work, I take a nap or walk down the street or look at illustrated books. The process is really agonizing, and I've never been able to take it for granted that I will eventually get a good idea.

Do you find that you go back to old ideas? I remember some of the drawings I did when I was a boy, like that steamship crossing the ocean. More than twenty years later, I am still drawing it.

Your humor is not slapstick; it's more subtle, probably because you don't use gags. How did that evolve? I've always been attracted by understatement, the kind of humor that requires a little attention to get.

I think my best work, in that vein, has been in the page I do for the *Atlantic*. Sometimes, though, the editor finds me too obscure, and I have gotten letters from readers asking me what I meant by something.

You're very free to deal with paradoxes and ironies—it's become a trademark for you. Would you say that you perceive the world in contrasts? I think I am afraid of the world, always expecting something awful to happen. As soon as I am given carte blanche, the same obsessions arise, cliffs, precipices, snakes, and, of course, catastrophes.

Finish for The Rescue, *an illustration featured on* The Atlantic's *page regularly devoted to the artist's musings. 1985. Watercolor and airbrush. Art director: Judy Garlan.*

You do ominous situations in a way that isn't frightening, though. On the contrary, you evoke a sense of recognition. Perhaps because there is a need to counterbalance that sense of horror with humor.

Let's go back to what you were saying about landscape drawing from nature. How did that change the way you were working as an illustrator? I remember years ago doing a drawing of Central Park for *New York*. I drew the trees in a very stylized, simplified way, because I did not know how to draw them. Observing their foliage, I became fascinated with the textures; when I began to draw trees from nature, my style started to change.

So it got to be richer in a sense. Before that you simplified more. From trees, I went to houses and then bigger structures. I used to draw skyscrapers making lines as eyes for the windows. Like for the trees, I was aware of my limits but it did not occur to me to go out and look at the real thing. When I finally did, along with drawing, I started to take Polaroids to help me finish a drawing at home. Now I just shoot pictures and draw entirely from them.

You appear to do much less freehand now. Yes, and I miss the unpredictable nature of the handmade work, but I also like the kind of control given by the airbrush. However, I am not really interested in developing more skill with the airbrush.

Then why do you prefer the airbrush now? I've always been impressed by the smoothness of the Japanese woodblock. Also, the use of flat tones by Hergé, the creator of "Tin Tin," a comic strip I started to read when I was twelve and which influenced me, I believe, in a very deep way. Hergé in his time was one of the very few who cared about colors.

So Hergé's influence played a part in your acceptance of airbrush? It could be that. I've done some of these flat tones by hand, and they look pretty good. But I like very much the perfection and fullness of tone given by the airbrush.

For some illustrators, the airbrush is a step removed, because you're never really touching the paper. Yes, but the basic process remains the same—even more complicated with the airbrush. You work half-blind when using the frisket film. You cannot see how two colors match before you peel off the frisket.

What tools do you like using? With the airbrush, usually I use the straight line of a triple-zero Rapidograph pen. When drawing from nature I use a pointed-nib magic marker, which gives me a thick line with many "accidents." Because this type of ink is waterproof, I can use watercolor directly on it.

I applied that technique to a series of illustrations about Miami, commissioned by *Vogue* magazine. Once published, the style seemed so different that I could act out an old fantasy. I bought a page in the Graphic Artists Guild annual and showed my drawings under a nom de plume, hoping to sell a style nobody would recognize.

On the contrary, I remember that we all thought, "Here's some guy ripping off Guy Billout." Do you prefer selling total concepts? Were the children's books your own ideas? Yes, they were. Prentice-Hall made me an offer that was irresistible: to create a series of books on any topics I chose. Once again, given total freedom, I made more progress in one book than in many regular assignments.

The books that you've done have all won awards and all been highly praised. But one of the things that some critics say about them is that they are adult books, not meant for kids. I am not aware of my audience as children. I just illustrate moods and feelings, and I think that grownups are

Top: Minots Ledge Lighthouse of
the Boston Bay, U.S.A. *from* Stone
and Steel, *published by Prentice-Hall.
1980. Watercolor and airbrush. Art
director/editor: Ellen Roberts.* Bottom: Nature *from* Thunderbolt and
Rainbow, *a children's book written
and illustrated by the artist, published
by Prentice-Hall. 1981. Watercolor
and airbrush. Art director/editor:
Barbara Francis.*

wrong to believe that they don't relate to children. However, I wish there were such a thing as an illustrated grownup's book.

Are there things that you wouldn't do? Subjects that you wouldn't tackle? As a professional, I used to consider that there was no bad assignment. I worked on these dry, abstract stories for corporate magazines; today, I tend to pick stories that seem to match my obsessions.

You say you're trying not to overuse your "little man." I am just not so interested in that vision. It comes back because in the past it has been really important for me.

Your drawing seems so perfect that I can picture you seeing an imperfection and just going crazy. I do get crazy when I don't meet some of my own expectations. Usually it happens with the choice of colors. After hours on a job, very often I have these depressions, believing I have ruined the painting. A few hours of rest give me a better perspective. Without deadlines I would redo many pieces.

Is that why you do not do "personal" work? I need the structure of the assignment to function. Right now, I am unable to finish a book project because I have no written contract nor a deadline.

What are some of your significant jobs in the last year or so? The *Atlantic* pages. The covers for the *New Republic.* A page for *Rolling Stone,* because I ended up with a drawing I could have seen in one of my books. It was interesting for another reason: the art director did not like the first proposal. It is strange that every time that I have had an idea turned down, it has been for the better.

Really? So you don't mind that kind of collaboration. At first I do. I go back to the drawing board, furious. This lasts until I start to work, usually leading to a better solution. This worries me a little bit; it seems that I need the participation of the art director to go further.

What are the limits of the relationship with the art director? Very early on, when I was a beginner not even speaking English, I made sure that I was going to work on my own ideas. I may have been arrogant about it. On the other hand, I have no problem with the art director coming up with an idea, if I like this idea. Very rarely does an art director want to impose a bad idea.

You sometimes work in a loose linear style. Do you enjoy working in an unfinished manner? I usually save that style for black-and-white spots, trying to keep the first drawing I make, before I become self-conscious. I still feel a little guilty giving for publication such an "unfinished" drawing. But experience shows me that trying to perfect that initial line destroys its liveliness.

Earthquake, *an illustration featured on the artist's regular page in* The Atlantic. *1984. Watercolor with airbrush. Art directors: Terry Brown and Judy Garlan.*

BASCOVE

Bascove *(born on April 4, 1946, in Philadelphia, Pennsylvania) received her first assignment while still at the Philadelphia College of Art. Being a woman in a then predominantly male profession, she was briefly relegated to rendering food for women's magazines. However, she soon marshalled expressionist influences and devised a distinctive woodcut approach that was as much a celebration of content as of design. Now she does book jacket illustration for some of the world's most important authors.*

When I was younger, I went to Saturday classes at the Philadelphia College of Art. But my best education came from my grandfather, who painted as a hobby. He would do copies of old masters and hang them in different relatives' houses. I used to sit by his side and watch.

Was he good? I think he was. The most extraordinary thing about him was his passion for art and books. He introduced me to an enormous amount of knowledge and an enormous appreciation and delight in that same search for knowledge.

At what point did you decide you needed a formal art education? As soon as I showed some talent—or at least my grandfather and my mother thought I did. When I was nine or ten, I started that regular training.

What kind of pictures were you doing then? I really liked drawing animals and human anatomy. Since I didn't see art as a viable way of earning a living, I thought I'd go into medicine. When I was twelve, I started working at hospitals doing volunteer work. About the same time, I rendered medical drawings for my uncle, who was one of the department heads at Albert Einstein Hospital in Philadelphia.

What kind of medical drawings? When a new instrument was needed, he would get me to do drawings that showed the design of the instrument. He would also ask for drawings of the instrument in use so that slides could be made and the new process could be taught to other doctors at the hospital.

Where do you think that ability to do detailed drawing came from? Several of my uncles were doctors, my aunt was a nurse, and my dad was a dentist, so I grew up with medical books in the house. Years later, I worked for Yale University doing drawings for the anthropology department.

You went to the Philadelphia College of Art (PCA). Was that the point when you realized that a living could be made from your art? Not really. It was a concern for me, though, because I knew I wanted to be independent. My mother had at one time done some fashion illustration, but she

Illustration for an article in The Progressive *entitled "Tales of Apartheid." 1984. Linoleum cut. Art director: Patrick J.B. Flynn.*

hadn't taken it very seriously. She stopped after her marriage to become a full-time wife and mother. Listening to her speak of that time in such a wistful way made me certain that if this was really something I wanted to do, I should do it, regardless of the consequences.

Were there any female artists you admired and looked to as models? Not many. There was one English teacher in high school, though, who generously gave me some much needed direction. After classes we would read philosophy, literature, and drama together. I had such a passion for books already, and she further encouraged my reading and gave me some direction since, until that point I was reading a lot of books in a disorganized way. But it wasn't until college that I met a woman who became a role model. Her name is Claire Van Vliet, and she taught me printmaking at PCA and now runs Janus Press and teaches at the University of Vermont. She is someone who understands the passion to realize books artistically.

Did you have any idea before that you could wed image to word in fine hand-pressed books? I knew I wanted to do books, but it wasn't until I met Van Vliet that I realized I could do them in a way that would touch on my understanding of the history of the book. You see, printing was something that interested then intrigued me.

What kind of printmaking did you prefer? Although I learned how to do lithographs and etching, I didn't care for them the way I loved wood. Even before I took printing, I had a class in woodcutting and wood sculpture. My professor said that he thought I should continue, but I was terrified of the big saws. Regardless of the machinery, I loved the smell and feel of wood. When I began doing woodcuts, it was like coming home.

Making a woodcut is a very physical act, much more so than pencil drawing or painting. Did that physicality appeal to you? I like the fact that it's an indirect way of working. There is something unique about the quality of a line that has been cut on both sides. And you go through many stages before that surprising moment of pulling the first print.

Did German expressionism affect your work? Yes, the intensity of that imagery, which is similar to the feeling of a lot of German and Russian literature, dark, brooding, and astonishingly perceptive.

What happened when you got out of school? Did you get work right away, or was it difficult? During school, I did what was frowned upon; I took printmaking as well as illustration. My portfolio was mostly made up of prints, which was anathema to the illustration department. They

Book jackets. Top left: *Alan V. Hewat's*
Lady's Time, *published by Harper and Row.*
1984. Linoleum cut and watercolor. Art director:
Joe Montebello. Bottom left: *Mykhaylo Osaochy's*
Cataract, *published by Harcourt Brace Jovanovich.*
1975. Woodcut with overlays. Art director: Harris
Lewine. Top right: *Thomas Mann's* Black Swan,
published by Harcourt Brace Jovanovich. 1979.
Woodcut with overlays. Art director: Krystyna
Skalski. Bottom right: *Georges Simenon's* Aunt
Jeanne, *published by Harcourt Brace Jovanovich.*
1982. Woodcut with overlays. Art director:
Rubin Pfeffer.

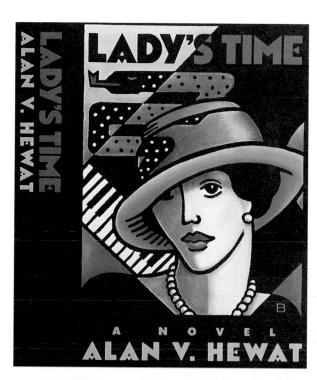

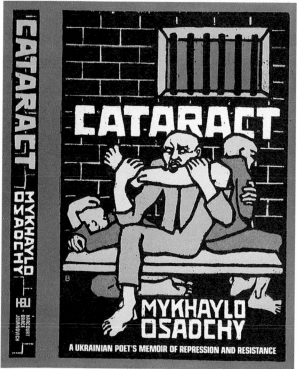

Sketches and finished book jacket for Robertson Davies's What's Bred in the Bone, *published by Viking. 1985. Marker (sketches); woodcut and watercolor (finish). Art director: Neil Stuart.*

said, "No one does prints for illustration." In fact, they often refused to accept a print solution to an illustration problem. Of course, that made me very concerned about my future. So in my junior year I went to New York with my portfolio to find out for myself how people would respond to the prints.

How did you do? I got a job right away. I came back and told my illustration teacher, who said that I would never get another one.

What was the assignment? It was a cover for a biography of D. H. Lawrence.

How did you respond to your instructor's comment? At that point, I considered just stopping and going into medicine. With my mother's encouragement, though, I continued to pursue illustration. At the beginning of my senior year, I thought I'd better go out into the world again. So I went to *Redbook* magazine and met Bob Ciano, who was then its art director. By chance, it turned out he loved doing woodcuts, and he gave me work immediately.

What kind of pictures were you doing? Working for *Redbook* meant I was doing mostly pictures of food and illustrating a few fiction pieces. The major difficulty I found was with what I felt were the limitations of *Redbook*'s writing. But, working with Bob and with Bill Cadge was terrific.

You were graduated and moved to New York. Did it go easily from there, or did you encounter problems because you are a woman? At that time, women were doing either children's book illustration or working for the women's mag-

Sketches and finished book jacket for Jan Willem van de Wetering's The Rattle Rat, *published by Pantheon Books. 1985. Marker (sketches); linoleum and watercolor (finish). Art director: Louise Fili.*

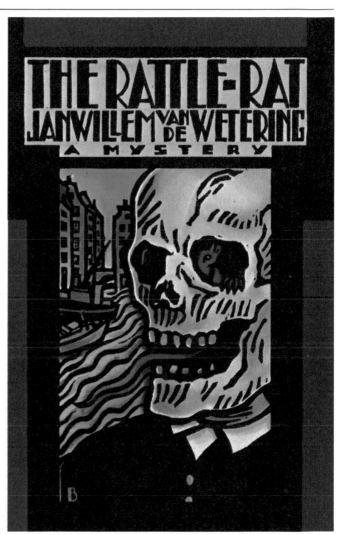

azines. Although I worked regularly for *Redbook,* it wasn't enough income to keep me afloat. So I did my share of children's book illustration too.

Did you derive satisfaction from any of them? It was odd, because I grew up in a black community, and when I started doing children's books, I rendered children of all different colors. I would get into a lot of trouble because of that and very often had fights with editors. I argued for my approach, stating that a particular story didn't *say* the kid was white or black. And I stood my ground. In a few years, I became known in the business for doing minority children. When Sam Antupit was doing the book *Free to Be You and Me,* he had seen several of my integrated-children efforts and brought me in on the project. It was

exciting. There wasn't anything like it at the time. Soon afterward, I started doing more adult-oriented work.

Were you working in an expressive mode for which you created a personal vocabulary? Yes. There were and still are a lot of recurring images in my work. Animals, birds, reptiles, skulls, and creatures from a rather personal bestiary.

When did you start doing book jackets? About 1972. I always wanted to do them, but my imagery was too dark for some people. I was literally told by publishers that if they had jobs needing a dark vision, which was rare, they'd rather give it to a man—a man, they said, has a family to support. Of course, no one would say that now, although there are probably people who still think it.

I'm amazed that sexism was so overt. This was at the

Illustration for a short story in Es-quire entitled "My Animal." 1974. Woodcut. Art director: Bob Ciano.

end of the sixties. Things have changed a great deal, but it was hard not to be discouraged then.

Was there any kind of bridge between the jobs that were woman-oriented and the more catholic subject matter? I had done a few mystery book covers that were qualitatively all right. Then, Andy Kner assigned me to do a Dostoevsky jacket. I was thrilled. Soon after I got the proofs, I saw Harris Lewine, a great publishing art director. He gave me a great many important jobs. That Harris responded so well to my work was encouraging; giving me the best authors helped build my reputation.

Were these book jackets all woodcuts? Most were. There were a few gouaches.

To a certain extent, doing book illustration is a decorative process. What is it that makes your prints different from decorative kinds of book illustration? First of all, it depends on the book. If I am working on a piece of literature, I am not simply embellishing it. I attempt to interpret the mood of the book visually, in my own vocabulary. There are some books where I must do a literal illustration, though when it's a good book, I am usually given the freedom of doing something interpretative.

Then you see being a book illustrator as a way to express yourself? The last few years, I've been very fortunate to have artistic freedom: I do book cover illustration almost exclusively, and I am given the good serious books to do. But there were many years where I did other types of illustration to pay the rent. I can do anything to survive, but unless I feel strongly about the material, it's ultimately meaningless to me—it's a job.

At what stage did you realize that you could do meaningful illustration and still make a living? I would say I've only felt confident about it within the last ten years. The first few years, although I knew I could conform and do something that people would be comfortable with, most of what I was given was so mundane that I didn't know if I could stand doing it. The only thing that would make it bearable, indeed pleasurable, was working with a good art director.

By this time, your stylistic as well as your thematic methodology was being formulated? It's hard to say. The problem with illustration is that you can only *respond* to what you're given. That is the limitation of being an illustrator.

But there is something that comes from you that no other illustrator can bring to an assignment. That's something I can't say.

Dostoevsky's Grand Inquisitor *was a benchmark piece for you. What was your influence?* A painting by Giotto influenced the part I decided to render, where Christ is

Illustration for a short story in Esquire about a Jewish man's identification with the sacrificial ram of Rosh Hashana. 1974. Woodcut. Art director: Bob Ciano.

talking to a priest. It is a passage that explores the cynicism of the priest. There is a painting by Giotto of a priest with a snake coming out of his mouth. I had admired it for years and have used it several times in different ways. It's incredible because it is medieval and yet has contemporary meaning.

What are you trying to say by using that image? Are you making a political or a personal statement? Is there something churning around inside of you that results in that kind of imagery? It's simply part of the visual language that many artists speak. It's just part of a historical vocabulary. I remember, as a child, being fascinated by similar images in books.

But is that entirely what you were saying? Merely culling from history, or is there something else more personal? I don't analyze my illustration that way.

Were you having any difficulty getting your imagery through? Although the late sixties and early seventies were political times, illustration was still a commercial field, and harsh, strong, graphic symbolism was not always easy for publishers to accept. Of course I had problems, and I had a lot of rejections until I met Lewine, who fought to get things through. I think after a few years of working with Harcourt Brace Jovanovich, where Lewine was art director, people became used to seeing the images that I did. Other art directors would then call me when they wanted that kind of look. Now I'm fortunate in that I rarely have that kind of trouble; people know what to expect from me.

Have you done political work? I worked with peace groups during the Vietnam War. But I haven't done too much of it recently. My rare political work is for *The Progressive.*

Do you feel that you can make some impact through your artwork? I don't believe I can; artists tend to be on the fringes of society anyway. First of all, it's a very isolated life, because one is in the studio alone most of the time. Second, I don't think we are politically powerful. At our best we illuminate and, on rare occasions, inspire.

Are there jobs that you refuse to take? I try not to do anything I think is racist or sexist. And being a vegetarian, I used to turn down things like barbecue cookbooks.

What's the difference between doing wood and linoleum cuts? It depends on the line that I want to achieve. There are times when I want it very simple and clean, so I'll use linoleum. Using wood takes a long time because I prefer hardwood, which can mean days of cutting.

Is there a different physical pleasure with each? Oh, definitely. I enjoy wood much more. I have much more control, and the wood has a character of its own.

Does the wood ever trouble you? Years ago, it did. But now I know what kind of wood to use to solve specific problems. For the most part, I use rock maple; it has a very light grain that doesn't fight. I can get a lot of detail, especially over a period of time.

When did you start carving letterforms? Was typography always part of your process? I think it was. With the early printed book, type was almost always inclusive. The German printmakers and Gauguin did it this way. Van Vliet showed me Antonio Frasconi's work, in which type was intrinsic. Because I don't think every job calls for it, I have learned to use set type too. But I'm willing to put a couple of extra days in if I think the job should have carved lettering.

Do you draw right onto the wood, or do you go through other preparatory work before cutting? Sketches and things like that? I always do tight sketches in which I use a heavy black line. I like doing tight sketches because I can't make changes afterward. I do a sketch on heavyweight vellum, which I can then reverse and tape down to the block; then after placing carbon paper underneath, I draw on it, lift it up, and have my drawing and my type reversed on the wood. The line begins to have its own character when it is carved.

Have you done color woodcuts? The traditional way of making a color print is to use as many blocks as necessary. But having been influenced by medieval prints, which were hand-colored, I elected to do it that way. Many printmaking experts feel this is very unorthodox, but Blake, Gauguin, and Max Beckmann worked this way.

Have you initiated work of your own, such as stories or books? I would like to do some books of woodcuts. But I started oil painting a few years ago, and that takes up much of the rest of my time.

Do you paint both as illustration and for yourself? The painting is mostly for myself. I do some gouache paintings as illustration. A couple of years ago I tried to do small oils for book covers, but a friend said it looked like someone was doing a caricature of my style, and I agree. There's no way for me to really do an oil painting because of the restrictions of commercial jobs.

Why is that? Because I don't want to think about specific characters, environments, or incidents when I paint. The painting is private, and the subjects are my own.

Does the painting influence the illustration? It definitely has. For example, there was a painting that I did a few years ago of a torso of a blue woman. I used that image as a woodcut illustration recently. In some ways, the woodcut has been very confrontational, but I think the painting has somehow made it even more so.

Top: *Paperback book cover for Julio Cortázar's* We All Loved Glenda So Much *and* A Change of Light, *published by Adventura/Vintage. 1982. Oil on canvas. Art director: Keith Sheridan.* Bottom: *Illustration for an article in* The Progressive *on censorship in the classroom entitled "Impaired Facilities." 1983. Pen and ink. Art director: Patrick J.B. Flynn.*

Do you work from models, from reference, or from imagination? From all of them. Especially for the painting, I take photographs or do sketches, and my friends have been kind enough to sit for me. For the illustration it is the same, but I add research for specific locations or the style of the country or era of the material. I love working with the human figure, so I enjoy sketching from life if I can.

I wonder whether artists who work in reductive forms, such as woodcut, miss drawing more realistically. Well, I do watercolors for myself, where I work from life and do realistic studies. You've seen several of those, and you know that if I'm doing a portrait, it looks like the person, is very anatomically correct, and is built from light and shadow. For me this is totally different from the line defining form, as it does with a woodcut.

Did you ever try to do that with a woodcut? I have but I prefer to paint that kind of thing. They are both different ways of expressing myself.

Do you ever have a hidden agenda with your illustrations? Sometimes a good piece of literature lets me do that. I mean one that speaks in a specific way about universal incidents and universal feelings. Inevitably, these will let a personal point of view emerge visually.

Who are some of the authors that you feel most kinship with? Well, I love doing authors that have a sympathetic political ideology, like the South Africans J. M. Coetzee and André Brink. I've also done a few books by Alice Walker. Of course, Thomas Mann and Dostoevsky are important to me.

Do you ever find that your interpretation is different from the author's? A lot of the work I do is with authors who are no longer alive. There are a few living authors I have worked for who seem really pleased and request me for subsequent books.

Do you ever illustrate a book on your own, just because you want to? I don't do that because I don't have the time. The books that are assigned to me take enough time. Because the book business has two seasons, there's a lull in between, and then I do my paintings. Even so, there are so many other things that I'd like to do that I don't have time to illustrate on my own.

What haven't you done that you would like to do? There are so many authors whose covers I wish I could just redo. Mostly the Russians, Germans, and some French. I must say, though, often, when I'm given a pile of books to read on my publisher's book list, there will be one or two that are such a pleasure to read and think about that it's hard to believe that I will be paid to do this.

JOHN COLLIER

*J*ohn Collier (born on June 26, 1948, in Dallas, Texas) followed in his father's footsteps as a commercial illustrator. However, his interest was less in the realistic modes that his father practiced and more in the modernist tradition. Although a brief sojourn in New York to sell his pop art–like collages did not result in great success, the resulting reevaluation of his art and himself proved invaluable. Collier returned to the palette and vocabulary of the Italian Renaissance and devised a renaissance of his own through the use of pastel. This medium, long out of fashion in illustration, was applied to his exquisite still lifes and portraits. Within a year of its introduction to the illustration arena, pastel was a medium of preference.

My father's work was respected in Texas, but it was difficult to make a reputation outside of the local area. Almost no work was sent out of New York at that time. I grew up in Dallas and went to college in Kansas and to the University of Texas in Arlington for a while.

Were you drawing all along? No. I studied religion and philosophy. At first, I thought I was going to teach philosophy. Then when I went to the university at Arlington, I thought I was going to be an engineer. College made me realize that I didn't want to be an engineer either. So I went to North Texas State University because it was the only school in the area that taught art.

Had your father encouraged or discouraged you in art? Actually, he did neither. My dad was always hesitant to encourage me to go into art, because he saw how difficult it was to get started, and he felt it would be really terrible to have your heart set on something that was so hard to do. Nevertheless, he was happy when I decided to be an artist.

At what point did illustration come into the picture? I had always thought of art in terms of illustration, because I knew the field existed. I think a lot of people who become illustrators start out thinking of themselves as painters because of limited exposure to what's available. I couldn't see making a living at anything else. Moreover, most people who want to be fine artists, which I suppose includes me, have to do something at the outset. So they either teach or become illustrators or designers.

When you finished school, was it your intent to do editorial work? The idea of illustration had been limited to my experience with my father, and a lot of the jobs that my father worked on didn't seem very exciting to me. So I thought about being a children's book illustrator. I realized, though, that to do that, I would have to go to New York, at least

A Russell-Manning Show.

initially, and since I wanted to stay in Dallas, I got a job as an assistant art director at an ad agency. I did the illustration work that they couldn't afford to give other illustrators. Which is how I got my portfolio together.

From there, I went to Minneapolis and became a staff illustrator at a studio, and got a little better portfolio together. From there I went on to Houston.

You were a peripatetic artist. Well, just running ahead of the wolf, really. There wasn't a lot of craft in the way I moved; I just kept trying to pay the rent. In Houston, I started freelancing, and from Houston I went to New York.

I remember your New York portfolio very well. There was a profound Robert Rauschenberg influence. When I began, my work was more abstract and gradually became more objective. I liked Rauschenberg and Cy Twombley a lot. It's funny, because initially that type of work was meant to explore the deepest feelings, but to me, and I suppose the art world in general, it became just a design exercise. So two things happened. First I wanted to achieve a wider range of expression. And second, no one would buy the type of work that I was doing at the time. Since then, a lot of that is bought for editorial use.

You mean New Wave illustration? Yeah. I was New Wave a long time ago. I don't mean this to sound like I changed because I couldn't sell the other (although that influenced my decision), but at the same time, I was feeling kind of dead about my work.

So what was the bridge that connected your old and new? That first year in New York, I didn't make any money at all. I had a lot of time to sit, think, and experiment with the direction I wanted to head in. Even though my work was somewhat abstract, it was still objective. I like to draw, and I would include elements that were drawn somewhat realistically. Gradually, I guess the drawing started taking over.

My recollection is that you dropped out of sight for a time and then emerged again with this beautiful pastel approach. Of course, I didn't think I had dropped out of sight. I was trying like crazy to be known by as many people as I could. It was really a hard decision, but I just felt that I wasn't expressing the things that I really wanted to express.

What were those things? This isn't really an answer to that question, but it has something to do with my emotional makeup, and that's got a lot to do with my being a Christian. So emotionally, I've always equated artistic transition with commitment. The work I was doing before had a connotation of sarcasm, but in reality I didn't feel that way about people. I didn't see the outside world in terms of institutions, to

be slandered or assailed. I saw things in terms of individual people who were just trying to do the best they could. I think just by being objective, I was able to describe people and events in ways that I couldn't have with that former style.

So was using pastel a way of digging below the surface, then? Well, the pastel came about for two reasons. One was mercenary, the other was artistic. The mercenary reason was that I wanted to have a style that was unique, and at the time nobody was using pastel. The other reason was that I felt I could draw better than I could paint. Only in the last few years have I been able to do some good paintings. So pastel allowed me to do what I did best.

Did you find that art directors were predisposed to the medium? Well, they were. Not to my surprise but to my happiness, they seemed to feel the same things that I was feeling when I was drawing. The initial problem, when you start out and your work doesn't look like anyone else's, is

that usually art directors will praise your work but won't know what to do with it. If you start out and your work does look like someone else's—let's say you imitate Mark English or someone like that, as so many people do—then you'll get work right away, because they know what to do with you (and, of course, because they couldn't get Mark to do it). But you're limited as to how high you can go, because Mark English is obviously always going to get the cream, and you're just going to get what's left. On the other hand, if your work is not like anyone else's, then you may have a really difficult time at first, but once you become accepted, then there's no limit.

Who and what influenced the approach that you're now known for? When I was beginning I think I was influenced by the *Illustrators' Annual*—it was like a Bible. I just devoured everything I could see. Gradually, though, if for no other reason than I'd looked at it so much, I became bored with it and started looking at the history of painting—starting with contemporary art and going backward, back to Giotto, who is still one of my favorite painters. I think the painters of the early Italian Renaissance and before were most influential on my recent work.

Well, I would categorize your work as proclaiming a pastel renaissance. There's a double meaning to that for me now. By studying as much art history as I could find and by *living* in the twentieth century, what I've tried to do is create a style that's built on the past. After you've studied something for a long time, it's not just a style that's mimicked; it becomes internalized.

When you broke away from your New Wave form and started working in pastels, how did you direct yourself? One of the first pieces that people became aware of was of a woman in a silk blouse with a bird in the corner of the picture. It was in the *Illustrators' Annual* and was done as a promotion mailer. It was awarded a gold medal in the Society of Illustrators show. So people started giving me assignments requiring me to draw women from the waist up. It's funny the way it works. In a way, it was a Renaissance-type portrait, although not completely. And that allowed me to play around with that early Italian portrait idea. It wasn't something I was crazy about, but people were associating me with an old way of painting. I wasn't associating it that way. I was painting the pictures that I liked to paint. Unfortunately, what would happen afterward is that people would give me assignments, using phrases like, "We're looking for a fine art look." That always makes me cringe. People would also say, "Now, we don't really want you to do it like a Renaissance painting, but you know the piece

Cover for Post Graduate Medicine,
illustrating an article on facial pain.
1984. Oil on Masonite. Art director:
Tina Adamack.

that you did that was like a Renaissance painting? Kind of make it like that." Again, I don't really look at what I do as being an old way of doing things. It's just using the old vernacular.

What from the vernacular of the past do you use most? Pop artists take a vernacular from bad commercial art and do something much more profound with it. I take a vocabulary from what has gone before, and I kind of shake it up and rearrange it.

Do you deal with your illustrations in terms of the form of the picture or the specific content? When I approach a painting, two things have to happen. The first, of course, is that it has to be useful to the client—that goes without saying. But besides that, I don't really think about any of the intellectualizing. I think about what would be a satisfying emotional statement, if not directly about the subject, at least that includes the subject. To get that, I'll often look through a lot of books. I might see some colors by Gauguin that cause me to think in a certain way. Another thing I've tried to do more consciously is give a contemporary subject a timeless feeling. So I take the palette of early painters— let's say in Pompeii—and use the colors that are in those frescoes, and paint a contemporary subject, sometimes including compositional approaches that they would use. It's an interesting juxtaposition of times.

What jobs don't interest you or are not appropriate? There are some skin magazines that I probably wouldn't want to work for, even though I have. But subject matter doesn't determine what I want to deal with. If I can make a satisfying emotional statement using the subject that's been assigned, that's important to me. I rarely get excited by subjects. The subject is curiously secondary to the emotional statement I'm trying to make, which brings me to what I was trying to think of before. With a lot of contemporary illustration, especially going back about fifteen years, there has been a lot of conceptualizing. It's like taking a political cartoon where different objects represent things and are orchestrated to communicate verbally with visual elements. With my work, things like that aren't really important. If we're talking about pet peeves and things that I don't want to do, *that's* something I don't want to do, because that kind of talk bores me. Words tell literal truths really well. On the other hand, paintings can communicate an emotion—sometimes highly complex emotions—quickly and do a great job of it. That's what I want to do. I think that essentially what's called conceptual illustration is trying to tell only a literal truth. That's such an indirect way of doing what you're doing. I'd rather go right to the heart of the matter. Give

people an emotional feeling, if not about the subject, then about painting at least. Boy, it seems really silly to talk about some advertising illustration in these terms, but I have to do that. I have a hard time doing a painting, let's say, that has to include the product. It's not satisfying enough. If that's all they want, I'll give them that, but I have to add something extra to the painting. I want to make a picture into an experience. I hope that someone will be able to look at my picture later and forget the fact that it might be of a jam jar.

How do you do that? Through composition? Light? Application of color? It's through manipulation of all the elements of design—texture and composition and color. The way I usually start is to do a lot of thumbnails, until something feels right. It's as if while I'm rendering the thing, I'm also the observer. I'm my own audience, and I decide whether it feels right. It's not an easy process, because with a lot of illustration, the artist actually traces the composition onto

Illustrations for the unexpurgated
Sleeping Beauty, *published by Crea-*
tive Education. 1983. Lithograph with
watercolor wash. 1983. Art directors:
Etienne Delessert and Rita Marshall.

the illustration board, then shows the client, "This is what it's going to be like," and comes back and paints by numbers. It's hard for me to do that, because it just seems like pulling teeth all the time. I keep pushing and shoving the picture around until it comes out right emotionally.

The sketch is the finish, is that it? No. Usually, in the process of doing the piece of art, I think of a hundred other possibilities, and the more tied I am to a sketch, the less the client benefits. Which is another reason why I like to be in on the beginning stages with the art director. A give-and-take of ideas helps a lot.

How much of your work is advertising? The bulk of it is noneditorial now. But if by advertising you mean consumer advertising, it is probably 25 percent. The bulk of my work is probably what some call institutional—annual reports and work for corporations.

I recently saw the Sleeping Beauty *book you did for the Etienne Delessert series. That was uncharacteristic. The illustrations looked like monoprints.* They were lithographs. Essentially what happened was, the fee on the book wasn't large, but it was enough to finance doing a suite of eleven lithographs. I thought, well, if I'm not going to make very much from actually doing this illustration, at least if I can sell the lithographs, then I'll be able to make enough to make it worth my while. But it also allowed me to pursue an interest in lithography that has been growing. Fortunately, there is a small place in Lawrence, Kansas, owned by a really talented lithographer. He taught me while I was doing the illustrations.

Why did you choose lithography? For two reasons. First, emotionally, I was excited about trying it, and this seemed like a good time to do it. Second, with a classic fairy tale like *Sleeping Beauty,* the lithograph is kind of an antique way of illustrating a book.

And you also illustrated it without it being fairy-taleish. I didn't want to make a Walt Disney tale, with lots of happy, smiling animals and people. It doesn't seem that difficult, but it was really hard to get away from that approach, because when I think of *Sleeping Beauty,* I think of Walt Disney's movie that I've seen probably three times since I was four years old. The original story was actually not at all a Disney-type story. In Disney's tale, they get married and live happily ever after. But that's only the middle of the real *Sleeping Beauty.* In the original, the prince's mother is an ogre and eats children. The Prince and Sleeping Beauty have to get married in secret so that his mother won't find out. But the truth comes out when his father dies and he becomes king. Anyway, when the prince goes away to war,

his mother tries to eat the grandchildren. The cook saves them. Then the mother decides she wants to eat Sleeping Beauty. So the cook substitutes a deer for Sleeping Beauty. Finally, when the mother realizes she's been deceived, she tries to kill the lot of them, and the prince comes back, and she's so mad that she falls into her own trap and dies. So it's really not the delightful, happy-ever-after story.

Most of the illustrations are not like the typical ones that you would expect. I wanted something that was accessible to children but interesting enough to hold an adult's attention.

When were you part of Push Pin Studios? I was represented by Push Pin in the mid-seventies. I wasn't there in the glory days.

But you did a lot of work for Push Pin's Graphics. I worked at my studio, and they were my agent. I think that experience helped get my name known a little bit. Then I started getting a lot of institutional work, which offered as much freedom as the typical editorial assignment. And it paid a lot more. So I just raised my prices. I would still love to do editorial work and do it occasionally—but it's hard to justify, when you get as much satisfaction out of doing an annual report as you do out of doing a job for a magazine, and corporate work pays three times more. Anyway, I broke with Push Pin.

Do you work from the figure or from your imagination? It's almost always from life. It's really rare to make up something, even though I often take a lot of liberties. I don't trace anything. Sometimes, I'll work directly from life, particularly if it's something like a still life. Usually I'll have a friend stand while I take the photographs, but I really hate photographs. In order to get a good photograph, I have to spend so much time in the darkroom that it doesn't make it worthwhile.

Do you look for spontaneity? The lithographs are incredibly spontaneous. Yes. The way I work with lithographs is to tone the surface of the stone with tush, then as it dries I push it around, trying to get as much action as I can. Then I draw with a lithographic crayon on that. After that's done, I scrape out with razor blades, needles, and things like that, then take steel wool and brush it down.

Do you take a similar approach to lithography as you do to pastel? No, actually it's more in keeping with the monoprint. That's really what I try to do with lithography.

Well, that's what they look like, so you've succeeded. I like the wide range of tones and values you can get in pastel and monoprint. But lithography comes closer than any other way for me to get that tone. And emotionally it's very satisfying.

Illustration for an article on Alzheimer's disease in TWA's Ambassador *magazine. 1982. Oil on Masonite.*

JAMES GRASHOW

James Grashow (born on January 16, 1942, in Brooklyn, New York) was influenced by pop art and sixteenth-century northern woodblock prints. He has blended these two forms into both original illustrations and unique sculptures. His woodcuts are metamorphic flights of fancy, and his larger, nonillustrational, three-dimensional constructions are massive cartoons. Though his approaches are too difficult to mimic, as a teacher at Pratt Institute in New York he influenced scores of pupils simply by exemplifying the fun in creating art.

When I was a boy, I loved the *Saturday Evening Post* and the "Farmer Gray" cartoons on TV. I made monsters, walking around holding the heads of their decapitated victims. In the schoolyard, I used to draw dirty pictures for all my friends.

What did you do with this unbridled drawing talent? I took a couple of classes at the Brooklyn Museum. At some level in high school, all my peers were achieving success with other things, in sports or studies—getting good grades. The only skill that I had was drawing, and it wasn't really a skill to expand or take a chance with. Rather, it was something to play safe with—to get applause with, not to grow with.

Were you a bad student? I was terrible. I was graduated with a cumulative sixty-eight average. I went for four years to summer school. I don't think I ever passed a math or an English class in my life. And nothing ever helped, even though I worked hard! But I know now that one of the problems was that I was dyslexic.

Did you go to art school? I went to Pratt. And as soon as I put my foot in the door, everything was fantastic. All of a sudden, everything came together. Everything made sense. I was graduated third in my class.

What specifically did you get out of Pratt? I got to understand that being an artist wasn't something bad. It had seemed to me that everybody else had *smarts* and that art was *talent,* it was something god-given and had nothing to do with intelligence. I started to understand that intelligence and talent made the best art. And, moreover, I got to compete with people I thought were extraordinary. I found that I could compete very successfully.

Were you studying to be an illustrator at that point? When I first walked into Pratt, I was going to be an advertising artist. My parents had convinced me that I could either fall back on my degree and be a teacher, or that in advertising I could make a middle-class living. But after the first year I realized I wanted to be a painter or a graphic artist.

Illustration for an article on the New York Times *Op-Ed page describing the birth of a new populist movement. 1977. Woodcut. Art director: Steven Heller.*

Top: *Illustration for an article in the* New York Times Magazine *about duplicity in the medical profession. 1976. Woodcut. Art directors: Ruth Ansel and Steven Heller.* Bottom: *Illustration promoting book advertising in* Vanity Fair. *1982. Woodcut. Art director: Bob Bartholemews.*

Were your drawings then as anthropomorphic and metaphoric as they are today? They always were. From the beginning, all my drawings had some kind of allegory. Sometimes I would make up my own symbols, which were often very obtuse. At some point, though, I realized that it wasn't really storytelling that was the most important thing, but it was the *media*—the *process* and the *materials*—that made the *work* fantastic. It was the sheer *doing* of it.

Getting back to the content of the narratives, were there specific themes? All the themes were based on my own emotional problems. The basic one was croaking. Death has been the single prime force in everything that I've ever done. I look now and see it very clearly. It seems to me that the medium that an artist chooses is more a statement of what the person is like than the images that he draws. I've always been drawn to paper, papier mâché, fabrics, things like that: paper and the cardboard speak to mortality, to a more transient state. I think the woodcuts are also part of that. They don't speak so much to mortality as they do to a slowing-down process. In a regular drawing on paper, I think so quickly—and with the woodcut I think slowly. It makes me seal the image and think from detail to detail, section to section. It becomes like weaving. I had a student in my class once who would do incredibly contemplative work, and every month he would bring a piece in, and it was never finished. I would wait for it to be finished, but it never was. I realized what he was doing; the work was a talisman against death. As long as he had that work, he would never have to face the world—he always had that obligation to that work, which made him safe. In a way, that's what the woodcuts are for me.

But they have an end. You have to meet deadlines (forgive the pun). I think the ending is the healthy part of my life. There is so much that's unhealthy, but I've been able to bring work to a conclusion, to say, "Enough of this craziness, let's move on."

What other work absorbed you at Pratt? I wasn't really doing anything extraordinarily well, but I was doing everything. I got a Fulbright at the end of school for painting and graphics. So then my time was really very much divided between painting and woodcutting. All the work was, indeed, mostly about mortality. They were metaphors about my own passage through life. They were figurative and full of my own symbols. I did a giant piece in which there were two horses racing, and a man was straddled between them. It seems so stupid now, but it was a race for life. It was one of these giant epics, of which I was very proud. Until my teacher, Stephen Green, who was one of the best

Illustration for an article on the New York Times *Op-Ed page analyzing recent urban sprawl and its effects on the suburbs. 1977. Woodcut. Art director: Steven Heller.*

teachers I've every had, told me it was one of the most atrocious pieces that he had ever seen. He said that it wasn't the metaphor that made it crummy, it was just a lousy painting. It took me a day-and-a-half of sticking to what I thought was right to understand that he was right.

So, how did that affect your work afterward? It made me understand what was important in my work. That process and contact with media was pivotal to good art.

Your work is involved with making the ordinary into something extraordinary, in the manner of the pop artists. Were you inspired by the pop movement? When I got the Fulbright and went to Europe, it was just as the pop movement really began to explode. At that time, I went through every church and I saw every painting. I was up to my palette in art. At the very end of my trip, I went to the Venice Biennale, where pop art was exhibited for the first time. I walked into the room with a gigantic tube of toothpaste and saw a huge Rauschenberg and a Claes Oldenburg hamburger. And God, man, I was home. I was back in Brooklyn. And I knew that that's what I wanted to know. That I had absorbed everything that I could absorb, and now it was time for me to be me.

Did that supplant the intellectual need to deal with death? I don't think anything ever supplants that. While I used to

Illustrations for a special section of American Artist *on information for artists, entitled "The Wedding of Art and Process." 1981. Woodcut. Art director/editor: Stephen Dougherty.*

think about it every minute, now I think of it once every couple of days.

When you returned from Italy, was it then you decided to become an illustrator? It was before I left, as soon as I started doing woodcuts. In class, when the other kids were pushing their tools through a piece of wood splintering cross-grain, my tools, for some reason, cut like magic. I loved Dürer and the Northern European printmakers. I couldn't understand how they could cut so much better than I could. Surely, I was as dexterous as they. So I set out to find out. I went to Long Island to see Gene Yerganian, who showed me what a great piece of wood is. And the same magic that made the tools cut beautifully in the first place, wed to a great piece of wood, started a chain reaction. Every time I did a cut, people would clap their hands. So I knew immediately that it was something that I could sell. It went directly to that middle-class logic that told me I had to make a living. A lot of friends of mine could live like artists in their lofts, but I wanted to live in a loft and make a living too.

Was your facility with woodcutting directly related to your dyslexia? It's interesting to me that the dyslexia and the woodcutting seem to go hand-in-hand. I don't think that's really important, though. The most important fact is the sensuality of the wood. That thickness, the way it feels when you're cutting into it. If it looks good backward, it looks good frontward.

When one thinks of a modern woodcutter, one thinks German expressionist—heavy blacks, minimal whites, not much detail. But you cut wood very much like an engraving. Where did that come from? When I started, I loved wood engraving more than anything. I've always loved doing really tight, detailed, congested drawings. Engraving was more satisfying because it was more detailed. But I also appreciate the German expressionists; I've always loved their directness. So sometimes, I have felt guilty that I was denying the surface of the wood by imposing my will on it so much, by making it so much like an intricate composition, where in fact blackness is so important to the nature of the wood.

The reason I think there's so much similarity in woodcuts is that so many people allow the wood to dictate. What you did, though, was create an engraving style without engraving. In the beginning, I felt that I was just trying to learn as much as I could. But then, when I started getting jobs, I would do engravings for everyone and quickly learned an invaluable lesson from doing a very early issue of *Fact* magazine. I was thrilled with the way the prints came out, then a month later, when the magazine came out, each

Tree in Bondage, *an unpublished piece derived from the artist's* Man and Nature *series. 1981. Woodcut.*

Sketch and finished poster commemorating the Statue of Liberty centennial for the Book of the Month Club. 1985. Woodcut and watercolor. Art director: Al Silverman.

reproduction was a blob; I realized that the wood engraving wasn't going to make it commercially. So I investigated media and found a good pearwood. Then I went to a toolmaker and had him make new gougers that were smaller than any conventional woodcut tools. I cut the handles off the tools, adapting them to my palm, in order to find a middle ground between the engraving and the woodcut. It worked perfectly. I now prefer it to woodcuts and to straight engraving.

Your woodcut technique seems as effortless as drawing. When an idea comes, it doesn't come totally. I get a feeling about it—just half an idea. I put it on the block as a half-idea and allow it to grow. One of the big differences between illustration and fine art is that with an illustration you really understand exactly where the piece is going; in other words, it has to meet the world at some point. You put a cap on the process. In fine art, there's no cap. You just have to trust that process right through to whatever magical conclusion comes. So what I do in the illustration is to keep the process open as long as possible, so that the preliminary drawing on the wood is very, very raw.

With the woodcut, though, you're forced by the nature of the material to be more controlled than you would be with a drawing. Once you're into the woodcut and you make an error of judgment or of process, there is no turning back, is there? There's only one thing that's really critical in a woodcut. It's a relationship between you and the piece of wood. Every piece of wood has a different temperament. Sometimes you're not in tune with that piece of wood. Sometimes that piece of wood doesn't want to be treated tenderly—it doesn't respond to a little namby-pamby chicken scratch. You have to feel the temperament of the wood. The mistake comes in choosing a wrong piece of wood for a particular job. Then, you have to fight the wood all the way. When you're working with broad and giant strokes for a crude woodcut, the mistakes may be greater, but the process covers up a lot of mistakes. But if you're working in an intricate, line-by-line technique, like I do, the mistakes are not as great.

Do you ever finish a piece that is unacceptable to you, that you're forced by time constraints to hand in, regardless? Time is not the only constraining factor. A woodcut, by its nature, is a kind of compromise. A block's surface is not passive like paper or canvas; it is an active participant in the work. What deadlines do is short-circuit the process, sometimes they prevent me from executing all the textural intricacies that I want to do. I think that often what I do in terms of texture and detail isn't called for anyway, it's just a reflection of my own insanity.

What is your insanity? Well, in the Statue of Liberty poster, it's doing a billion faces. It wasn't asked for. They always say that the worst thing about Albrecht Dürer, if he had a problem at all, was his compulsion to fill up every damned bit of space. I feel the same way. When I cut out an enormous white and leave a section blank, there's something in me that says, "Cheat—fill it in."

When illustrating, do you religiously interpret a text? I am always adding to my vocabulary. When I started working for the Op-Ed page, the first job I did was an illustration about a guy who had a disease in which one part of his body was frozen and one part of his body was terribly hot. I did a woodcut of a guy, showing one-half of his body in Bermuda shorts, entombed in ice cubes, and the other part was all in furs and earmuffs. The art director said, "I don't want this. I want you to go back and think of what this thing *really* means. I want you to be yourself with the problem." So I went back and I made a caduceus, one snake devouring the other. It looked fantastic, and it reproduced really well. But the words "be yourself" have always stuck with me. In a weird way, that first cartoon was myself. But the other was also me. It has been difficult for me to justify the cartoon that lives inside of me—that's always there and always ready—and to adapt it more intelligently.

What does that cartoon mean to you? It means all those things from the beginning; my ineptness, stupidity, not being sophisticated, my insecurity. I think it means Brooklyn.

What's interesting, then, is that your sculptural work, which you don't do as illustration although it certainly could be, is like an epic cartoon. One of the first shows that I had, I did what was called *Cottage in the Woods*. It was a big house with all kinds of cartoon figures. It was a life-sized suburban house that fit inside the gallery—with trees and a giant tongue that beckoned viewers to enter. When a viewer walked on the tongue and into the house, there was a family sitting around having a turkey dinner. After I showed the piece, I was at a party and heard people say, "Did you see that crazy environment that Grashow was exhibiting?" So I walked up and down Madison Avenue, looking at all the third-generation abstract work being shown at the time—I'm not saying anything bad about it, I love abstract work. De Kooning and all those guys are like gods to me. But I was unbelievably proud of myself. I felt that I had done something courageous, knowing, as I did it, that my work had the root of a cartoon and that I wasn't running away from it.

You did other shows, as well, that could be considered

Details from and composite of A City, *a multipiece sculpture installation. 1980. Dyed fabric, plywood, cardboard and fabric mâché (largest piece is 13 feet).*

part of the pop aesthetic. What made you do these epic sculptural "cartoons?" I've always held that the key to a work was that it had to have an entry point, like the theme of a book. But once in, the *painting* would take over. I started showing at Allan Stone Gallery in 1966. The first show was *The Cottage in the Woods,* and then I did *The Party,* in which the eight principal figures were about fourteen feet high. They were in a room drinking and smoking. People could walk in under the figures' legs and arms. On one level, it was a large cartoon, but on another there were unbelievable painterly things happening, like in the passage from the pants to the shirt. What I was really doing, once the structures were built, was using them almost as a canvas. But the idea itself sometimes becomes more important, and people can't see the painting. The next show I did was a riot in

the gallery, called *Murder Mâché,* with eight-foot-high figures beating each other up. The rationale for that was to activate the space in the room; I thought that the fighting figures would be a good vehicle. But again, the cartoon statement was overly powerful. Next, I decided to go directly to the cartoon and not be so precious about the process. So I built a show called *Metamorphosis,* in which figures turned into animals. This was done in papier mâché, and I started using fabric mâché. The genesis of this piece came from when I used to watch those "Farmer Gray" cartoons; they would always have some guy who would slip on a banana peel or something, and there'd be a pan to the audience. All these animals would be clapping their hands. I don't know exactly what it was, but something about them stuck in my mind. So I thought it would be interesting to have

Seated Tree, from a multipiece sculpture installation entitled The Woods. *1977. Threat and yarn with Elmer's glue on wire armature.*

a gallery of people metamorphosizing into animals. But essentially, I really wanted to make them into paintings— piece by piece, thread by thread, they would become very intricate compositions.

Making a cartoon for its own sake doesn't interest you? It's not that interesting to make *only* cartoons. You play with words and you make jokes, puns, and metaphors— I've heard that a pun is the final refuge of a truly humorless person. The thing is to make each piece rich. And it's possible to use cartoon metaphors as the entry point, but there has to be more.

A City *appears to be your most successful blend of cartoon and process. What was the idea for this metamorphic extravaganza?* Up to the point I started *A City,* I had been doing very amorphous things, and I wanted to do something more geometric. And there's always been a parallel between my personal and commercial work. They are two arms of the same body: the sculpture is more physical, the woodcuts more contemplative. The show before *A City* was called *The Woods.* It was a group of anthropomorphized trees all sitting in chairs. The entire show was made from yarns and thread—chairs, clothes, bark, everything. The process for this show was so slow, so contemplative, that it was exactly like the woodcuts. I wanted to do an epic thing that would be physical. I decided to work with cardboard and fabric and actually build a city. Making it anthropomorphic just seemed like a wonderful entry point. I wanted also to do something that was primal, like an Easter Island totem.

A City *seems to be a monument to your perseverance. Some of these things are as high as fifteen feet, and each one has so much detail. How long did the project take you?* Four years. A work of this kind, or like any long-term project, is like a spiral. The first steps are long and sluggish, but as you get down to the core, the work moves quickly.

From A City *or other gallery projects, do you derive inspiration for your woodcuts or illustrations?* I think everything comes back. The art director calling while I'm working on the tree show would get flower metaphors. It makes the experience of doing the illustration richer and more meaningful. I want illustrations that, after the piece is shown, will have integrity. So I'm always looking for a chance to do something that fits directly into my current vocabulary.

Is your editorial illustration becoming more realistic and considerably less symbolic? This mammoth Statue of Liberty is like Grashow's socialist realism. It's only a pause. I've always had this compulsion to do really epic things. But after I've finished with the Statue poster, I'm not going to

do another epic for a long time. Still, the opportunity comes along so rarely to do something really challenging on a level that's different from the ordinary work. This piece is the most difficult that I've ever done, because every section is critical. In an editorial, there's always room to take license. But with this, there is no place where I could make an exaggeration.

Do you see using sculpture in illustration? I can't. I don't want to compromise in any way with the sculptural work. As illustration, it would be inevitable.

So as you get more successful, more widely known, as a sculptor—as is the case now—will you give up illustration? I can't. It's part of me. When the phone rings, I run like a racehorse. Of course, I'd like to be able to select my jobs more. But even so, I want to do the crap, too.

191

JULIAN ALLEN

Julian Allen (born on September 2, 1942, in Cambridge, England) came to the United States in 1972 as a staff illustrator for New York *magazine. His watercolor re-creations of odd, but not impossible, historical and news events earned him a reputation as a journalist/illustrator. Since then, in addition to doing more conventional illustration assignments, he has covered many significant news stories, including the Arab-Israeli Seven-Day War.*

At Cambridge College of Art I made a deliberate decision to reject fine art in favor of commercial art. It was probably a working class attitude. After all, one could get "a job" as a draftsman, not as a painter.

Were you the first artist to come from your family? Yes. I was brought up by a guardian in a house that seemed to be constantly at war. I spent a great deal of time in my own room copying from American comics, sketching old paintings reproduced in books, and drawing people as I remembered them. Learning to draw was a way of escape for me.

Is that what made you choose art school over college? I don't think I could have gotten into a real college under the British school system—my education was very limited, but I did manage to pass an entrance exam to the local technical college, which was affiliated with the Cambridge School of Art. I was actually too young to enter that year but the head of the art school saw a bunch of my drawings, thought they were better than most of his students', and asked me to join that year. I was fourteen.

Did you already have the impetus at that time to do commercial work? Yes, but it was a municipal training course with a fine art department. We drew from plaster casts and other artifacts in the museums around Cambridge. We had courses in strange, archaic skills such as heraldry, illuminated manuscripts, and calligraphy, which became my specialty. Curiously, there was a course called illustration, but that was pretty archaic too: old-style wood engravings, vignettes, chapter endings—that kind of thing. There was some magazine illustration around at that time, but I always imagined it was the art editor who did it.

That's interesting, since there's a rich tradition of English illustration. Yes—book illustration and advertising. There was the Radio Times, and there were Penguin covers, but not very much magazine illustration. I can remember magazines called *John Bull* and *Illustrated*, which carried very poor imitations of American illustration.

What made you enter this netherworld of illustration? In

One of a series of illustrations for Newsweek's *reprint of H.R. Haldeman's memoirs. This illustration shows Nixon, pressured by Watergate, retreating to a favorite haunt, a diner near the White House. 1978. Watercolor on paper. Art director: Peter Blank.*

Illustration for an article in New York *entitled "The War Watchers," sketched while covering the Arab/Israeli war in the Sinai. 1973. Pencil. Art director: Walter Bernard.*

my third year, Paul Hogarth joined the staff—he moved some colleagues in, and things began to change. I was studying along with Roger Law and Peter Fluck and David Driver and other good people. It was a good time to be at Cambridge Art School. Hogarth already had a tremendous reputation as a traveling artist-reporter and book illustrator. He taught us a tradition of satirical drawing and introduced us to *L'Assiette au Beurre* and *Simplicissimus* and Ben Shahn. It was then that I saw that drawing could be an end in itself, that it could convey a message.

Was the work you were doing then, as an outgrowth of these studies, similar to what you're doing now? Or was it more sketchy like Hogarth? It was both. Paul changed my attitude toward drawing. He was a stylist, and that went contrary to the academic teaching I got elsewhere in school. I began to draw like Ben Shahn, for instance.

What was it about Ben Shahn's work that appealed to you? It was journalistic. I was intrigued that he used a camera as a sketchbook, for instance. Also, the pop artists who were emerging at that time were interesting to me— David Hockney, Peter Blake, Kitaj, and others. I used to go to their exhibitions in London. They were, of course, very influenced by the American pop movement but their subject matter was less dynamic—cuter—more English. Movies were my other great influence. I spent a great deal of my childhood in the cinema. I had an American accent when I was twelve.

What did the movies do for you? I used to be a great collector of movie photo albums and stills, and I've often thought that I am trying to invent movie scenes in my illustrations. I've learned a great deal about composition from Welles and Hitchcock, for instance, and a great deal about color from Bertolucci.

What was the next step in your career once out of art school? I did a one-year post-graduate course at the Central College of Art in 1963. At that time the magazine boom had begun. There were *Queen, Town, Nova,* and the Sunday color supplements, and they all needed illustration. My portfolio was made up almost entirely of movie portraits— pop-art influenced. I did a number of very stark woodcuts of silent-movie stars and a few rips-offs of some American illustrators I admired, like Harvey Schmidt and Robert Weaver. I was pretty lucky. In my first week of going around with my work I was given a huge job by the art director of *Queen* magazine. He wanted some 1930s-style fashion illustrations. So I took a suitcase full of clothes home, got my girlfriend to pose in them, and did drawings using thirties movie star faces. They were a great success. About two weeks after publication I received telegrams from *Elle* and *Marie Claire* asking me to go to Paris, where I spent a few days drawing girls in underwear.

Did you see these jobs as stepping stones or as ends in themselves? At that age, I don't think one thinks about means or ends. I was happy to get the work. However, as time went on, I became more and more frustrated because as I became involved in fashion, the clothes got more boring. Moreover, I was not a very good fashion artist. I wanted to paint again and to work as an editorial illustrator.

How did this transition take place? Gradually. By 1968 I had pretty well turned it around.

Once you made the switch, what were your creative goals? I wanted to paint like Peter Blake, but I also was very interested in approximating newspaper photographs. For instance, there would be a photograph in the paper of Mick Jagger having just been arrested on a drug charge; I was drawn to the picture because of all the spontaneous cropping and the frozen expressions. It was the perfect subject matter for a painting.

Were you interested with it as a pop art convention, or was there some other motivation? These images made a statement about the time I was living in. Moreover, I was busy just trying to fill my portfolio with conceptual illustration. The first breaks I got were at the *Observer* and the *London Times Magazine*. They used me as a kind of "easel" photographer. In other words, a re-creator of something that

had already taken place, when there was no chance of a photograph.

Were you working in watercolor? I didn't know the difference between watercolor, opaque color, or acrylic. I used acrylic, but in a very light watercolor manner. I was studying Peter Blake's pictures, trying to figure out how he did it.

From all those years of fashion work, I realized I had a facility to compose a picture made up of any number of different people. I tried various things. For instance, I collaborated with Nik Cohn on a *Zelig*-like comic strip about a lawyer (played by Gary Cooper) who was as old as the century and always managed to be in the best place at the best time: Berlin in the early thirties; defending a country boy rock-and-roll singer in Tennessee in the fifties; etc. It was a lot like making movies. It was published in *Queen*, though only for two episodes. At the same time Michael Rand at the *London Times Magazine* started using illustrated journalism, and I was often assigned to do reportage pieces and sometimes I would interview the people involved in the events, for details.

Did Rand invent this form of journalism? I don't know if anyone actually invented it. It was a form that evolved. For instance, I worked on a story about James Cross, a British diplomat who was kidnapped by terrorists in Canada. In that I used a comic strip device, where I had one central image of the kidnappers bursting into his bathroom, then

Sketches and finished illustration for a critical article in Vanity Fair on Rupert Murdoch, the renegade publisher. 1983. Pencil (sketches); water-color on paper (finish). Art director: Ruth Ansel.

Sun-Times

Red Streak
Latest Market

CHICAGO, WEDNESDAY, NOVEMBER 2, 1983

Sun-Times sold for $90 million

Murdoch o... local group

Field Enterprises Inc. has announced that it has accepted an offer from News America Publishing Incorporated to acquire the Chicago Sun-Times and the Field Newspaper Syndicate.

News America is a subsidiary of the News Corporation Limited, an Australian public company with newspapers in the United States, Britain and Australia.

According to Lee M. Mitchell, pre... and chief executive officer of Fie... prises, the purchase price offere... America is $90 million to be... at the closing of the transacti...

The offer is subject to the ne... definitive agreements, which ar... to be completed by Dec. 15, and to... legal requirements. The parties an... being able to close the transacti... 3, 1984.

The sale of the Sun-Times resu... the decision made last April to... Field Enterprises. At that time... terprises announced that the... voting shareholders, Marshall... chairman, and Frederick Field... man, wished to sell the comp... and to pursue future business... ties separately.

In announcing that an offer... been accepted for the Sun Tim... Field brothers issued the following... ment:

"In seeking a purchaser for the S... Times since last April, our manag... has spoken to many interested partie... we have considered a number of fie... and informal offers. We have now s... ed the News America offer because of... parties who contacted us, News Am... expressed the greatest confidence...

...y Marshall Field (right... ...irman of Field Enterprises... ...nd James Hoge, Sun-Times... publisher.

around it there were separate images in frames telling the
rest of the story. I later made that device look like photographic contact strips.

Was it similar to some of the work you were doing for
New York *magazine?* Yes, although the field had its limits
in England. There were just two magazines that could use
me in that way, and they couldn't use me all the time. It
took another kind of editorial imagination to push that potential
further. It wasn't until I came to the U.S. that I saw the
possibilities of photorealistic journalism.

*Did you do conceptual illustrations, using symbol or
metaphor?* No. My interest has always been to make scenes
that had photographic conviction. To make the impossible
photograph possible.

What brought you to New York? Clay Felker, then editor
of *New York,* wanted someone on staff, or someone who
would always be available whenever he needed a naturalistic
re-creation of a particular news event. For me, it was the
perfect opportunity, since I was planning to come to America
anyway. I had a romantic conception of New York, and I
admired a lot of the illustrators here.

*It's fortunate that Felker was so astute about the pos-
sibilities of illustration.* He was one of the last editors with
any real vision, in the graphic sense. He sent Milton Glaser,

his design director, to London. They were interested in
having me come over for a six-month contract. And the
thing was that I wasn't going to have to schlepp the streets
of New York with my portfolio. I would get priceless exposure
through working for the magazine. Despite some battles,
Clay and I hit it off pretty well.

*Were you heavily directed or did you come up with your
own ideas?* It was collaboration. Our first cover, for instance,
was a story entitled "When Cops Get Caught." I sketched
out an idea showing two policemen in the back of a police
car, handcuffed—strong Ludwig Hohlwein shadowy faces.
Milton said, "No, this is the cover," and proceeded to crop
right in on just the faces and hands. I learned a lot from
that. Sometimes the collaboration worked well, sometimes
not, but the main thing is that Felker saw the possibilities
of using an illustrator where a photographer couldn't go.

*A case in point must be when you covered the Yom Kippur
War for* New York. That's probably the best example. The
Yom Kippur War broke out in 1973 and, because the Israelis
were hit pretty hard in the first offensive, they were very
sensitive about pictures leaving the country uncensored.
So, excellent war photographers like Don McCullen were
presumably getting some incredible battle shots that were
not getting printed. Clay and I discussed the idea of re-

creating the battle scenes in paintings. I had in mind the paintings of battles, some by well-known artists, that hang in the Imperial War Museum of London.

So he agreed with your suggestion? Yes. He got me accreditation to visit the Golan Heights and the Sinai desert, where I observed what fighting was left. I took photographs, for instance, of an entire Syrian column that had been pulverized by Israeli aircraft, and I thought of bringing it to life as a painting. A few days of looking at war debris has a profound effect. I felt like a voyeur. We'd be on the battlefront during the day and back in the Hilton bar in the evening, sipping cocktails, talking about the war. While I was there I did a drawing of Nora Ephron (who was also doing a story for Clay), and I was looking down through the turret of a blown-out Syrian tank. As it happened, I did not do the story as planned because I got injured in an explosion on a bus in the Sinai desert and subsequently spent two weeks in an Israeli military hospital getting over a leg wound.

Did you do any paintings before or after? There was no way. I kept a journal and I made a lot of drawings of wounded Israelis and of Egyptian prisoners. Clay printed the story I wrote, along with some of the drawings.

Did this lead to other journalistic assignments? Yes, but not quite as dangerous. Our next big story was Watergate. When I first arrived in New York in June 1973, the Watergate daily soap opera was being played out on television. I was an avid follower of the hearings.

Did you respond to it in partisan fashion? No, I was an observer. In England I was partisan, not here.

You did a number of striking Watergate-related pictures for New York *at that time.* We did a huge variety of stories . . . including Watergate, as you say. When I was sent to travel to Israel, I was halfway through a series of paintings of New York neighborhoods that I finished when I got back. We did a lot of crime stuff, in particular one with Peter Maas called "The King of the Gypsies." And I remember one day Clay was storming through the offices, ranting on about the oil cartel. After the Arab oil boycott, of course, Americans were having to line up for hours in gas lines. That led to the "Secret History of the Oil Cartel," where again, we used a number of illustrators. The story was about the origins of the oil cartel, right back to the original capitalists who, under the pretext of grouse hunting in Scotland, formed the first oil monopoly and fixed the price of oil.

These were re-creations of historical events. Yes. I was reminded of the Victorian historical paintings I used to copy

when I was a kid. They were an indirect influence.

By this time you were working in watercolor. Yes, and acrylic. I like using watercolor. It's an art of understatement; very English. What you leave out is as important as what you put down.

How do you mean, "what you leave out"? You work from light to dark as opposed to opaque painting, where you work from dark to highlight. In other words, in watercolor, your initial base color is your lightest tone, and you work down from there.

Speaking of process, do you sketch things first, or do you draw *with the watercolor?* I sketch my compositions out, often on a luciograph. Then I'll transfer the composition onto the paper.

Some of the pictures—the one I remember most fondly has Nixon in a luncheonette, sobbing into his coffee—are totally credible. What did you do to make it so believable? That was an illustration for a section of Haldeman's book. During the time the Watergate story was breaking, everyone was phoning Nixon, and Haldeman always knew he could find him at some local diner in Washington. There used to be a diner around the corner from me called Dave's Luncheonette, which I used in that picture. The rest of it is just me doing my graphic tricks.

Do you ever have the desire to go beyond illustration? Well, I sometimes have a desire to go way beyond, but I want to take illustration with me. I have a desire to *change* illustration, in general, and my own illustration specifically. I'm talking about taking journalistic illustration much further.

What's interesting about journalistic illustration is that you are dealing with the real and the imagined. How can that be expanded upon? I think one can take what is possible much further. There's a strong emotional element in a lot of my work. It doesn't just stop at a re-creation of a scene. Very often there is a definite mood with which I try to provoke reactions.

You also do portraiture. What makes a good portrait? It's a matter of mood as much as likeness. If you capture a mood, you also capture a viewpoint. I don't necessarily start off with a particular point of view, but if there isn't one by the time I've finished, I've failed.

Do you find your profession too solitary? Sometimes. There are times, in my studio, I'm working on a picture wondering if it is a good picture or whether I've just gone utterly mad. Only later, perhaps, when I am giving a talk at an art college, I discover that someone has remembered a picture I did, studied it, and wants to talk about it. That's when I know someone is listening.

ELWOOD H. SMITH

Elwood H. Smith (born on May 23, 1941, in Alpina, Michigan) has resuscitated the comic conceits of the early-twentieth-century masters, giving them new life. Although from his childhood he loved the work of George Herriman and Bud Fisher, it wasn't until he arrived in New York City, after having been an advertising art director in Chicago, that his sprightly and animated cartoon style took form and took off. Smith maintains and builds upon the comics legacy, applying it to illustration rather than to the comic strip.

Mickey Mouse, Donald Duck, and all the comic characters brought me to the drawing board. I read "Pogo" and didn't understand any of it but liked the drawings. When I was young, the *Detroit Free Press* had "Krazy Kat," one of my biggest influences today.

Were comic books also an influence? Very much. I was a very discerning fan. I decided that "Pogo" was really well drawn, compared to some of the other strips. I knew that Jack Davis's work in *Mad* magazine was drawn better than others. It's interesting that I've come full circle; as I got older, I moved away from the comics and more toward Seymour Chwast, Milton Glaser, and Heinz Edelman—who were influences on my early style—and now I've come back to the artists who influenced me when I was a kid.

Since you came from Michigan, were you aware of the regionalists? Not much. My father read Max Brand novels, so I liked the cowboy art that was on the jackets. My parents were not interested in art; we had one reproduction of a painting on the wall. They were *very* supportive of my drawing ability, however. There was no art exposure until my third year of high school. Because my father thought drafting would be something I could use to get a job at the plant where he worked, I took two years of drafting. By the third year my grades weren't good enough to continue. I decided, instead, to take an art class. I hadn't taken it earlier because the instructor was kind of a meatball. When I signed up, however, I discovered that he had gone, and the new teacher turned out to be terrific. She introduced me to Daumier and Paul Klee and to art beyond cartoons.

She took my work to Toledo and showed it to the artist who did the comic strip "Mary Worth." She also showed it to the creator of "Judge Parker," who, in fact, called me to encourage me to keep drawing.

So you never worked in the factory? I worked for a year in the foundry to get money to go away to art school. Also during that year, I took the Famous Artists School cartoon course. There were twenty-four lessons and I think I did

Illustration for article in Fortune
entitled "The GM of Fast Foods."
1985. Ink and watercolor on paper.
Art director: Margery Peters.

Drawings for greeting cards. 1979. Ink and watercolor on paper. Titanic Publications.

twelve of them. Meanwhile, my teacher searched around to find me a real art school and discovered that cartooning was taught at the Chicago Academy of Fine Arts. I owe her my greatest debt, and my first kids' book is dedicated to her.

Did you like the Chicago Academy of Arts? It was a mediocre school. There were no real prerequisites for admission. Almost anyone could get in. We had a life-drawing instructor who wasn't a great teacher, but he was very enthusiastic, and I think I was influenced by him just because he had real drive and enthusiasm. He would lean over your shoulder, onto your drawing pad, saying, "The gesture! You have to have the gesture."

If school was basically a bust, how did you learn? On the job. In those days, I had never heard of freelancing as an artist. I was working as a stock boy at a supermarket making just enough money to get by, through the remainder of school. My first art job was with a trade publishing house that issued *Super Service Stations* and *Jobber Topics.* I did mechanicals, layouts, worked with type. I fell in love with type. I also got to do little spot cartoons for the magazines.

What was your drawing like in those days? Like John Gallagher, who did work for *Argosy* and the old *Saturday Evening Post.* They were just nebbishlike characters with big noses. My next job was at Marshall Field, the department store in Chicago; I worked there for six months, and then

in several smaller advertising agencies. All along, I occasionally did little drawings for promotions, but basically I was a designer and art director. I worked at a nice little agency called Arthur Wilke Advertising where, after a while, I realized I was very unhappy—for one thing, I had an ulcer due to the stress of the advertising business. I knew if I stayed much longer, I wouldn't be able to be an illustrator. Curiously, I would commission *other* people to do humorous illustration. And the more I would commission, the more I would think, "I don't think I can ever do it as well as they do." Still, I knew that I wanted to do the drawings *myself.* So I quit the job, helped out on a freelance basis, and started freelancing illustration until I got up a strong portfolio. Actually it was all over the place stylistically—I always had trouble finding the right style, probably until I was thirty-four years old.

How important was style to you? It was very important. There are people, like Glaser, who can successfully work in various styles, but for most people a strong single-minded style is what helps you to get established.

Did you want to deal with content? Did you want to do satire? All along, I just wanted to be an illustrator of articles. I don't think I have ever had a real strong point of view, which is why I never considered myself a real cartoonist. Once I am given an assignment, I can add wit and personality, but I must work off outside stimuli. I was called by *Atlantic,*

Illustration for an article in New York *about the opera. 1978. Pen and ink. Art director: Wendy Palitz.*

when Walter Bernard was redesigning it a few years ago, and asked to come up with any idea that could run on its own. I realized that I couldn't do it. I don't have a real strong idea orientation.

Is this something that upsets you or are you comfortable with it? Would you like to be able to conceptualize? I think I'm capable of doing something with more substance. I can do work that is expressive, that comes from a deeper part of me. The humor and the whimsy that I put into my work is very much a part of me. I would like to think that there's a deeper side. Certainly, I know I have imagination that doesn't get tapped because of the constrictions of the commercial field. I have, however, established myself as having a certain style and can produce work under quick deadlines—especially when the client is just asking for technique. Technique, however, is second or third or fourth down the line of importance. I really think that my concepts, and my characters, are most important.

What was it that brought you to New York? Illustration. I really wanted to be like Norman Rockwell—not work like him but be a well-known illustrator. Maybe it comes from primal insecurity; I was shy and was bullied in school. Yet I drew in my books all the time, and it was the one thing I could do well. I wanted to be recognized for it, and in this society, that means being respected by your peers. When I arrived in New York City, it fell into place.

But let me just backtrack: I was very frustrated at the end of my Chicago days. Chicago was not a very good town for me to work in. It's mostly straight-laced advertising. If you do realistic work, you can do very well there. I stayed busy as an illustrator, but I was very frustrated because of the conservative mentality of the town. I was playing in a bluegrass band, and that was my saving grace at the time.

Is music something you have done throughout your life? I studied trumpet when I was very little and didn't do well with it. My parents owned a resort for a while in Michigan, and in the summer of 1957, this unusual couple, Clarence and Mable Couture, stayed there. She played Hawaiian guitar, and he sang and played rhythm on acoustic Spanish guitar. They stayed for two weeks, and during that time I fell in love with their music. My parents paid for me to take guitar lessons with them, and after the lesson, we'd sit, and I would accompany them while they sang songs, with whatever I had learned in the way of chords. That was heaven. I played guitar off and on over the years, and then as my interest broadened to classical music, I learned to play Renaissance music on the lute. I even built a clavichord from a kit; never learned to play it, though.

Why didn't you go into music? During my first year of art school, I was torn about going into music. I played in a band in 1958–59, and it was a rough life. As much as I loved it, I realized I was a better artist than I was a musician. I think I made the right choice.

Did you derive any inspiration for your art from the music? I suppose that one influences the other. Certainly, I drew a lot of characters playing music; on my business card is the guy playing a pen/flute. One could talk about the rhythm of my work, but I'm not the one who's going to talk about that. So, I consider the two as separate. Still, I think music has given me a greater idea of what's available out in the world. I often think, if there were a fire, and I could only grab a couple of things, it would be musical instruments, not my artwork.

Let's go back to what happened when you came to New York. Were you still trying to find a graphic voice? I was thirty-five when I came to Manhattan, and when I was thirty-four, I sat down and I formulated "a style." I tried to converge my various influences into one, and what resulted was a very cartoony thing done with tight cross-hatching. My first New York stylistic incarnation was a very mannered line, very stiff but in a cartoon vein. I got work right away because art directors could see something that was a little different.

Cover of the Push Pin Graphic, for the special Hero issue. 1979. Ink and watercolor on paper. Art director: Seymour Chwast.

Sketches for miscellaneous catalog spots. 1985. Pencil. Workshop Records; art director: Dan Huckabee.

Your style changed radically—and loosened considerably—from the first months in New York. Since you were getting work and were becoming known, why did you change? About a year after I was in the city, I got *bored* with my style. It still wasn't me. I got interested in the "old masters" from the late nineteenth and early twentieth centuries. I started studying the comics, like "Mutt and Jeff," "Krazy Kat," and "Popeye." I would go out to a store in Queens called Little Nemo and buy original art, old comic books, little booklets, and any kind of reproductions. I tried to draw like them and simply couldn't. So I read articles about them and in the older magazines would find an occasional ad for a new cartoon course by Elzie Seeger who created "Popeye." Sometimes these ads would show a page from the cartoon course, which would say, "Use the Gilette Number 1290 cartoonist's pen." So I'd run out and buy the pen nibs—fortunately, they are still available.

So you were entering a time warp. Did this experimentation affect your work right away? Yes. And fortunately, there were art directors who were open to the idea. I injected this new-found information into my work. I didn't sit down

and fully develop it; I just started making the drawings more cartoony; the gestures became exaggerated, and certain kinds of cartoon things started. Then it just flowered. I continued to study the masters. I filled sketchbooks with copies of their work. It was the only way I could learn, since there was no one around to show me how to do it. I didn't use the copies in jobs.

What is it about "Smokey Stover" or Rube Goldberg, to name only two examples of what you're talking about, that appealed to you? I can't sit with anything too long. If I can't get it done in a sitting, chances are it won't get done—it's just my nature. So this comic style is perfect; especially strips like "Krazy Kat." The idea is to get in there and do it fast, and do it with a lot of snap.

Did you have any guilt about borrowing, or one might call it stealing, from these masters? I was excited about it. I felt like I was carrying on a tradition. One reason was because when you look at "The Family Upstairs" or "Baron Bean" by George Herrimann, it looks very much like Bud Fisher's "Mutt and Jeff." I always thought that Herrimann, who is considered an original, took from Fisher and refined it.

Top: *Sketches for more catalog spots. 1985. Pen and ink. Workshop Records; art director: Dan Huckabee.* Bottom: *Sketch for a satirical column by "Professor Kennilworth" in the* National Lampoon. *1982. Pencil. Art director: Michael Grossman.*

QUARTET HARMONY

SUGGESTION BABE

Illustration for article in Mother Jones *entitled "Looking for Mr. Goodwrench." 1985. Ink and water-color on paper. Art director: Louise Kollenbaum.*

So you felt you were playing leapfrog, reviving a venerable approach? I felt it was absolutely natural that I should work in that style. The more I got into it, the more excited I got, and the more I realized that my whole childhood was spent observing these artists.

At what point in this development did you start creating stories or even ideas of your own? I never created stories because I'm an illustrator. The strip artists did something very different; they created a strip and a troupe of characters. I have always been an illustrator, so all I use is their technique. I have my own sense of humor, but I'm not a narrative artist.

You're being too modest. You may not do narratives, but you do create situations that are filled with humor and have odd, almost surreal things going on. Yes, I do. And, in fact, I have written and illustrated a couple of kids' books.

Do you think that you're doing inventive things with this tradition? Only in that I'm using the approach in illustration in a way that strip artists wouldn't do it. I think my concepts are very strong. So I'm taking something from them and using it in a way that they wouldn't have been able to use it. That makes my work original. Although, I must say, there have been other contemporary artists, like Bobby London, who do the old comic style nicely.

Actually, I *have* worked up a strip called "Uncle Dowdy." Although the syndicates I've heard from like it, they don't quite seem to know what to do with it. My style is either too early or too late.

Do you keep a sketchbook? Yes. I fill it with doodles that are character studies. In addition, I draw *organic* things; *inorganic* things like architecture hold no interest for me. Unless, for example, I can draw an airplane with real floppy wings so it looks like a soft sculpture.

Well, you must love to draw people. Your work is replete with zany types. The images I truly enjoy making for myself are very limited. But, because I have to make a living, and I get assignments, I can't limit what I do too much.

The thing that interests me about your work is that it has a storybook feel. It's art that is sophisticated, yet accessible, and often makes one relate to pedantic subjects in a lighthearted way. I think the greatest virtue of my work is its loving quality. When, for example, I use a worried dog or a worried cat, I think that the viewer's heart goes out—my heart does, when I'm drawing them. I think that if there's one thing I'm able to do, it's to draw upon the child in all of us that's being bullied and make that work in illustration. I am capable of making very sympathetic drawings without being saccharine.

What drawings are you proudest of? The cover for the *Westward* magazine with a little cat holding a brush that says, "Joy." It's all me. I made it all up. All I was told was to "come up with a Christmas cover." It's my character, there's nothing in there that's dictated by the client. I guess that's what it comes down to: I want to do what I want to do. But when I get an assignment for which the clients know exactly what it is they want, occasionally I'll do a job that I'm pleased with, but more often, it's something of a compromise.

Do you find there are times when once you have a picture in your head, you cannot render it? Oh, yes, quite often. What I usually do is, I get a concept that's very much like, say, a Disney idea. I create a certain action for a character. And what happens, interestingly, is if I can't draw it, I struggle to come up with a different idea that's invariably more original. Usually, the first thing I come up with is just an extension of something I've seen in the past.

You draw in ink and then you add watercolor. Where did your color craft come from? Actually, I think it came from close friends who were really venturesome in wearing interesting clothing, earth tones together with sparkle color. The woman I lived with also wore all kinds of wonderful color combinations. Before that, all my colors had been *Yellow Submarine* oriented, like real bright magentas and bright oranges. I never felt that I had a handle on color. Thanks to what my friends wore, I started getting interested in earth-tone colors, and that's still my palette. In addition to that influence, the washed-out reproductions in magazines of old comic art, like Sunday pages, really appeal to me. I've become a little braver, and I use bolder touches.

Are you satisfied with the work you're doing now, or are you going further? I'm pretty satisfied right now, but I'm refining my approach. There are still days when I feel I'm nowhere near the quality of the masters, but I would say I'm at a point where the style is down. I always feel I have to move in new directions, but I think such a direction is not as drastic as it was. This time it will be a subtle change. It's going to be in the form of more energy and a looser style.

Is that impetus coming from within, or elsewhere? Well, some of it is because of the New Wave illustration I see emerging. However, Francis Bacon is my favorite painter, and I have done some work over the past few years that smacks a little of his. Years ago, I did some drawings called "daymares." It's day-by-day dreaming—streams of diverse images, coming from deep-seated feelings. I believe this could propel me in an interesting direction.

Top: *Sketch and finished cover for* Sunday, *the* Chicago Tribune *magazine, for "The 1984 News is Stranger Than Fiction Scrapbook." 1984. Pen and watercolor. Art directors: Dan Jursa and John Twohey.* Bottom right: *Cover for* Chicago Tribune Magazine *for an article about hot dogs entitled "Hot Diggety Dogs." 1983. Ink and watercolor. Art director: Dan Jursa.* Bottom left: *Sketch for an advertisement for Hunter fans. 1985. Pencil. Agency: Young and Rubicam; art director: Jill Hohannan.*

SUE COE

Sue Coe (born on February 21, 1951, in London, England) had already made a stir in art circles at the Royal College of Art before coming to the United States in 1974. Here she was feared and admired by art directors who were never quite certain what she might produce. In recent years the decidedly political heart of her drawings caught the eyes and minds of many young illustrators, many of whom mimicked the style but not the content. Lately she has turned passionately to painting. Her evocative images of rape, crime in the streets, and genocide are personal cathartics for a world run amuck. The art world has also taken notice, and recently three of her paintings were purchased by the Metropolitan Museum of Art.

When I was about four, I found some books around the house. One was *Sex and Marriage*. One was a cookbook. Another was *Airplanes of World War I*. I copied all the pictures from those books and also drew comic strips from the newspaper. That's how I got interested in art.

Did you go to art school? Yes. But when I first told my Mum and Dad my plans, they said, "No, there's no money in it." So I had a choice: work in a candy factory that made Mars bars or be a shorthand typist engaged to be married. But I didn't want to be engaged. So I went to work for Mars. I was quickly removed from the job, and then decided to go to art school on my own. I was living just outside London, so I went to the Guildford School of Art. This was in 1968, at the time of the French student rebellion, and trouble was brewing in England too. Right after I got to Guildford, the students took over the college. That was my first dose of enlightenment; we were fighting a corrupt class system. You see, it wasn't really acceptable for working-class kids to go to college; they are needed for factory fodder and the army.

Did you know anything about illustration? At the time I went to art school, there was absolutely no choice for me: I couldn't be a fine artist, because I was a girl. That meant I had to do children's books. I was put into the illustration department, and that was that. I never thought about doing anything else, but I didn't really want to do children's books.

What kind of drawings were you doing then? Drawings that were unacceptable to the eyes of children.

Were you influenced by any artists? I was influenced by the other students.

As I remember it, you became a major force at the Royal College of Art. When I was twenty years old, I said, "Oh, God, I'm going to go on the dole"—you know, unemploy-

U.S. Military Bombs Mental Hospital
in Grenada, *exhibited at P.P.O.W.
Gallery in New York. 1985. Oil on
paper.*

Mugging 3, *a page from sketchbook, created in response to the artist's own mugging. 1982. Photographs, pencil drawings, and pages from "crime-stoppers" manual.*

FILL IN ALL THE BLANKS

GIVE TO THE FIRST POLICE OFFICER ON THE SCENE

crime

MUGGING 3

Be able to describe size, type, and color of guns or other weapons that are used.

Take a good look at the suspects. Notice any details which will aid you to describe them and their mannerisms. When trying to determine age, height, weight, and appearance make comparisons between them and yourself or people you know.

Memorize peculiarities such as tattoos, scars, and prominent physical features.

You are gonna wish you were never born motherfucker

Remain calm. Robbers usually are excited and may be provoked easily or might be under the influence of drugs.

Vary the route and not always go at a scheduled time.

Discuss only business with the tellers. The next person in line may be getting familiar with your routine.

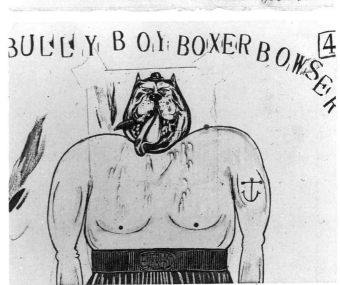

Drawings from sketchbook. Top: Cow on the Marshes. *1980. Pencil.* Bottom: Bully Boy Boxer Bowser. *1980. Pencil and rubber stamp lettering.*

ment—"if I don't do something about work." So I applied and got into the Royal College—women had a bit more freedom by then. I met people there who were middle class, highly educated, and Marxist. We got involved in politics and in political art—studying work by Goya, John Heartfield, and George Grosz. After the first year I left and came to New York, to work.

What got you politically motivated? The French student rebellion was only one thing, experiencing that didn't change you entirely, did it? No. Getting an education helped me to understand why there were massive inequalities. I learned why those things were perpetrated.

The artists that you were associated with at the Royal College all practiced a kind of rage-inspired expressionism. Were you working for any political publications while you were in college? No. We made our own magazines. There were only a few publications that had any content, and those were very underground press things, like *Oz*, which was actually before me—they were the old school. I just went to work for *Nova*, and that was that. And it was only when I got to America, at twenty-one, that things came together for me artistically.

The drawings you were doing early on still had an edge. They were expressive. There was emotion but not *contradiction*, and that's different. There was an emotive, subjective rage, but there wasn't any struggle or any conflict, which has to be in socially conscious art.

Your approach was quite different from what Americans understood as illustration. Where did this work stylistically come from? People have said David Hockney or George Grosz or Richard Lindner. But I don't think so—all German expressionism and Soviet art have influenced me, and most especially Goya and Käthe Kollwitz. My roots basically go to the tradition of caricature in England and to black-and-white illustration of the *London Illustrated News*. And, of course, all the people who taught me filtered through.

You never worked in line, did you? You always worked in tone. Somewhere you made a decision to use different media. I cannot honestly remember where it came from. I've always done drawings like this, since I was drawing in my Mum's house. I used pencil because we didn't have enough money for paint.

Once you realized that you could put politics into your art, how did that affect your commercial illustration? I don't think art directors or editors ever liked my work, whether it's political or not. I've hardly been used in America. It has always amused me that people say they see my work everywhere, because in reality I have, maybe, three drawings

Greed, *a page from sketchbook, chronicling an illustration published in* Design *magazine. 1979. Watercolor, collage, designer's gouache, and photographs.*

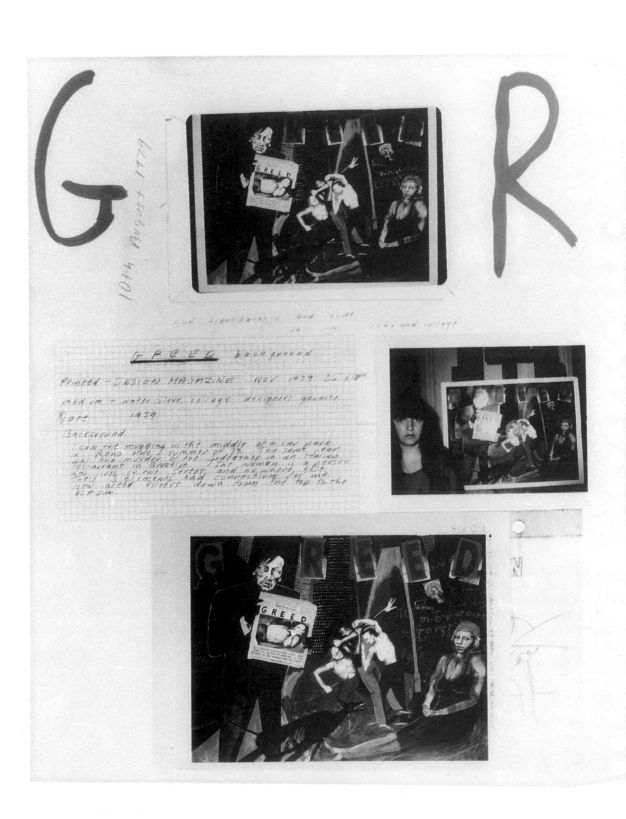

An illustration for Mother Jones *entitled* Bobby Sands, *depicting a member of the IRA who died after a hunger strike in a Northern Ireland prison. 1982. Oil on paper. Art director: Louise Kollenbaum.*

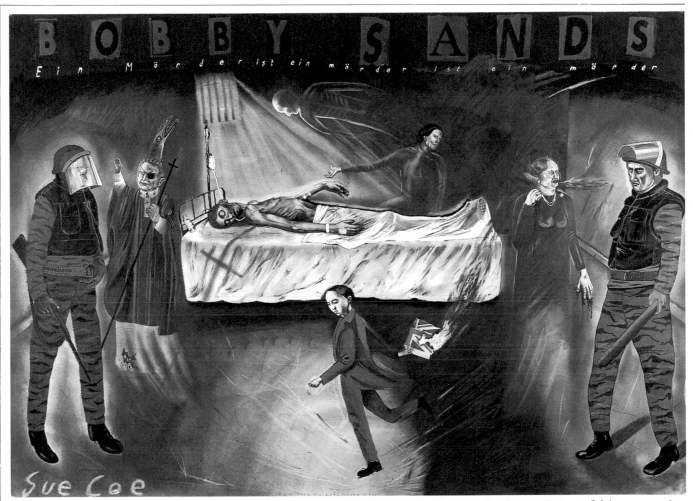

a year. There have been only two or three art directors who have ever given me any encouragement and consistent support. I imagine I am used by art directors to give them a sort of veneer of *"I can take risks"* (but not this year).

Usually, editors are afraid of this work, and employ someone who uses style without content. But, if I have the opportunity, then I'll take it. I won't hold back, and I'll try to do the best I can do, without self-censorship.

Given that, in the time you've been in the United States, have you been satisfied with the editorial work that you've done? I think I've achieved what I set out to do in illustration. Go for broke, and make it as truthful as I possibly can, holding to the content of the article, without holding myself back and without giving in to the look of the magazine or newspaper. Sometimes, I do really bad work, but about three or four drawings have made it all worthwhile. Like

the rape picture in *Mother Jones*, that one I felt was worthy.

Was that an illustration, or was it self-motivated? The art director told me I could do what I wanted to do, as long as it referred to the Reagan era. I simply personalized my feelings about this period. To get it published was very important and, I think, very important to a lot of people who saw it, because the magazine got so much response from that one painting.

Speaking of response, do you realize that you have had an impact on illustrators in this country, as well as in England? If I have had an impact, I would like it to be in the way Goya had an impact on me—in making me closer to myself, not in any stylistic imitation. In fact, if you influence someone, you are influencing them to be closer to their own truth. Stylistic influence alone doesn't interest me at all.

Some illustrators, painters, and sculptors who have a

217

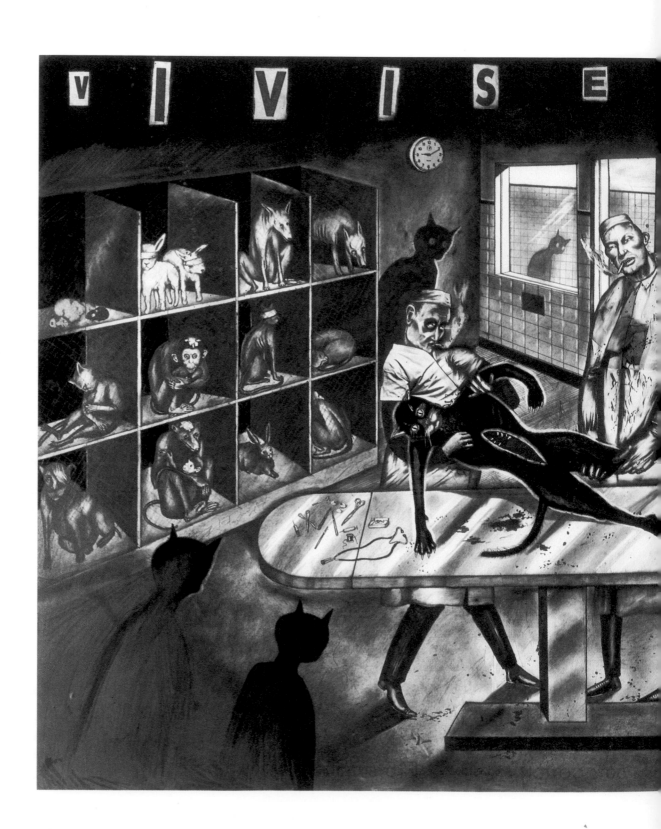

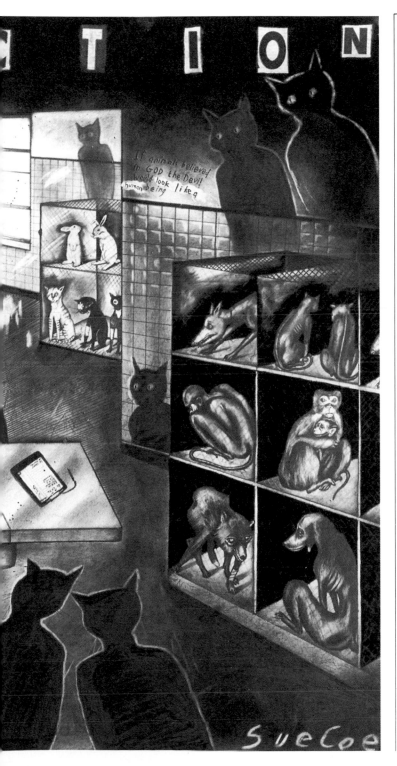

personal vocabulary go to it all the time, reworking their symbols over and over again. Do you ever have that problem? In hours of weakness, I do. I think that has to do with being exhausted and overworked.

Are you doing less illustration in favor of more personal art? I would prefer to do more illustrations; illustration can be personal art. I never particularly wanted to be in galleries, but it's become my way of making a living. I'd prefer to make a living doing illustration.

What is it about illustration that gives you the most satisfaction? It is the fact that one is instantly communicating and that one gets immediate response from people. It's a special thing when you can buy a newspaper, see a drawing in it, and have a relationship with that drawing on the subway or a bus. I've seen people look at newspaper drawings very closely. It's an intimate exchange, which rarely happens in an art gallery, rarely happens in museums, and doesn't happen when artists are painting for rich people.

What are some of the themes that you've dealt with intimately? I'm working on a series now about war resisters. People who are forgotten by the regular media. I'm just trying to keep the idea alive.

Are you a journalist to some extent? Was it a journalistic impulse that prompted the South Africa series? It was about Steve Biko. I was sitting with the publishers of *Raw* magazine, and I said, "Why don't you give me the money to do a bloody book?" And they said, "All right, then, here's the money. We'll do it."

How did you come up with those striking images? I try to stick to an area of truth: I just tapped the feelings I have on the street in New York; the new material wasn't totally about South Africa. But it *was* about Biko being tortured, and innocent people in Johannesburg being victimized, which happens in America, too.

Are there subjects you won't tackle? We obviously wouldn't expect you to do a campaign poster for Ronald Reagan. I wouldn't do anything that I hadn't really researched and didn't feel was honest for me to do. I'm always asked to do things like that; like, quickly whip out pictures about El Salvador, or do ten things about dissidents. I can't, because I don't have the information. The information has to be whirring around in my head for months before I'll even start to talk about it.

Do you get excited when you're doing a picture? Ralph Steadman once said that when he gets someone in his gunsights, he does a war dance. Yeah. He doesn't play by the numbers, and that's what I like. I give the same amount of thought and energy to something that pays $50 as to something that pays $10,000. In other words, I get excited but only by inherent contradiction.

Do you have rituals about working? There's all the equipment; it can't be touched by anyone but me. Like the sable brushes that are never, ever used, even by me. They're just bought to be looked at. Moreover, I work every day, because I'd go insane if I didn't work. Work is the organization of sanity. There's nothing else as important to me. If I'm not painting, I get physically sick. All the people I know in England and America that come from working families put a great deal of emphasis on labor, on craftsmanship, and on technique. I understand that, because the insecure thing for me is, if I don't put in five thousand hours of work on a painting, I come to doubt it. But I should have left that behind by now.

Why should you leave it behind when it's part of a process? Because less is more, and I've got to learn to leave stuff out. Because my work is sometimes so overstated. I've just got to trust myself more.

Once you make an overstated painting, and you know it, what do you do? You think I should rip it up?

You've done some beautifully economical pictures, too. That's more the direction I want to go, but I'm scared because it's difficult.

Is that why you put words in so many of your pictures? No. I *love* the shape of letters, and a lot of times they add graphic impact. Sometimes, I use them to get at the political edge so there is no ambiguity.

How do you feel about the paucity of strong female artists? You are one among only a handful. Women are oppressed in every way and have been through history. Women have never been together as a group. The reason why Western imagery is so superficial is that it removes the images that involve a woman's experience. A woman's experience living in this society is totally different from a man's. Women, and that includes female artists, are bombarded with male imagery in all the media. Any human that is not a white middle-class man is depicted as a caricature, a distorted stereotype. Why? Because white men in a majority control the media, and therefore perpetuate the idea of what is real—for them. Women are only encouraged to participate in the images that men find acceptable and nonthreatening. Sexism flourishes where a tiny minority of men control the wealth and the media. Great art, male or female, comes from an intelligent artist. An intelligent artist understands what is real for all. Maybe the question should be, "Why are there so many 'weak' male artists filling up the magazines and art galleries?" and, "Why can I think of only a handful whose work has a concern for humanity?"

You've taught art and lecture often. What do you share with the students? I show them my work, and then I see them personally. Female students show me drawings that they don't show their teachers. They show me what they'll call "personal" work, as though there's a difference. And I find that work more powerful than anything in their slick illustration or fine arts portfolio. I try to encourage them in any way I can, but there is no support system for these women. When I started doing illustration, I was told that my work had balls, which was some sort of compliment.

Do you think being able to draw is important? Anybody can draw. It's the amount of energy and thought put into it. Like, Munch's *The Scream.* That has to do with something so pure. It has everything to do with vision and perception. You can take anyone off the street and make them into an artist, if they have the will to express their vision.

But that comes head-to-horn in conflict with the prerequisites of commercial art, and commercial art means a picture has to be finished. Well, I taught at a prison for a couple of weeks. The question they asked—the only question— was, "Now we have the content. How much should we concern ourselves with form?" And I said, "You have to know about form. But the content comes first. I don't give a damn how well you can do form. If you haven't got truth, you've got nothing." And I'm not mistaking truth for emotion here.

The system says otherwise. How does one circumvent the system? People will have to change the system, because the system is artificial and destructive. That's why we hear about it day and night, because it is a lie. But you only have to whisper the truth once, and someone gets it. And that's all you have to do. Whisper it. You don't need to be MTV or NBC or the *New York Times.* You just whisper it to someone, it will carry.

Are your most successful pictures the whispers? My existence is a whisper.

Don't you think some people are best suited to do other things? Maybe there are people out there who can't form images. People are best suited to somehow relate to the world and themselves in a way that makes them very happy. People are best suited to be themselves and then somehow change the rest of the world to be about life and reality.

Does your work make you happy? It reconfirms feelings. My work is about trying to grasp a reflection. It's not what it appears to be. It's not about violence, and it's not about a direct political ideology. It's not about the past and it never will be.

Top: Riot, *in the collection of the Brooklyn Museum. 1981. Graphite on paper.* Bottom: Dancing Bear, *exhibited at P.P.O.W. Gallery in New York. 1981. Graphite on paper.*

INDEX